EXPERIENCING GOD'S POWER AND MIRACLES

EXPERIENCING GOD'S POWER AND MIRACLES

GOD USES ORDINARY PEOPLE FOR DIVINE PURPOSES

A MEMOIR

PASTOR SABRINA R. HUGHES

XULON ELITE

Xulon Press Elite
2301 Lucien Way #415
Maitland, FL 32751
407.339.4217
www.xulonpress.com

© 2022 by Pastor Sabrina R. Hughes

Contribution by: Michelle Y. Blakely PhD, Black_artts

All rights reserved solely by the author. The author guarantees all contents are original and do not infringe upon the legal rights of any other person or work. No part of this book may be reproduced in any form without the permission of the author. The views expressed in this book are not necessarily those of the publisher.

Due to the changing nature of the Internet, if there are any web addresses, links, or URLs included in this manuscript, these may have been altered and may no longer be accessible. The views and opinions shared in this book belong solely to the author and do not necessarily reflect those of the publisher. The publisher, therefore, disclaims responsibility for the views or opinions expressed within the work.

Unless otherwise indicated, Scripture quotations taken from the Holy Bible, New International Version (NIV). Copyright © 1973, 1978, 1984, 2011 by Biblica, Inc.™. Used by permission. All rights reserved.

Scripture quotations taken from the King James Version (KJV) – *public domain.*

Scripture quotations taken from the Holy Bible, New Living Translation (NLT). Copyright ©1996, 2004, 2007 by Tyndale House Foundation. Used by permission of Tyndale House Publishers, Inc.

Library of Congress Control Number:

Paperback ISBN-13: 978-1-66284-882-7
Ebook ISBN-13: 978-1-66284-883-4

TABLE OF CONTENTS

Acknowledgments vii
Foreword ix
Preface xi

Chapter I: Whom Shall I Use 1
Chapter II: When God Speaks 27
Chapter III: A New Beginning 59
Chapter IV: Moving With The Master 91
Chapter V: A Place Called Wetumpka 129
Chapter VI: When The Hanks Come Marching In 177
Chapter VII: Carmen's Way 201
Chapter VIII: Raging Storms 235
Chapter IX: The New Frontier 261
Chapter X: The Wrap Up 287

About the Author 293
Endnotes 295

ACKNOWLEDGEMENTS

First and foremost, I want to acknowledge my Father in Heaven. God, there is nothing or no one greater, more powerful, or more loving than you. To you, I owe my undying love, gratitude, and service. I am so thankful for the Bridegroom who took my place on the cross and made it possible for me to live throughout eternity with you. Lord, I also want to acknowledge and thank you for my blessings and thorns that have produced an abundance of growth and fruit in my life. Lastly, Lord, words cannot adequately express my heartfelt thanksgiving for using me as a vessel of your divine and miraculous work!

I would like to give an enormous thank you to my husband, my love, best friend, and life partner, Larry T. Hughes for his support and selflessness. Whatever, I need or whisper he provides without complaining. I am very blessed that he is a God-fearing man who is full of wisdom and provides sound direction.

Finally, I would like to thank my sisters, all of my friends, and church families far and wide for their infinite prayers, encouragement, and willingness to assist with the evolution of this book.

FOREWORD

Have you ever met someone who you know that God placed in your life? To take this a step further, the connection is so incredibly special that you have a difficult time wrapping your head around what is happening. Well, that is who Pastor Sabrina Hughes is for me. I simply never ever met anyone like her. Her relationship with God places me in a state of wonder.

She is the epitome of an obedient servant of GOD. She is an evangelist and pastor. More importantly, she is a true Christian! I am blessed to call her friend.

God sometimes places people in your life, and you do not know what will happen next, but you know He is orchestrating something special. Sabrina Hughes and I met when I arrived to a new assignment at a hospital in Tennessee. She was and is from the first moment we met a strong force. She spoke into my life shortly after we met, revealing a truth that she had no way of knowing within her own power. It was in that moment that I began to wonder who she was. I never questioned her connection to God and the way that He used her to speak into my life. I was growing in my maturity with God and hungry for connections with those who had a strong relationship with Him.

For the next twenty-plus years, God has continued to use my friend and confidant Sabrina to speak into my life. She is obedient to the voice of God and fearless. The truths in this book will at times leave you wondering if they could possibly be true. I assure you; they are. God loves when we are obedient to His direction. When we are, He trusts us with more. This book punctuates this phenomenon. I am excited that you will have the opportunity to learn from Sabrina's walk with God. I am proud to have been an eyewitness to facets of her walk and the benefactor of her Godly warnings.

As a Christian on the journey to ensure that I am in service to God, I am excited to have a road map like this book to highlight what an obedient life looks like that I could emulate. I truly believe that once one sees what is possible, it propels us forward into action with God. I am thrilled that you too will have this opportunity to go on this journey with Pastor Sabrina Hughes. I pray that it causes you to think, stretch and grow. It will change your life!

Michelle Y. Blakely, PhD, MHSA, FACHE

PREFACE

In 2004, the co-pastor of the church I was attending in Cary North Carolina, prophesized and indicated that the scripture Jeremiah 33:3 would be magnified in my life. The King James' (KJV) version of the scripture she uttered says: Call unto me, and I will answer thee, and show thee great and mighty things, which thou knowest not. That scripture has truly been a high tower in my life. The majesty of God shows up in the most interesting ways in our lives. Everything He does is to expand His kingdom and glorify His name.

My bucket list or desired accomplishments never included experiencing God's power, miracles, and wonders. Yet, throughout my life, He has afforded me countless opportunities to see and be an active partner of His divine work, power, miracles, and wonders across the globe. My experiences with the Lord have led to many valuable lessons which have been shared with innumerable people from all walks of life who are either entering, amid, or coming through a storm.

The first profound lesson I received from the Lord is that He reveals His divine power and performs miracles so that others may believe. For whatever reason, miraculous statements do not often move to our hearts or souls, but visualizing something miraculous or breath-taking forms an indelible place in the depths of our hearts and souls instantaneously. The impact of the phenomenon leads to a burning desire to share with someone what you have experienced. Hence, His Story (The Lord) becomes a part of your story, your truth and before you know it, the gospel has been shared in some form or fashion.

My second greatest life lesson from God is: He is not looking to partner with a perfect person. Sabrina would not be in His equation if He were looking for human perfection. Let me share a secret with you, there is no perfect human being on the planet and, there never will be one. The Lord is not concerned with your material gain, titles, your beauty, or your educational level. God is after willing vessels eager to provide genuine humble service.

One time, my parents planned a Thanksgiving holiday visit with us when we lived in Alabama. When your parents visit, you want everything in your home to be immaculate and the food you prepare savory. I worked my fingers to the bone before they arrived. While I was finalizing dinner and awaiting their arrival, God said: Sabrina, this is what I require of you for me. You need to press through your fatigue and your perceived pain for the good (Phil. 3:12). God spoke very clearly and gave me a real-life example that I could relate to in short order. He did this so I would not misconstrue what He meant. He desires that we have perpetual perseverance (James 1:4 and, Rom. 5:4, New International Version, ([NIV]).

Consider the way that Jesus entered the world. Was He wearing a majestic robe? Was He adorned with jewels? Was He riding in a beautiful chariot or riding an animal fit for royalty? In all of the scenarios, the answer is no. Jesus entered the world as the king riding on a donkey. His chosen transportation was designed for an average human being. Some would say that His entrance portrayed someone who lived meagerly. Through His entrance and His appearance, the Lord revealed humility and portrayed that He is for all mankind.

Preface

He is without question the Lord of inclusion (John 3:17, 1 Pet. 1:17 and, Acts 10:34, NIV).

This book is indeed God's book. He designed it with every one of you in mind. I am the transcriber and the person who witnessed all the accounts in the book as a believer, a backslider, a servant, an ordained evangelist, and an ordained pastor. However, you will find out that others were integral to my miraculous life journey.

The Lord began to nudge me about authoring this book two years ago. At the beginning of 2021, His voice became louder. When the pandemic swept through our country, many people became homebound. Because of this, many people acquired the time that they never had to author several books. I remember watching CNN and hearing of several interesting books that were being published. I said to God, everyone is authoring a book and many of the authors are famous people. God said to me, yes, many books are being written, but they are not about me. Satan almost gained a foot hole of deterrence. As we know, God's power is greater and, this book began to take root. God's purpose for authoring this book is to gain you as His partner in expanding His kingdom, provide modern-day accounts of His power, wonders, and miracles so others may believe. Nothing that man can produce can ever overshadow God's grace or His power (Col. 1:16 and, Acts 17:24-26).

Most of all, this book is being written to let you know that God loves you deeply and wants to use you for His magnificent work despite what you look like, what you possess, or what you are going through. Everything said and depicted in this book is real. Some of the truths may appear far-fetched, but they happened. After all, God's power and wonders may seem fictitious and unbelievable when told or seen. We also know that a miracle is such because it is something that generally would not occur or be thought of in the natural world or carnal mind. I stand here today professing that

God uses ordinary people for divine purposes and miracles. There is nothing special about me. My life is a living testament to the fact that the Lord can mend you and use you at the same time for His divine work if you allow Him. Yes, you can be a part of the miracles that He continues to perform in the twenty-first century and beyond if you call on Him.

Each day as a Christian, I am going through the firing process. Like the making of pure gold, my impurities and traits that do not reflect the Lord's image are being removed throughout this process. I am, and you are, valuable as imperfect beings and, we are much more precious when God uses us (1 Pet. 1:7). My roses, your roses, my thorns, and your thorns are experiences that will heal the brokenhearted, create eternal partnerships with the Lord, encourage the heart, and restore hope, love, and self-esteem. Let God use you today. He is waiting on your call.

Preface

CHAPTER I

WHOM SHALL I USE?

Have you ever wondered why and how God chooses someone to be an instrument of His work? As a child and a young adult, I was glued to my seat and mesmerized by the ministers delivering God's Word amid packed pews either on television (TV) or in a church building. Those ministers were able to glide through the pulpit, the aisles and speak with authority concerning God's power and miracles that manifested in their lives, while seamlessly connecting their manifestations to scripture. As I looked around the buildings, there was not a disengaged person present. It seemed as though these ministers were speaking directly to me and, I am sure that was true for others because, I could see and hear people weeping, clapping, shouting for joy, dancing, and praising the Lord with vigor.

Being the analytical thinker that I am, it dawned on me that the actions of these ministers led to the outcomes of those in the pews. Exactly what the ministers said and what they did through the Holy Spirit touched the audience in a way that made them bear witness to what was being said, and their emotions and thanksgiving to God poured like a river. I said to myself, these ministers have a straight line to God and are capable of entering into a Holy realm that those in the pews including myself could not. In my mind, they were divine beings and everyone else was measly mortals.

But then, I began to read the Holy Bible and realized this was not the truth. Moses, King David, Apostle Paul, Peter, John, and others committed many sins that were unpleasing to God. King David himself was a womanizer and a murderer. Yet, after his repentance, God said that David had a heart like His (1 Sam. 13:14). Despite their flaws and sin patterns, God used all of them as an instrument for His glory. God's power was released, and His miracles were manifested through them for countless people to see (Acts 4:13).

My a-ha moment was realizing that the disciples, other great people in the Bible, and the world are no different than me. They are ordinary people that you interact with every day like your family member, next-door neighbors, grocery store clerks co-workers, friends, and me. Although my sin pattern differs from the prominent figures in the Bible, the point is that I am an imperfect being like them. Guess what? so are the ministers that amazed me. If God can use them, then, He can use me too. God's power and miracles are infinite. The Bible, which is inspired by God Himself, tells us that He is not a respecter of a person (Rom. 2:11 and, Acts 10:34). What does that mean? Simply put, it means that God does not play the game of favoritism. He loves each one of us unconditionally and, we are all on equal footing with Him. What a Hallelujah!! This was surely not my belief forty years ago.

I emerged and evolved from humble beginnings that started in Motown. As my mother would say teasingly, well, Sabrina, you were not the prettiest baby. After spending my toddler years in Detroit, my mother decided to pack up and move us to Wilmington, Delaware. Our father and her husband remained in Detroit. At the time, I was four years old, and my sisters were ages six, three, and two. I can still remember that greyhound bus ride. It was exciting to pass through and see various cities and towns while enjoying fried chicken and bologna sandwiches that our mother prepared for us along the way.

The Power of Influence

Little did I know that my new destination in Delaware would be the beginning of my journey with God the Almighty. My mother and friend named Beatrice (Lumpkin) Thomas was a great woman of God by many accounts. She moved to Delaware with four young girls and no job. Truly she took a leap of faith. She had a sister who resided in Delaware and, we lived with her for a brief period. In the latter part of 1964, we moved to a neighborhood that would be considered low-income. We lived there for a long time even though my mom was financially stable to move. She refused to leave until she was able to find a house that she could afford and be proud to call home. Santa came regularly and filled the tree with sparkling new toys, clothes, and candies. Not a single birthday went uncelebrated, and we strutted in our new school clothes every year. If we were poor, I never knew it because we always got the things we needed; most of all lots of love.

My mother was a child of Elder Lenster Lumpkin, the presiding elder/pastor of the Primitive Baptist Church Association. His grandkids called him Big Daddy. His church was on Lumpkin Street which we believe gave us bragging rights. Two of my mother's three brothers were ministers in the same Primitive Baptist circle (one still is). Going to church was embedded in my mom's routine as a child. She would say with a hearty laugh that she was in church every time the door opened and stayed until it closed, which was often late in the evening. I remember traveling to Ohio and Michigan to attend some of Big Daddy's church functions. All of the music was Acappella and, everyone hummed, patted their feet, and rocked while singing. The audience was so in sync with the pulpit it seemed that the entire audience was the choir. From the outside of the church building, you would think that there were actual instruments in the room, but it was not one. My mother never required or forced us to go to church as kids, but she found a way to incorporate praise and worship to the Lord in the kitchen!

Cooking was a big ordeal growing up. I can remember learning to cook as early as nine years old. Sunday dinners were always a feast, but cleaning the kitchen afterward was brutal. My sisters including myself were summoned to the kitchen to cook and we would cook one or more dishes, with our mother watching over us until we got it right. Every time we cooked anything at home we would sing or shall I say make a joyful noise. The only songs that were sung were very old Christian hymns and, my mother knew all the words and verses to each one of them.

The hymns were so old that as children we thought our mother made them up herself. Because we sang them very often, my sisters and I knew every verse in an abbreviated period. In 2016, we googled them and found out that they are real songs. Of course, my mom was always the lead singer and, we were the mighty chorus. Singing with my mother and sisters made me feel good and lighthearted as laughter and the Primitive Baptist rocking filled the room every time we sang. Without a doubt, I know God's presence ushered in the room when we sang. Singing kitchen songs was my mother's way of threading praise and worship in the home and, the lyrics penetrated our souls (Ps. 150:6). They have become so contagious that our kids, and their kids, are now singing them and praising the Lord when they cook. Besides being a family tradition, kitchen songs became a key influencer that ignited my desire to go to church.

The distance of the church in our neighborhood was a good rock's throw away from our house. Every Sunday morning and some Friday nights, you could hear that Pentecostal church rocking. From my bedroom, I could hear the different piano keys, the strings of the guitar thumping, the beats of the drum, and the vocalists. If I did not know any better, I would have sworn that the church band was right downstairs in our living room. Although I could often hear the church when they were in session, it was never seen as a nuisance or bother. I would sway back and forth and simply enjoy the music. If I knew the songs, I could sing along with the church choir from my bedroom or any place in the house. Like the music, the preacher's sermon was crystal clear, and my bed became a church pew as I remained still, listening, but not understanding the content. After all, I was six through ten years old when this was taking place.

My mother never took us to the church near our home. Instead, she took us to the church that her sister was a member of about ten minutes away. It was something peculiar about the church that was a rock away from our home. This church named The Church of the Living God was drawing me. At the age of ten, I became interested in going to this church instead of my aunt's church. The funny thing is that I was not the only one interested in going to it. My sisters felt the same way. Our mother honored our request to attend this church and was incredibly happy that we were interested in going.

After going to the Church of the Living God for two years, I gave my life to the Lord and was twelve years old. I had no idea what I was to do with this new salvation and what it meant. Yet, I told everyone I knew about my conversion. Unfortunately, it took some time before I became rooted in Christianity and God's Word. Puberty came early for me. At the age of ten, all of my feminine attributes were in full bloom, making me appear older. At the age of twelve, I was 4'11" with a big deep voice and was the tallest student in my sixth-grade class. That did not last long. My full godly design was received at twelve and, I did not grow a single iota after this age. Even today, people look around me when they hear me speak for the first time in search of someone else. They do not believe that such a big voice is coming out of a tiny body like mine. This always makes me chuckle. God has a profound sense of humor and certainly had fun with my design.

During the ages of thirteen through fourteen, I was simply mischievous and did many things that I know were not pleasing to God. My friends and I would get the telephone book and randomly make prank calls to people. We would disguise our voices to appear more mature and tell the person on the telephone that they won a prize. After they would get extremely excited and inquire as to what they won, we would say something like you won an acre of cow manure, giggle and abruptly hang up the telephone.

After these types of pranks became boring, I sought other ways to get a laugh at someone else's expense. My pranks became crueler. Sometimes my mother would bring some of her nursing supplies home. She would take the supplies out of her uniform pocket and place them on her bedroom dresser. One day, I noticed an ammonia capsule on her dresser. After determining its' purpose, I stashed one for later use. I learned that this capsule was used to arouse unconscious or passed out people. My intrigue started to run wild. I thought it would be fun to see how a conscious person would respond to this ammonia capsule. Early one Saturday morning when my sister was in a deep sleep, I cracked the capsule open, eased across the bed where she was, and gently placed it under her nose. She nearly jumped to the ceiling and chased me out of the house and around the community until she caught me. I paid dearly from both my sister and mother for pulling this stunt. There were no thoughts of possible injury or side effects on my mind, but there should have been.

First Encounter with God's Power, The First Dance

At the age of fourteen, my conscience was getting the best of me. I started shying away from some of the activities that my teenage friends were doing that I knew were wrong. To not participate in pranks any longer, I pretended that my mother grounded me. At the same time, I was aware that God saved me, and, I was in a backslidden state. I was not finding comfort with my friends or in what I was doing as a teenager. The pranks were not funny anymore. Frankly, I became ashamed.

I went back to the Living God church. The day I returned to church was the first time I entered any church doors in two years. When I entered the church, it felt like every eye and head in the building was on me as I walked down the aisle to be seated. A heavy sense of shame overcame me as it appeared everybody was continually watching me, pointing at me, and ridiculing me. I thought, did they know the things that I did? With shame written all over my face, I bowed my head, closed my eyes, and tuned into the music being played. Then, the vocalist began to sing a song called It's like Holy Ghost and fire, shut up in my bones. Instantly, my feet started to pat the floor and move with delight. Certainly, this is customary when a good song and/or music is playing. Shortly after that, I started clapping and my body began to sway on its own! Something was moving inside of me that was outside of my control! Signals, like a jolt of lightning, were being sent to every part of my body and causing movement everywhere these signals went.

I took my hands and put them on my lap to halt their movement which did not work. They kept moving upward as in praise to God. My feet began to pat the floor and move more rapidly from side to side. I leaned forward, grabbed the top of the pew in front of me very tightly, and planted my feet firmly on the floor, hoping that this would restrain me. It did not! Before I knew it, my body was erect and was moving swiftly from the back of the church to the center aisle. My feet swayed from side to side very rhythmically with the beat of the music. I danced from the beginning of the center aisle, all the way to the end of it, and back until I reached my seat again. **For the first time, I realized and experienced the power of God and the Holy Spirit!**

I did not want to dance, but I was powerless in controlling this movement. As I reflect upon this period of my life, a few questions come to mind that may surface in the minds of others. Why could I not control my movement? As a child of the King, I can do all things through Christ who gives me strength (Phil. 4:13). Where was the self-control that is reiterated in the Bible that Christians are supposed to have? (1 Pet. 4:7, 1 Cor. 9:27 and, Prov. 25:28). God had a different intention this time. He knew that I did not know anything about Him or the power of the Holy Spirit. God also knew that He would be able to connect with me on a physical level because I was in tune with my body. He wanted me to see and feel how powerful He is and understand that His power is greater than mine and anything I could ever comprehend. On a deeper level, the dance reveals that God never left me despite my sin. **Beyond realizing God's great and infinite power for the first time, this dance is also the first miracle I experienced with God!**

I was definitely on an emotional high after having this miraculous experience with the Lord. My sisters witnessed my dance but had no inkling of what I was experiencing sitting in my pew. We never talked about it, nor did I ever share it with my mother when it happened. My mom did not get the full beauty of my experience until I was an adult and, my sisters received the full description when I was in my fifties.

It was not that I was embarrassed or anything. I did not know what to make of it and how profound it was at the age of fourteen. God reminded me of this dance and its meaning when I was in my forties. The work of the spirit within me before and, during the dance was so phenomenal that it was almost unbelievable. The shame produced by my childhood antics vanished with repentance. Do you think that my sisters who were sixteen, thirteen, and eleven at the time would have believed me? I do not. Did you forget that I had a history of being a practical joker? What I have come to know is that God's work is purposeful and masterful. With that being said, I do not believe that the dance was just about me. There was someone in the audience that God may have freed from a hurtful event or touched in some mighty way at the same time that He touched me.

Abandonment

Considering my miraculous event, one would think that the dance experience would be my catalyst to learning more about God and serving Him. Except, I was not bubbling with enthusiasm to do so; there was not a fizz of interest. Surprisingly, I went backward. Instead of moving closer to God, He became a distant thought. I was a germinated Christian seed on a spiritual rollercoaster from the ages of sixteen through twenty.

In the ninth grade, I jelled well with a girl in my neighborhood. She and I became besties, and it was hard to separate us. One of the best things that we had going for us was education. Both of us excelled academically from middle through high school. As a college-bound "A" student, I was involved in many activities and clubs. We were also assistant coaches for the girls' high school basketball team. Because of my engagement in many school activities along with my scholastic achievements, my integrity was never in question. If someone implicated us in any wrongdoing, it was discounted and never believed. Oh! We were not the good girls that we were portrayed to be. When we acquired marijuana which was often, we would simply tell our teachers that we had a meeting or activity to leave class early. Once we left a specific class, we would go to our secret location under a remote stairwell in the school and puff away. After smoking to our hearts were content, we returned to our class higher than a kite with no questions asked.

Aside from the activities and classroom work that I had in high school, my summer months were always tied up with something linked to education. I was chosen to represent my school in several different things, or my mother would enroll me in programs that included learning about legislation, music, attending summer enrichment programs for gifted students, Christian youth camps, and others. Of course, I had fun and gained a considerable amount of knowledge. My mother wanted to ensure that I was exposed to as many educational opportunities as possible. By the time I got to the twelfth grade, I was exhausted from the ongoing educational activities. You can say that I was burned out.

The climax to my high school years came with a four-year academic scholarship! My mother jumped for joy with this news. I was happy that my work in high school paid off, but quietly I was not thrilled about going to college at this time. Being thrust into so many sequential educational programs was draining for me and, I wanted to do something different going forward. Do not get me wrong, a college degree was something I desired, but just not now. There were documents that I needed to complete to receive my scholarship. With zero desire to attend college at this time, I hemmed and hawed as long as I could, and finally, I got the nerve to tell my mother that I did not want to go to college right now. I told her that I wanted to see the world and join the military. This broke my mother's heart. She fussed for a while, tried to convince me otherwise, and cried. I embraced her and assured my mom that I would get my degree.

After speaking with the recruiters, my mother was eventually at peace with my decision.

My challenge in seizing my opportunity to see the world was my weight. I only weighed eighty-five pounds and needed to weigh ninety-five pounds to enter the military. Bananas and potatoes became my friend. I guzzled a lot of them regularly to gain ten pounds. By the age of twenty-five, bananas and potatoes were no longer my friends. God was the furthest thing from my mind as a teenager. I did not consult Him about my decision. At this point in my life, I was unaware that I should. To boot, my prayer life was abysmal. This downward spiral continued for a few years.

In June 1978, I graduated with honors and began to pursue my military career in February 1979. My career choice was military intelligence (MI) which made my mother so proud. After completing basic training, I headed off to Fort Devens, Massachusetts for my MI training. When I was not in the classroom learning, I was at the pub partying and dancing the night away. You could not tell me that I was not the best dancer on the base. My trophies from dance competitions were proof of my dancing skills and also helped to swell my head. I never took the time to evaluate the lyrics to the music that I was dancing to either. I did not have a care in the world, I was singing the songs as much as I was dancing to them. Looking back, some of the lyrics were perverse.

During my stay at Fort Devens, I met Boom-Boom Washington who later joined the Women's Army Basketball team. She got that name because of her basketball skills as a point guard. Boom-Boom's incredible rhythm on the court led to back-to-back points. She would blow up the basketball hoop frequently. Boom-Boom and I were roommates. Like my close high school friend, she and I became besties at Fort Devens. You would think that the rhythm she had on the basketball court would translate on the dance floor. Well, she could not dance a lick or follow a beat and would turn down dance requests from attractive guys because of it. I helped her to learn some of the latest dance moves which tightened our friendship. Our training was completed in six months. At the end of it, Boom-Boom and I parted ways. She and I went to different permanent military duty stations and lost touch with one another. I thought, will I ever see Boom-Boom again? Sometimes people are in your lives for just a season. Yet, there are times when people from your past reappear for a deeper purpose in life (Eccles. 3:1-2).

Desolation

My first permanent duty station was overseas in the country of Korea. I was initially assigned to a strategic military site called Camp Humphreys in the city of Pyeongtaek. This was seen as a great assignment with many opportunities to gain experience, learn about a new culture, and explore a new horizon. The surroundings are picturesque and close to the big, exciting city of Seoul which is full of bright lights, nightlife, and theatres that mimic New York City. Wow! I was going to begin my new journey of seeing the world. My heart was skipping with happiness as I envisioned my journey until a disaster took place. At the processing station for incoming soldiers, I was informed that my orders have been changed and I was going to be diverted to a MI unit in the 2nd Infantry Division (2ndID) located on Camp Hovey. When I asked why, an officer that towered over me, emphatically stated that the 2ndID had priority over all soldiers entering the country. I was being moved to a tactical division instead of a strategic one. What a huge disappointment to say the least!

It was a two hours journey from the processing station to Camp Hovey. Within thirty minutes of the bus ride, civilization began to fade away. Skyscrapers, business-related buildings, stores, and attractions of any kind disappeared in thin air. The closer I got to Camp Hovey the more rural and desolate the surroundings became. The only visible thing was miles of rugged terrain and trees. Because the roads were tremendously rocky, my head was bobbing and weaving, and my body was bouncing toward the ceiling of the bus about every other mile. I felt like I was on a teeter-totter instead of a bus. As my body descended from the bounce, my back would hit a spring that was protruding from the back of my seat. At last, we got to my MI unit at Camp Hovey. The rough ride made me feel like I just got out of a brawl and, boy was my body sore from the fight.

Whom Shall I Use?

When I got off the bus, I could not believe my eyes and thought that my sense of smell was playing tricks on me. The air quality was unbelievably horrid. The smell of raw sewage on a sizzling summer day filled the air and remained a constant. As the saying goes, the stench was so bad, it knocked me to my knees. I gagged and held my stomach to keep from vomiting. There were no picturesque views. The base was filled with Quonset huts that looked like igloos. This was a structure I had never seen before; thus, their appearance was quite shocking to me. After briefly being greeted, I was taken to the place that was to be my humble abode for at least a year.

When I entered my new home, none of the women present said hello. Someone said, hey, your sleeping area is over there and pointed to it. In the area designated for me were a dilapidated, rusty twin bed frame and a makeshift closet. Where was the mattress? I asked someone if I was in the wrong place since the area designated for me seemed to be incomplete. Someone giggled and, another female soldier yelled you should be glad you got a bed frame, when I got here, I did not have that.

Then the person responsible for the barracks which were open bays (meaning no privacy) arrived. She told me where to locate a mattress. I had to go up a high hill to a destination about a mile away to get this mattress and bring it back down the hill to my new home. Where was the help? I was it! This was not an easy feat. Picture a ninety-five-pound 4'11" woman lifting and carrying a mattress longer than her body a mile down a hill. I was out of breath about midway home (if you want to call it home).

At one point, I sat that mattress on the ground and rested. When I got back up, I decided I was not going to carry this thing anymore. I began to drag it on one side down the rest of the hill. My rationale was if I drag the mattress only on one side, I will only need to clean one side when I arrive. About a block away from my Quonset hut, a male soldier offered to help me the rest of the way and, I accepted his offer because I was out of breath again. Where was he about an hour ago? He also spruced up my bed frame. There was a twinkle of expectation in his eyes and, I extended my hand and said thank you. Later, I acquired a dresser that mirrored the condition of my bed (dilapidated).

Following a thorough cleaning of my area and bed, I reviewed documents containing my instructions and requirements for the week. I did not have any energy left after the bus ride and the mattress exhibition, so I zonked out for a while. I awakened to take a shower and go to the bathroom. I walked around the hut two times to locate the shower and bathroom. Then, I found out that I had to go outside to a building to use the bathroom and shower. To get there, I had to walk over a long wooden plank with a Benjo ditch containing floating sewage beneath it. Early one morning, I was walking on this plank and turned my head to respond to someone. I slipped off the plank and fell in the ditch! I was covered with raw sewage from head to toe and felt violated. How disgusting it was! Scrubbing my body took on a whole new meaning following the fall and, I discarded my clothing. I wished I could have removed my skin too! Crossing the Benjo ditch was a daily necessity. I decided to spare your eyes from the graphic contents of the ditches. Your depiction is what the surroundings look like after God's intervention.

In September 1979, I had been in Korea for a month and got to know my fellow soldiers very well. Many of them wanted to show me a fun time and took me to Korean villages to explore the Korean nightlife. En route, I witnessed some despicable events. Some of the things that I saw were unconscionable to occur in the United States. Prostitution was legal and, there was a wide array of deplorable activities occurring in broad daylight every single day. People would openly urinate and defecate on the street. Multiple times, I would see men riding a three-speed bike with a refrigerator tied to their back and baskets on their heads full of food or objects. In my mind, I said that they are missing out on their calling; they should be making money performing acrobatics.

It was common for a female to confront you for sex and, I was not excluded. The sheer approach toward me by a prostitute was detestable to me and, they received some of my choice verbiage when they did. Considering the gravity of the events, I thought to myself, this is surely a God-forsaken place. This is not what I had in mind when I decided to see the world. How did I get myself in this predicament and how am I going to get myself out of it? I decided to suck it up and not let anyone see my disgust. My tour in Korea was thirteen months and, I was going to make the best of it.

Three months into my tour, I became a trusted member of the team and quite proficient in my job. This fostered my candidacy and selection for an elite position with the S-5 after being in Korea for six months. The S-5 team was responsible for assessing the condition and activities of communities, nightclubs, checking venereal disease cards of known prostitutes, eliminating black marketing, and, more. My new role meant that I no longer did the job I was originally assigned to do at my MI unit. My hours were often in the late afternoon and throughout the evening hours when events were at their peak.

We wore specialized jackets that permitted us in places prohibited for others and, this gave us power. With this power, we had the authority to close down establishments if they were not meeting requirements. Can you imagine how inflated my chest was? At the age of nineteen, I did not have to follow any traditional military rules and, I created my schedule. My chest was so big that I could easily inflate the big year blimp. Eliminating black marketing was a primary role of the team, except the team did far more black marketing themselves than eliminating it. Although I did not participate in black marketing, over time I became complicit. This is similar to being an accessory to a crime.

Because I was in an environment that was vile, You would think that I would have become a recluse. Well, that did not happen. I normalized my environment, elevated my party life, and silenced the Holy Spirit. The only women stationed at Camp Hovey were in my unit. The majority of the male soldiers behaved like fleas on a dog. I did not succumb to their repeated sexual enticements, so they retreated. The same soldiers began to function as my bodyguards. Whenever I would go to social events, someone was there looking after me. My S-5 position coupled with the protection of the male soldiers gave me a false sense of invincibility and protection until one night the unthinkable happened.

Turning Point

After showering one evening in March 1980, I started styling my hair and primping in the mirror. Then, I began to make funny faces in the mirror, simply having fun by myself. As I leaned my face closer to the mirror, my face became distorted. All of a sudden, my face resembled a monster far worse than any monster I had seen in a spooky movie. I scared myself and screamed. Quickly, I ran out of the bathroom to my hut, running as fast as I could while being mindful of the plank and Benjo ditch. I did not want to fall into that stinky ditch again. When I got to my area, I sat down with my head slumped over in total shock and disbelief. Did someone slip a drug of some sort into my food or drink? This could not have occurred since I was off duty and did not consume any alcohol or drugs. My socialization for the day was very limited. No, my monster face was not a hallucination.

With my head bowed, I grabbed my head and said to God what in the world is going on? What have I become? Had I become a quasit (demonic figure) in a Quonset hut? Lord, I know that you saved me. I picked up the Bible and begin to read and talk to God simultaneously. Through His Word, God started talking to me, slowly but surely. Over the next week, I received some divine revelations and chastisement that I needed from God. He revealed to me that the face I saw in the mirror was me. The word quasit is a new addition to my vocabulary provided by God in October 2021 to illustrate how I appeared in the mirror. You will not like what you see if you google the word. God indicated that I was vile and wicked. He allowed me to go thousands of miles from home to see it. Indeed, God revealed to me in His Word that apart from Him the best I could present is filthy rags (Isa. 64:6). He rebuked my self-righteousness, conceit, and pride that I paraded every day (2 Tim. 3:4). Then, God guided me to scriptures to show how much He loves me and, the steps I needed to take to reach a turning point.

The turning point started with my knees on the floor in my Quonset hut and my hands raised high in praise to God. My weeping saturated my blouse as I repented to God every time something I needed forgiveness for came into my spirit. My cup of repentance overflowed multiple times. Like King David, I gained a repenting heart. I was determined to humble myself and serve God (Acts 20:19, 1 Pet. 5:6, and, James 4:10). How could something so ugly (my monstrous face in the mirror) become a thing of beauty? God shared that the beauty was in the recognition and knowledge. I recognized that I had changed drastically and knew that the Lord was the only one who could transform me. The sewage that I thought I scrubbed from my body was entrenched in my character. Lord change me! Through His Word, I heard His voice and listened. This episode allowed me to acquire the knowledge of the truth (2 Tim.

3:7). God's forgiveness is immeasurable. Your repenting heart will never be ignored (Ps. 51:17).

It was now mid-March of 1980, and my departure from Korea was quickly approaching. Throughout the next month, I immersed myself in the Word of God. After work, I resisted the urge to attend any social events to reduce the chances of reverting to my old self (Eph. 4:27). It worked. My new orders arrived and, I was now going to a MI unit in Fort Bragg, North Carolina. My peers knew I was leaving soon, but I did not share the actual date. I flew out of Korea in April 1980 without saying goodbye. As extraverted as I am, I desired to leave quietly and tiptoe out of the country without fan fair. I did just that. This behavior is atypical of me. I simply wanted to end this chapter of my life discretely.

After leaving Korea, I was looking forward to relaxing and spending time with my family in Delaware. I could not wait to share my Korean experiences with my family. My sisters were bursting with laughter as I told detailed accounts of the events I witnessed. I am sure they thought that I was joking about my experiences. My mother looked straight into my eyes and knew it was real. She patted me on my back as she walked into another room as if to say, I'm glad you got through it.

My two-week vacation ended and my journey with God started to bud in May 1980. It seems like only yesterday that I was stationed at Fort Bragg, North Carolina. My recollection of this period of my life is very vivid. First of all, I arrived at this base a few days before my twentieth birthday. As I evaluated my environment this time, my assessment was the polar opposite of Korea. Spring crisply filled the air with aromatic flowers, lush trees, and dark green grass. As the wind blew, the aroma of the trees and flowers traveled to my nose and was such a welcoming scent. Wow! No more wilderness (at least I thought). I completed several briefings and a routine orientation in two days. Following this, I was assigned a room with two roommates. We were all assigned to the same MI unit. This abode was very much like a college dormitory (dorm). Each person had their own private space and, we shared a bathroom. Outside of the room, there was a communal living area. In this space, there was a TV, table, and chairs for individuals or groups to socialize, relax and have group-related functions.

On May 13th, I was informed that our MI unit had a new Command Sergeant Major (CSM) whose background was special forces. The gossip mill indicated that he was not happy with the caliber of the soldiers in my unit and planned to make some radical changes. The same day, I was told that I would be going to training for two weeks in the field (the woods) on the following day which would be my birthday. Of course, I did not want to celebrate my birthday in the woods. I asked if I could speak with the CSM to hopefully appeal to his good graces. He agreed to speak with me. I shared that I had recently arrived at the base and that tomorrow was my birthday so, I was not ready to go to the field. The CSM sneered, opened his desk drawer, gave me a candy bar, and said, Happy Birthday soldier, you will learn a lot in the field. Under my breath, I said are you kidding me! I just left the woods and the wilderness. I could not catch a break!

Off to the field I went, toting a rucksack containing fifty pounds of gear on my back until we set up the site. The weight of the gear pushed my little body into a downward position. This forced me to walk looking at the ground. Every now and then, a soldier that was walking behind me would lift my rucksack so I could walk upright. Despite being in the woods on my birthday and beyond, the stay in the woods turned out okay. I learned that there were many Christians in my unit, and some were eager to start a Bible study group when we returned to base. At night, I was able to read my Word, memorize scripture and get closer to God. There were times in the field when I was able to talk to others about God and the scriptures which was a pleasure.

Face to Face with the Enemy

Because I left the base for the field shortly after my arrival, I did not get to know my roommates. During the summer months, I spent some time with them at lunch, dinner, military or community events. At the same time, I was making observations regarding their behavior and mannerisms. There was no judgment of any kind. However, I could not ignore the peculiarity of one of my roommates. One, in particular, walked like Morticia from an old TV show called The Addams family. Whether she was walking or remained stationary, she murmured to herself and, there was always something white oozing from the sides of her mouth. Rarely did she look you straight in the eye when speaking to you. Either her head was bowed or turned to one side when she conversed. Initially, I thought she was shy, but by and by I learned differently.

In mid-July, the Bible study group formed and, we alternated places to study. The communal area located right outside of my room was the place chosen when it was my turn to lead. Bible study became a constant in my life and, we had the group study every week. One Bible study evening at my place, the group was in the middle of a deep dialogue about the meaning of some scriptures. In addition, we took turns reading various passages of scripture. All of a sudden, my roommate who walked like Morticia, stormed out of the dorm room to our location dressed in full satanic witch attire, bellowing some chants that were unrecognizable to us. She had on a long black robe that extended past her shoes, a black hat, and some sort of scroll or stick in her hand.

I stood up in disbelief with my eyes bulging out of my head and began quoting scriptures and the others in the Bible study group did the same. Scriptures came from the depth of my soul that I did not know were there. Studying the Word of God and memorizing scripture paid off (2 Tim. 2:15). The Holy Spirit rebuked her spirit repeatedly and the white oozing was no longer just from the sides of her mouth. It was now foam and flowing from her entire mouth and drooling down her chin. The foaming proliferated with the continued utterance of the scriptures. God was dealing with this demonic force. **Oh my God! My roommate was a real witch!**

Never, in my wildest dream would I have imagined that I would be confronted by the enemy in this manner! Living with a witch is unthinkable.

Unlike my face in the mirror in Korea, I had no fear of my roommate or any demonic force dwelling in her. This ordeal led to the beginning of my understanding of the scripture: For we wrestle not against flesh and blood, but against principalities, against powers, against the rulers of the darkness of this world, against spiritual wickedness in high places (Eph. 6:12). Like me, you may wonder what made her storm out of the room? Although I do not know it to be true, I believe that the scriptures we were sharing in our study group penetrated through the walls of my room and, her demonic spirit was being tormented and vexed to the point of intolerance.

What happened to my roommate the rest of the evening or the next day is a blur, but I do know when I saw her at work a couple of days afterward, she was not the same. She did not ooze anymore and held decent conversations with a smile while looking you straight in your eyes. **Halleluiah, God set her free!** The miracle in this event was the Holy Spirit's intervention and action. God used us to quote scripture to defeat this demon and revealed to me yet again how powerful and mighty He is!

Reflections and Movement Forward (Chapter I)

God had you in mind before this book was written. It is His desire and mine that there be interaction with you throughout the book. Below are some thoughts and or questions about the preceding chapter for you to introspectively examine and determine with Jesus how to move forward. Some scriptures have been added after the questions or thoughts to assist you with your internal assessment. It is recommended that you pray either before or after reading the questions to allow God to speak to your heart. The Lord will respond. Focus on the Lord during this time as much as possible.

Question 1: Lord search the reigns of my heart and reveal any unconfessed sin (Ps. 26:2 and, 1 John 1:9).

_____

_____

_____

Question 2: Lord reveal to me any aspect of my life that makes me feel unworthy to serve and be used by you (Job 22:2).

_____

_____

_____

Question 3: Lord am I blocking your ability to use me (2 Tim. 2:21)? If so, how?

_____

_____

_____

Question 4: Lord manifest any form or feeling of abandonment and rejection that has wounded me to a point that you are not able to use me (2 Cor. 4:8-10).

_____

_____

_____

Question 5: Lord, where do I go from here (Ps. 32:8)?

_____

_____

_____

CHAPTER II

WHEN GOD SPEAKS

A New Season

My Christian walk became less feeble at Fort Bragg. I felt God's presence, but my maturation appeared to be a light-year away. Fellowship at a local church became an essential part and highlight of my week. Bible study continued and the group expanded. An opportunity to learn my role at a strategic base in Misawa, Japan was offered to me. If I said yes, I would be assigned to Misawa on an interim basis for three months. There was much to gain by going and nothing to lose. Going to Japan would mean that at last, I would get to learn the strategic component of my job that I yearned for since 1979. Going to Japan would also expand my quest to see the world so, I said yes!

In January 1981, I boarded the aircraft bound for Misawa Japan which was 6,628 miles away from Fort Bragg and over a thirteen-hour flight. After the take-off, I got fairly comfortable in my seat while glancing out of the window periodically. About mid-way, God began to boldly speak to me. He called my name to get my attention. I was in tune and ready to listen. God said when you get to Misawa, Boom-Boom was going to be there and, you are to share the gospel of Jesus Christ with her. As Christians, we are all called to do the work of an evangelist (2 Tim. 4:5). There is no requirement to be an evangelist or a minister to share the gospel of Jesus Christ.

There was never any doubt that the Lord was speaking nor was there any doubt that Boom-Boom was going to be there. The Lord expects us to follow His instructions out of love for Him and obedience (Luke 6:46 and, 2 John 1:6). It was over three years since I had seen or spoken to Boom-Boom Washington. As my life progressed and new horizons developed, Boom-Boom Washington was forgotten. Nevertheless, she was on God's heart and now rekindled in mine. After God finished giving me my instructions, I had flashbacks of our time at Fort Devens, Massachusetts. I was no longer the fly party girl, but a budding Christian seeking to follow and serve God. Was Boom-Boom going to be the same? A person's life experiences have a way of shaping or reshaping belief systems and behavior. After putting my curiosity to bed, I relaxed and enjoyed the festivities on the flight.

After a long flight that included an unexpected delay in Toyoko, the plane landed in Misawa and, it was the dead of winter. The military assigned someone to pick me up from the airport who was present when I arrived. It was bitterly cold when I went outside. The sky was hastily showering snow with razor-sharp wind gusts that could cut your skin. Korea was a very cold place, however, Misawa topped it considerably. Since it was the weekend, I was taken to my temporary quarters after checking in at their headquarters. My housing was suitable (Thank the Lord)! After unpacking my bags, I decided to venture outside with hopes of having a much-needed walk after sitting on the plane for a long time. In several areas, the snowdrifts were deeper than five feet. Do you know what would happen to me? It means that the snowdrifts would bury me alive.

If I wanted to walk on the sidewalk or in principal areas, it was trial and error. At one point, the snow in my pathway was up to my neck. To survive, I walked on the edge of the street to get to my destination. Because I just arrived, no one knew me. If I were swallowed by a snowdrift, I would not have been missed. My buried little body would have resembled a snowman that some child made and remained unnoticed.

The weekend ended and now, it was time to go to work. Overjoyed with the opportunity to learn the strategic component of my profession, a smile stayed on my face for days. I was transported from my temporary quarters to work for the duration of my three months stay. When I arrived at this strategic site, I was star-struck. The building, equipment, and electronics were far more sophisticated than my tactical assignments. I was like a kid in a candy store during my initial training. A few days passed and there was no sight of Boom. Where was she? Once her name re-emerged in my heart and mind, there she appeared. We both screamed out of pure joy and embraced! Boom said, I just found out that you were here. At this point, I did not let her know that God told me that she would be in Misawa. I kept this a secret for a while. Likewise, the timing was not right to share the gospel.

We decided to meet after work to become reacquainted with one another. This was a new season that I did not expect Boom to be a part of at all. God had this reunion planned long ago and, what He had in store for Boom was even better! She introduced me to a restaurant called Ubagami which is still operating today. I can still smell and taste the blend of their grilled shrimp and pasta dish with a sauce that adhered to the pasta perfectly. Ubagami became our meeting place and dinner site. Within a month, it seemed like old times minus the pub. The nightlife never surfaced as an interest; our conversations focused on our career paths for a while.

One night, Boom came to my quarters. This night was different. Something was on her mind or troubling her. God pricked me and let me know that tonight is the night to share the gospel. To determine who or what she was trusting in for her salvation, I asked her some questions. The responses made it apparent that she was basing her trust on what she believed to be good works, but she was not sure if she was going to heaven. **Shortly thereafter, I had my first out-of-body experience with the Lord!** The Holy Spirit started sharing many scriptures that led to her repentance and acceptance of Jesus Christ as Lord and her Savior! I was there, the scriptures were coming out of my mouth, but God took over and performed all of the work.

The Lord was doing the speaking but using my voice. I was the chosen vessel used to deliver the gospel. God knew what she needed. I did not. Glory to God! After she accepted the Lord, I told her Happy Birthday and gave her some information relating to her conversion. She became extremely thirsty for the Word of God. Her thirst kept me on my toes and sharpened my reading and understanding of the scriptures. There was mutual excitement in exploring the Word of God.

During lunch, we would discuss scriptures that we had previously agreed to read. Sometimes, others would quietly listen. We intended to penetrate the souls of those who were listening. The Lord wants us to make effective use of every opportunity (Col. 4:5). Our discussions of the Word branched into the work section. We verbally gave one another an uplifting scripture each day that others could hear. Then, all hell broke loose and, Satan began his attack. From the onset, there were rolling of the eyes and hand gestures that signaled unacceptance when we would share a scripture either face to face or by passing a leaflet to each other(1 Thess. 5:11). Most assuredly, there were atheists among us who snarled as we walked by or would say that God did not exist loud enough to ensure that we would hear them (Ps. 53:1).

Boom and I continued to praise the Lord! Nothing stopped us (Ps. 34:1 and, Heb. 13:15)! The devil was angry and raised his level of attack with a specific target in mind. The target was me! False accusations against me became insurmountable. They were never proven and dispelled as gossip. Because that did not work, my professionalism and competence were now under heavy scrutiny. Those who made verbal and nonverbal gestures regarding Christianity were the source of the attacks. They painted a picture that I was incompetent and incapable of intercepting and analyzing the far eastern intelligence that I was well trained to perform. Some of the leaders were buying what they were selling.

Based on these false claims, someone was assigned to evaluate everything I did and fabricated erroneous errors. None of it was true and, I was being set up to fail. They were on a mission to make me second guess myself, become fearful of them, and send me back to Fort Bragg early with egg on my face. Their actions were blatant persecution, directly linked to my profession of faith and Boom's new conversion (Matt. 5:11). I had become their problem. For about a month, I was subjected to repeated sarcastic remarks in an open forum, treated as inept, and ostracized. My concerns regarding their biases were communicated to leadership and, they responded accordingly. The God we serve will never let Satan win despite what it looks like. The collective goal was to devour me, but my enemies who were the Lord's enemies stumbled and fell before me(Ps. 27:2).

A new proctor who happened to be a strong Christian was assigned to evaluate my work. He piped into my system from another desk and intercepted the same intelligence data at the same time that I intercepted it. Afterward, he evaluated my work in comparison to his. He did this day after day. His work mirrored mine every day and he shared his findings with the upper leadership who realized the prior litany of fabrication. I received an apology and understood that administrative action was taken against the perpetrators. God rescued me from the persecution (2 Tim. 3:11). Although I was wronged, there was no vengeance in my heart and, I did not desire or pray for something to happen to any of them. Our flesh wants to repay evil with evil. This is not God's way (Rom. 12:17). Vengeance belongs to God alone (Heb. 10:30 and, Deut. 32:35). God let me know that Satan was at work, and, he will use anyone that will allow him to operate. Be not mistaken, God's work is always superior!

It is remarkable to note that God took me 6,628 miles to be a part of someone's new birth. God reminded me of this event in September 2021. Certainly, I will never forget it again. I cannot ignore the aftermath. God wanted to reveal His power in defeating the enemy and demonstrated that His love never fails us (Lam. 3:33, 1 Cor. 13:8, and, Ps. 136:12-13). Boom-Boom was surrounded by atheists in Misawa for a long time before my arrival with no armor. God used me like a ram in the bush. She is now endowed with salvation, the Holy Spirit, and equipped for spiritual warfare (2 Tim. 3:16-17). Indeed, she entered into a new season and, there was a new season blossoming for someone else (Eccles. 3:1).

Remember the Christian proctor that was assigned to evaluate my work? He and I became friends and I got to know his wife very well. Both of them were strong Christians with two young children. I began to fellowship with them and attend their church.

His wife and I became such great friends that they offered me to stay at their home instead of my temporary quarters. Being a single woman, I was reluctant. Her husband's shift did not coincide with mine, therefore, his wife convinced me to stay. Although she worked part-time, we spent a lot of time together while her husband worked. When she worked, I was the babysitter. Doing our time together, she poured her heart out to me. Many nights she cried like a baby and, all I could do was hold her.

The source of her pain was the previous infidelity in her marriage. She remained with her husband for the sake of the children, but she never forgave him. This led to bitterness and distrust. Based on some of the examples she conveyed, Satan had set up shop in their home and was doing all he could to destroy their marriage (Eph. 4:26-27). God used me to delicately minister to her. As a single woman, I could not advise her on marriage. What I could provide was my testimony and supporting scriptures relating to the circumstances that God brought me through when I was struggling with unforgiveness and relationships. Forgiveness is without limits or boundaries (Matt. 18:21-27).

She began to petition God for guidance. What about her husband? Bringing anything to his attention would give the appearance that I was prying. I chose to pray. God revealed to her the aspects of her life that required repentance. Within a few weeks, she started laughing more and singing around the house; leaving the impression that the heavy burden she was carrying was lighter. Before long, she stopped throwing verbal stones at her husband and became fixated on self-restoration. Her partnership with God led to forgiveness and reconciliation of their marriage. God used me as a mediator toward their reconciliation. Satan's shop was destroyed. Praise the Lord!

If we do not forgive others, God will not forgive our sins (Matt. 6:14-15). Confronting his sin as his wife is grounded in scripture. If he repents, God also requires that she forgive him (Luke 17:3 and, Matt. 18:15). If someone expresses sincere sorrow and asks for forgiveness, will you forgive them? Unforgiveness will torture your soul and destroy your mental wellness.

As my time began to wind down in Misawa, my soul was overjoyed with God the Father, God the Son, and God the Holy Spirit (the trinity). What a mighty God we serve! God manifested Himself in every form during my stay in Misawa. God was and is omnipotent, omniscient, and omnipresent. God is all-powerful, all-knowing, and present everywhere (Rom. 11:33, Ps. 145:3, and, Ps. 46:1). If God is all of this, why does He need any assistance? He does not. God does not need anyone or anything to accomplish His mission. Instead, He wants to partner with His children to advance His kingdom. Here is the thing, His children must want to partner with Him. Think about that for a minute. The God we serve is after our hearts. He desires willing vessels who love Him. He does not force Himself on us or treat us like a puppet. God desires a reciprocal love relationship which we see expressed in a good marriage (1Chron. 28:9, Luke 9:23, and, John 3:39).

Why did God use me to witness to Boom? There is nothing particularly special about me. As the Bible says, He searches and examines the heart. Despite my hiccups, He knows my heart and mind (Jer. 17:10). Secondly, He tested me. I did not know that this event was a test until October 16, 2021. Remember when I was on the plane headed to Misawa? He gave me specific instructions. My mind was not cluttered at this time of my life; allowing me to hear and know His voice, hear and obey His instructions. In other words, I was and am readily available to be used by God. Is Jesus your Lord if you do not follow His instructions? (Luke 6:46). The Almighty is one of action. He set the captive free (Boom), exposed and dealt with demonic forces, and reconciled a marriage destined for divorce. Knowing my God, someone else in that military building repented and turned to the Lord as a result of hearing the Word of God, witnessing false persecution, and seeing the change God made in Boom's life. I like to think that God used me to start the fire and, I left Misawa on fire for the Lord!

After returning to Fort Bragg in late April 1981, I was wanting more of Jesus. How was I to keep this fire burning? I did not have a clue. A handsome man appeared at work that turned my head. He was a fine specimen of a man with hazel eyes and pecan-colored skin. He dressed impeccably and, if I did not know any better, I would have thought he was a runway model. Good looks were not the only thing he had going for him. He was a perfect gentleman with a beautiful tenor voice and could sing like a canary. Where in the world did he come from? He pursued me relentlessly and would sing to me in public. I successfully quelled the temptation for a little while but soon, I was like ice melting in his hands. I fell totally off the track, and you know the rest of the story. This is not the end of the saga. I was committed and engaged to someone else. My fiancé was stationed elsewhere, and Mr. Gorgeous knew of the engagement. Because of my commitment, this lustful relationship was severed.

In September of the same year, I got married. It took some time before I repented, but I did. Why did I delay my repentance? Did I think that God would not forgive me or was I enjoying the sin that I was in? In reality, it was the latter. In the end, neither fellow was an ideal mate for me.

In December 1981, Big Daddy (Elder Lenster Lumpkin) transitioned. My mother shared that when he was in the hospital, he predicted the date of his death and said to her that death had no sting (1 Cor. 15:55). Big Daddy went into a coma on the day he predicted and went to live with Jesus on the same day. I was granted the time off to attend my grandfather's services that were held at his church in Detroit on Lumpkin Street.

As a child of the King, the Bible tells us that when our spirit man leaves the body it joins the presence of the Lord (2 Cor. 5:8). Thus, the term funeral service is not preferred in my family. We typically use the term homegoing service. Big Daddy's services were not what I expected. I anticipated a lot of mourning and crying, but this was a service of celebration. My uncle Morris who was also an elder and a pastor kept moving me closer and closer to Big Daddy's casket and the heart of the praise and worship with our family. I resisted his movements somewhat, by slowly moving forward. Besides, I did not want to end up in the casket with my grandfather. My uncle kept telling me to look at my grandfather. For a few minutes, I was a little angry with the people present including my family. The nerve of them having an enjoyable time at the expense of my grandfather's death. I did not like it one bit. Once I heard his eulogy given by my uncles, I understood why everyone was rejoicing. He lived a life in service to God which was worth celebrating and emulating.

When I got back to Fort Bragg, I got an apartment off base. The celebration of my grandfather's transition stayed on my mind for a long time. I remember telling God when I was praying that I wanted Him to give me whatever it was that my grandfather possessed. Although it initially seemed awkward for people to be laughing and singing at his services, I said to myself what manner of man is this? He told his children when he was departing earth and he did, and now he is being celebrated as though he was a king. What did he have that made others behave like this? What he had was an intimate relationship with God. At the age of twenty-one, I could not say that I had this. Yet, I desperately wanted to have it, the sooner the better. God, how are you going to fill this void?

Living Manna

I went to the throne of grace more than once requesting to find a teaching church that was on fire for God and, one that would be an agent for my spiritual maturation and, relationship with God. The Word tells us that if any of you lacks wisdom, you should ask God, who gives generously to all without finding fault (James 1:5). This is definitely a scripture for me. I needed His guidance, most assuredly I lacked wisdom and was still full of faults (sin). After the new year of 1982, a new platoon sergeant by the name of Dean Graham came on the scene. Dean was a seasoned Christian who talked about Jesus often at work. He was well respected and quite a conversationalist.

He extended an invitation to his church called Manna. It was on Cliffdale Road, which was nearby my apartment. Therefore, my husband and I decided to attend. Walking to the church seemed foreign, the church did not have the customary presentation. Instead, it resembled a school or university. Later, I found out that they had a college and an elementary school on campus. Dean was waiting for us in the lobby area. As we entered the sanctuary, Dean walked off and left us. Why in the world did he leave us? We did not know these people. Within seconds, a countless number of saints introduced themselves with big bear hugs. Their embraces were awkward, as I was not accustomed to strangers hugging or touching me, nor did I want it. Nevertheless, everything they expressed was out of love.

To add to my discomfort, no one in the sanctuary looked like me except Dean and, he disappeared. Dean intentionally left us to see what our reaction would be to the saints and the church as a whole. He eventually joined us. The sermon for the day spoke to my heart and the pastor was on fire! The first checkmark was satisfied. Every Sunday, I looked forward to receiving manna. This was a great teaching church that fed me constantly. Homegroup studies throughout the week were an integral part of continual praise, worship, and my spiritual maturation. My active involvement in a homegroup increased my knowledge and understanding of the Bible exponentially. Finally, all of my checkmarks were fulfilled and, I joined the church. I was all in!

One Sunday, Pastor Fletcher was ministering on unforgiveness. There was a segment of the sermon whereby he asked everyone to bow their heads and ask God to reveal any unforgiveness in their hearts. I thought this event was useless. Out of obedience, I prayed and asked the Lord if I had any unforgiveness with the expectation of receiving nothing since I did not believe it existed. Without haste, God brought to my memory a big episode of unforgiveness. Not only did He bring it to my mind, but God also presented the full visual account in living color when I was praying. When I was a youngster, my stepdad gave me a spanking that I did not believe I deserved. Over time, I tucked the event away in my heart, forgot about it, and never forgave my stepdad. Repentance and forgiveness followed the conclusion of my prayer and, I stood in awe of God. God knows what is in the most sacred places of your heart. Did I deserve the spanking? The bottom line: I earned it. Is there any unforgiveness sequestered in your heart? Ask the Lord.

My willingness to repent and forgive unbridled the Holy Spirit mightily in my life. Like Boom, I had a thirst for God that was not easily quenched. God supplied all of my needs and we became friends. I talk to God like I talk to my earthly friends with straight and frank conversation. I remember telling God that I thought some of the books of the Bible were boring and, He needed to give me visuals and create some excitement when reading the Bible. The boredom I experienced made it difficult to finish the books in the Old Testament. God says in the latter part of James 4:2 that you have not because you ask not. Well, I asked and, He delivered beyond my expectations.

This time and even now, I can see and hear the plots in the Bible unfold and thicken. God has allowed me to hear the chariots in the streets, visualize the battles and see the characters. Some of the visuals that left permanent impressions in my mind are Abraham's foreshadowing of the sacrificial lamb, the battles between King David's sons, and the physical appearances of Nebekenezer and Jonah. Because God the Father knows us and relates to us on our level, He presented modern-day interpretations for me. The visual that God gave me of Nebekenezer reminds me somewhat of a boxing promoter. He had wild hair on the sides and the back of his head and, his head was bald in the center. His fingernails were long and curled under as he lay in the middle of a jungle on a bed of briar patches. Jonah resembled a Casanova. He was wearing a well-fitted polo shirt and slacks along with expensive gold chains on his neck with a neatly tapered haircut.

What a miraculous and uplifting experience! Just a few years ago, my girlfriend laughed when I shared with her how exciting the Book of Numbers is and what God allowed me to see. Not only did God make the Bible exciting to read, but He was also depositing the meaning and application of the scriptures deep in my spirit at the same time. The Lord's deposits were through Manna Church and my time with Him. God does actively listen to us and will honor our request if it is aligned with His will and purpose for your life. As a Christian, understanding the concept that God had a specific purpose, plan, and will for my life did not register with me for years. The scope of walking in my full will and purpose was not in the realm of my thinking for a decade. Yet, God's plan for me was unfolding without my recognition. If you were able to acquire this knowledge at an early age, good for you. Share your secret with a Christian that is struggling with this.

First the Demonstration

In 1982, I was on a spiritual high with the Lord that I did not want to end. You know, you can have as much of God as you want. If you come near to God, He will come near to you (James 4:8). I thirsted for more and, He was faithful to give me more of what I wanted and needed. Manna wanted to expand their outreach and equip their members to share the gospel. They chose a teaching approach called Evangelism Explosion (EE). The premise of the training was to learn an outline grounded in scripture that would lead a person to willingly accept Jesus Christ as Lord and their Savior. Those who completed the training would in turn become trainers and advance to a trainer of trainers with a certain level of experience under their belts.

The training seemed intriguing and, I became a student and subsequently a trainer. We would visit individuals who visited the church first. Out of all the things that I have ever done in my life, sharing the gospel of Jesus with others is the most enriching and gratifying. Every Saturday, I rushed to the church ready to go into the community. The first out-of-body experience that I shared with you concerning Boom-Boom Washington was woven into the fabric of my being. Thoughts of the Lord emerging the same way through this program crossed my mind. Prayer was the first component of witnessing. It took place before leaving the church and when God pricked me to begin witnessing.

Every time I share the gospel or a word from the Lord (past and present), the Holy Spirit takes over and, I fully surrender. When this occurs, I am acutely aware of the precise moment when the Holy

Spirit takes control. God tends to add or take from the planned outline. As always, He knows exactly what each person needs. At the end of the visitation timeline, each team would report back to the church and share what happened during their witnessing opportunities. The reports were always heartfelt and moving. Little did anyone know; I was holding onto the edge of my seat and close to exploding because I was very eager to share what God did through our team.

God was faithful in saving someone and usually more than one person every visitation that I can remember. Soon, the EE team at large anxiously awaited my report. Because God was faithful in saving people through my team and awesomely used me constantly, I was jokingly coined an evangelist. I laughed and never received the title in my spirit. There was no ordination planned and not an inkling of it in my mind.

On one particular Saturday morning, I skipped to church ready to continue what God started. Who will God save today? We had exhausted all of the prospects. Those we went to visit were not at home. Given that God had ordained this appointed time to witness, I was not going to forfeit this divine appointment. I prayed and asked God what to do and where to go. Yes, God was now my chief consultant. God put Hay Street on my heart. I told my team and, some of them reared their bodies backward in hesitation. You need to know why they hesitated. At the time, Hay Street was a street known for prostitution. Some of the team members were afraid of what they may encounter while others were simply embarrassed to be seen there. I was neither. What a change God made in my life.

The mere sight of a prostitute used to be repugnant to me. If you recall my days in Korea, a prostitute would receive a verbal lashing if she came near me. The same people that I once believed were an abomination and vile, I now wanted to express how much God loves them and, I was compelled to do it. Whether my team was on board or not, I had to follow God's instructions (Luke 6:46 and, Matt. 7:21). All of the team members got on board. As we speak, I am smiling as I think about how our God of action moved. He saved seven women on Hay Street that day. Glory to God!

We were late getting back to the church. There was no way I was going to disturb the Holy Spirit and disrupt what God was doing. When we returned to the church and shared our testimonies and God's performance, there was not a dry eye in the building. The icing on the cake was seeing some of the women from Hay Street visit the church and become active. Who am I to call a child of God in the making vile? Did I forget about that woman in the mirror and my vile state? Heaven forbids.

To the Rescue

Of course, Satan is always on the prowl. He is lurking to see what he could destroy or use as a source of ridicule. One of my younger sisters named Crystal moved to Fayetteville, North Carolina to live with me. She had hopes of starting a new life there. At the time, I did not have daily access to a car. Therefore, I had to walk to some of my destinations if a friend was not available to assist. The grocery store was across the highway on Fort Campbell Boulevard. It was about a mile away, but there was always heavy traffic on this road. We needed to pick up some groceries and decided to walk. Both of us were in decent shape and youthful. Walking a mile to the store did not appear to be a problem. We sprinted across the highway when it was safe. Once we exited the store with two bags each in our hands, the sky became pitch black. Unexpectedly, a downpouring of torrential rains like those that accompany a tornado came and began to flood the area. Crystal and I were drenched from head to toe. It took all that we had to hold on to the groceries that were saturated with as much water as we had on our bodies. It was a blessing that the bags did not completely collapse. We were in the middle of the store parking lot and had less than a mile to get home, but the heavy rain shut down our visibility making the destination seem like ten miles instead of one. Have you ever walked a mile in my shoes?

We got colder and wetter with every inch that we moved forward. Before we knew it, our bodies and teeth were shivering and chattering with chills. Our shoes were so soggy they could no longer keep our feet dry. Because of all of this, it was impossible to outrun the rain. It was like we were drowning while standing. We were miserable and at a loss as to how to do anything differently. Our focus was on getting home safely and, there was no way to circumvent the highway. To get home, crossing the busy highway with the added element of danger due to the weather was a must.

I could not ignore the feeling that someone was watching us and laughing. I realized that the enemy was enjoying our calamity. I did not say a word to give him any gratification. Out of nowhere, a cab came from the back of the Food Lion grocery store with its headlights on, heading directly toward us. Wait a minute. This was a grocery store, not an airport. Cabs do not hang out here. As much as I shopped at this grocery store, not once did I ever see a cab. **Then, I realized that God sent this cab to rescue us (Ps. 69:13-14)!** Neither one of us had a telephone to call a cab. Back then, I don't think cellular telephones existed. If they did, I could not afford one. Regardless, we did not call for or expect a cab.

We were going to walk at a snail's pace and get home whenever we could. How did the cab know to approach us? Who knows what God shared with the cab driver beforehand? The cab driver took us home without charging us a dime. I know that the cab was a divine rescue, and it was a gift to me for being a willing partner of His work on Hay Street (2 Sam. 22:19-20). Thank you, God, for using and gifting me with Manna Church and more. God awakened my spirit and put me on solid ground at Fort Bragg, Manna Church, and the city of Fayetteville. Greatest of all, He granted me a partnership with Him to expand His kingdom. I will be forever grateful. No longer am I a germinated seed or a Christian bud. My road to spiritual maturity was being paved.

The end of my four-year military commitment was nigh. Staying in the military was a glimmer of possibility for me. In my mind, the only way that I would be willing to stay in the military would be an assignment to Hawaii which seemed to be a needle in a haystack. As the Lord would have it, I received orders for Hawaii and, I reenlisted. I guess needles in haystacks can be found and, God hears your quietest whisper. Ultimately, my request was granted because it was aligned with the Lord's will (1 John 5:14 and, John 8:47). The sheer beauty of Hawaii had me pumped up and ready to continue on my journey. This time, I was going with God and wondered what He had in store.

I flew to Hawaii in the spring of 1983. My sponsor picked me up from the airport as planned. My spouse was finalizing some business matters so, I flew unaccompanied. Some of the friends I made at a prior MI unit were at my new unit in Hawaii. It did not take long to find a great church and start fellowshipping with other believers. Some of the believers that I fellowshipped with were co-workers. My acclimation to an unfamiliar environment was easier because of this. At last, I have a true strategic assignment that became a gift.

Approximately two months after my arrival, I was not feeling like my normal self. I had this light constant headache and some queasiness. On a hunch, I took a pregnancy test, and I was pregnant. My spouse and I were ecstatic. I was now twenty-three and going to be a mother. My fire for God was blazing hot. I clinched every opportunity that I received to share the gospel or my testimony.

From time to time, I had some discomfort that felt like something was pulling or stretching in my abdomen area. This was due to my pregnancy I thought. Perhaps, my cervix was expanding to accommodate the growth of the baby. Because the awkward feeling and discomfort did not subside, I went to see a doctor who said I had a cyst and what I was feeling would go away. With this diagnosis, I continued with my daily routine although it turned out to be a misdiagnosis.

Two of my co-workers moved to new apartments or homes within a brief period of each other. I helped both of them move which included deep cleaning, packing, and lifting. It was my pleasure to help. After dinner at my friend's house, his wife took me home since my car had not arrived in Hawaii yet. On that night, God started speaking to me in a very concerned tone. His words kept being repeated over and over again. This was something God wanted me to address quickly. His resounding words were Sabrina, you are bleeding, you are bleeding internally. I went to the bathroom and blood was coming from the two main exit points of my body. I quickly called my friend's wife who had just dropped me off to see if she would take me to the hospital. It was raining and, she shared that her windshield wipers were not working. She then asked her husband to drive, and she came with him to take me to the hospital.

I was taken to Tripler Army Hospital and wheeled into the Emergency Department (ED). While I was in the ED, a sudden urge to go to the bathroom emerged. Nothing but blood appeared in the toilet and, I alerted someone. I was rushed into a room where a procedure called a culdocentesis was performed. Immediately there was a big gushing sound similar to a water faucet running on full throttle. The noise I was hearing was blood pouring from my body into a syringe connected to an eighteen-gauge needle that they inserted in my body. Urgently, I was prepped for surgery. As I was being rushed to the operating room on the gurney, all I remember is shouting my blood type.

When I awakened, my bed was surrounded by a sea of white coats. Several doctors from various disciplines were marveling at my survival. One physician blatantly stated we do not know how you are still alive. I had a ruptured ectopic pregnancy that was present for three months or more, which the doctors stated was incompatible with life. I still remember the surgeon saying to me: "never take the medication scopolamine again because you were saying some strange things." Hallelujah, God rescued, saved, and healed me(Ps. 41:3 and, Matt. 19:2)! At a later time, the Lord revealed to me that I was not saying strange things on the operating room table. My spirit was crying out to God in my prayer language (Ps. 18:6, Ps. 40:1, and, Rom. 8:26). What seemed foreign to the clinicians was readily understood by the Lord. My spirit and mind were in synchronized prayer and, the Lord had mercy on me; His servant (Ps. 102:1 and, 1 Cor. 14:13-15).

Let us ponder over this event for a minute. Was my healing delayed? God could have healed me when He made me aware of the bleeding at my home. I believe and the Bible says that God performs miracles so others may believe (John 4:48). My friends, my healing and survival were indeed other miracles performed by God. My healing was not delayed. It was right on time! Somebody in that operating room or hospital became a believer or was divinely touched by God because of my healing. Everything God does is purposeful. How and why this happened to me is unclear, but He used me, nonetheless. One thing that is quite transparent is the fact that God still has plans for me and, those plans are bright (Jer. 29:11)! This miraculous event became a key element of my testimony about the Lord.

Within six weeks, I returned to work and my spouse arrived. From a technological standpoint, my work environment at Field Station Kunia in Hawaii was as swank as the arrangement in Misawa, Japan. If I had to select which place, I preferred, it would be Hawaii because there were more Christians in the environment. Where there are Christians, you can rest assured that Satan's cronies are among them portraying to be an angel of light while devising destructive schemes (2 Cor. 11:14).

The Nasty One

Hawaii was not exempt from the wiles of the devil (Acts 13:10). My work life was good and, my Christianity was well intact. Sharing the gospel became my passion and persisted throughout my life at work and in the community. One night in my dreams, the Lord appeared to me and spoke to me as a German Sheppard dog. He illuminated a picture of a pale-faced man of average height with brilliant red hair. God stated to stay away from him **he is the Nasty One!** His exact name for him was the Nasty One. God was saying that the red-headed man was aligned with Satan. He said that I was not to be combative toward him and to avoid him. The dream vanished and I forgot all about the vision. About a year later, a soldier who was more senior than I, approached me about my hairstyle that he believed to be inappropriate for my uniform. He received an unadulterated piece of my mind. My hair met the regulations. What was his problem? Secondly, I did not work with, or for this man. His soft-spoken presentation had many people fooled.

Immediately following this altercation, God gave me a vision that appeared before my eyes as a gigantic boomerang while I was at work and on my computer. It was the very man that God as a German Sheppard revealed to me a year ago in a dream! It was the Nasty One. Wow! Behind the scenes, this man went to great lengths to get me kicked out of the military over my hairstyle and other frivolous things. My spirit let me know that he was a God hater who was inventing ways to do evil (Rom. 1:30). Nevertheless, his efforts and weapons failed (Isa. 54:17). He must have forgotten whose child I am. Did he believe his actions would prevail against the Lord.? His arrogance clouded his judgment.

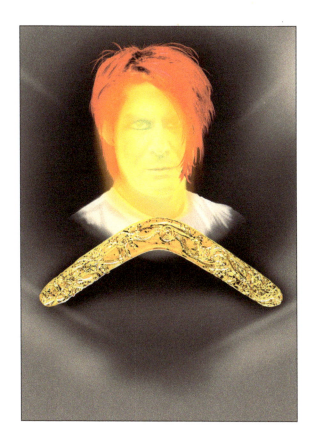

Shortly thereafter, it was discovered that this man had sworn allegiance to an Irish rebellious Christian hate group. Can you believe it? My hair was a scapegoat. I was being targeted because of my open belief in the Lord. You never know who you are among. God obliterated him from my life and that MI unit. The German Sheppard was indicative of God's continual protection over my life (Ps. 41:2 and, Prov. 2:8). There are several valuable lessons here. We are to be mindful of God's instructions and take heed to His warnings (Dan. 2:19, Job 33:15-16, and, Matt. 2:12). The removal of this man also meant that other Christians in the unit were not going to be attacked by him. Actions led by the Lord have a way of benefitting others without their knowledge.

There is also another angle for you to assess. Our roles, our actions, or inaction in a given situation will impact others in either a positive or negative way. Following the Lord's instruction is always the correct decision despite the outcome. God used me to expose Satan's protege. Some of the aggravation I faced could have been avoided if I had remembered and heeded God's instructions. Why did I not remember? My synopsis is that the event was not seen as important to me. If it were, the vision would have moved from my head to my heart and the appropriate actions would have followed. This failure was disobedience, sin and I repented. Again, we cannot call Jesus Lord if we do not follow His instructions (Luke 6:46). Sometimes the Lord will use someone or something to give you a message. When you know it is of the spirit, the expectation is the same.

Working with the Lord and being a vessel of His work is not always rosy. The persecution never feels good. The battle scars in the form of memories remain. From a carnal perspective, I stood alone many times to right a wrong (Eph. 6:13). Others witnessed wrongdoings and knew in their hearts that what was happening around them was egregious. Fear of losing their positions or ostracization paralyzed their willingness to act.

Some Christians were in the paralyzed group. A friend of mine once said that not everyone is willing to be a martyr, Sabrina. Paraphrasing the words of a wise man; evil flourishes when good men and women sit idly by and do nothing. Is any human good? No, but, the God that dwells in us through the Holy Spirit is (Rom. 8:8-11). If God uses you in a battle, He will bring you through it. I am still very much alive after many battles! As believers, we are to consider it pure joy whenever we face trials (James 1:2). This scripture provides an expectation of trials as a Christian. Furthermore, the Bible tells us that we are made in His image. God is not referencing physical attributes but His nature. He is a God of action. Each time we act out of obedience to God, He is using us.

My zeal for the Lord reached new heights in conjunction with an elevation of my professional skills. Unfortunately, my marriage was not going as smoothly as the rest of my life. A wedge formed between us, progressed to a rocky road, and, led to a divorce after I sought Godly counsel. My marriage to the Bridegroom became stronger.

The Sponsor's Secret

On December 3, 2021, The Lord awakened my memory to an event that began in 1983. Undoubtedly, the Lord wants this truth shared with someone who is wrestling with a secret that he or she is afraid to disclose because of potential repercussions. Your secret or indiscretion may not be the same as the event that will be shared shortly. Yet, the toll it is taking on your soul, mind, and body are the same. The military would often assign a sponsor to assist you when you reach a certain level. Shortly after receiving my orders for Hawaii, I was assigned a sponsor named Tammy. Once I was given her name, my spirit became heavy as it often does when turmoil is approaching my doorstep.

When Tammy telephoned me from Hawaii, the Lord revealed to me that Tammy had a secret that she was ashamed to disclose. He told me about the actual secret in the middle of my telephone conversation with her. What God's shared with me about her was not discussed with her until two years after we met. Building a relationship with my sponsor can be described as awkward. She was a very introverted person with very little conversation. Her defensive wall was very apparent. It took about six months before she would have a meaningful conversation with me. She had two small children that were darlings and extraverted. I got to know them very well.

After my sponsor and I became friends, I would babysit her children on occasion. One afternoon when I was babysitting Tammy's children, they wanted to play in my backyard which was fenced and full of fruit trees and pepper bushes. Before they started to play, I told them not to eat the peppers from a particular bush. The children acknowledged that they understood my instructions. The bush that I did not want them to bother was a habanero bush. My body will not tolerate half of a habanero pepper so I knew that this type of pepper would wreak havoc on their tiny bodies. One time, I put a whole habanero pepper in my chili and, it lit my digestive tract on fire for a long time.

The kids were having fun playing a game and I entered the kitchen from the patio door to prepare them a snack. I had just started preparing the food when I noticed from the kitchen window that the kids were jumping up and down and wailing at the same time. At first, I thought they had to go to the bathroom. Most children wait until the last possible minute to go to the bathroom when they are having fun and then, it becomes an urgent matter. Considering their motion and wailing, I went back outside to see what was happening. You probably already figured it out. The children were intrigued by the forbidden bush and decided to eat the peppers anyway. The moment I started to enter the door and my back was turned toward them; they must have rushed to the habanero bush. Immediately after they ingested them, they began to wail and asked for copious amounts of water. They gulped the water quickly and wanted more repeatedly.

If I had called the fire department, they could not have put that fire out! It took some time before the water did any good. Their little hands and faces were redder than a clown's nose and more than likely their digestive tracts were too. After two hours, they returned to normal and apologized with big puppy dog tears. Certainly, they learned a valuable lesson and, I bet their story lives on to this day. What about you? Given indisputable facts will you take no for an answer or risk potential harm or negative outcomes?

Tammy's arrival to pick up the kids could not come soon enough. Since there was no apparent harm, there was an internal chuckle for me and, I was eager to share the event with their mother. However, that event took a back seat to the story she had to share. Tammy informed me that she was going to be evicted from her apartment and needed somewhere to stay. At this time, I was living alone in a three-bedroom home. She asked if I would consider allowing her and her two kids to live with me for a while. I communicated that I would consider it. Tammy then said, well before you make your decision, I need to tell you something about me that you do not know. She indicated that once I made her aware of what I decided, she would then disclose her secret. Of course, I already knew the contents of her secret. I prayed about her request and called her to tell her the good news two days later. She wanted to share her secret in person and came to my home within an hour of our telephone conversation.

When she came through the door of my home, I gave her a big hug of acceptance. I told her that her family was welcome to stay at my home as long as needed. She lowered her head as a gesture of shame and said, I need to tell you something. I could tell she was struggling with the statement, thus, I interrupted her and said you want to tell me that you are gay right? Tammy looked at me with sheer amazement and said I cannot believe that you knew all of this time and never treated me differently. God permitted me to share with her that I knew her secret before I arrived in Hawaii. When she realized that God and I loved her, there was a sigh of relief in her voice and attitude.

The Military Intelligence positions that Tammy and I had required a top-secret clearance. In the 1980s, the Do Not Ask and Do Not Tell military provision relating to same-sex activity did not exist. Nor was there any tolerance for an alternate lifestyle in the military and most assuredly not in the Military Intelligence branch. Frankly, Tammy was in a catch 22 situation. Openly disclosing her same-sex activity would mean a surrender of her top-secret clearance and a dishonorable discharge from the military would rapidly ensue. An eviction would also add a wrinkle to maintaining her top-secret clearance and ultimately her job. The military was her only monetary means of providing for her children.

Tammy also informed me of her prior abusive heterosexual marriage and her husband's infidelity with her sister which resulted in a child. This scenario forced her into depression and low self-esteem. She explained that the only love she experienced was from another female, but that relationship was severed due to abuse as well. Tammy was given the best I could offer, the cross and unconditional love. Because she lived with me for a few months and saved some money to pay her past due rent, her looming eviction disappeared.

We prayed together often, and I invited her to join me at church. She became active in the church, experienced God's love, and accepted Jesus Christ as Lord and Savior. Tammy was discharged from the military. Did she disclose her secret to the military? She never informed me of the details surrounding her discharge and, I did not ask. Thank you, Lord, for loving Tammy and allowing me to help her during a tough time. Prayerfully, all things worked for the good. We know that with God all things work for the good of those who love Him and have been called according to His purpose (Rom. 8:28).

If you are struggling with a secret, an addiction, abuse, or in a dilemma riddled with risks and potential negative outcomes, talk to the Lord and seek godly counsel. The Lord will teach you and guide you toward the direction you should go. He will counsel you with His loving eye on you (Ps. 32:8 and, Prov. 11:14). Fear of rejection or shame of any kind can take us to a dark place and overtake us if, we allow it. The light and darkness do not co-exist (John 1:5). Satan has a permanent resting place in darkness and our secrets. God says in His Word that whatever is hidden is meant to be disclosed and, whatever is concealed is meant to be brought out into the open (Mark 4:22). Tammy's children thought they would be able to hide that they ate from the habanero bush. As you can see, their actions were exposed with dire consequences for them. This is what Satan does with our hidden indiscretions and secrets. He will expose them publicly to ensure that you are humiliated.

As the light of the world, the Lord calls us to be loving, compassionate, and understanding. Our love for others should be as great as the love we have for ourselves (Prov. 11:12 and, Matt. 22:39). Extending love and generosity without judgment to those in need is being used by God. It is so easy to love someone who loves you. Our challenge is to extend love and hope to those who despitefully mistreat us or those whose sin we determined in our mortal minds to be repulsive (Matt. 5:44 and, Luke 6:37). Do you remember the parable of the wedding banquet? In the end, the servant gathered guests far and wide who were both good and bad and the banquet was filled with guests. The Bible reminds us to be humble. In the book of Luke, it is said that when we have a luncheon or dinner do not invite those who can repay us like your relatives, friends, or rich neighbors. Instead, invite, the poor, the crippled, the blind, and the lame who cannot repay you. Your payment will be received at the resurrection of the righteous (Luke 14:12-14). Some of us will not be seen with the poor or afflicted and will sway others from meeting their needs. Our invitation to love or help anyone should not be based on their standing, but on their needs (Matt. 22:9-10).

Reflections and Movement Forward (**Chapter II**)

Question 1: Lord show me anything that is putting a wedge between us (Rom. 8:5-7 and, 1 John 2:15-16).

_____

_____

_____

Question 2: Lord reveal anything that the enemy has reign over in my life (Gal. 5:7-22).

_____

_____

_____

Question 3: Lord reveal to me any gifts that you have loaned to me that I am not using (Matt. 25:19-27 and, Luke 16:10).

_____

_____

_____

Question 4: Lord, am I walking in your will and purpose for my life (Eph. 1:9, 2 Cor. 13:5, and, James 1:23)?

_____

_____

_____

Question 5a: Lord identify anyone that needs help that I have avoided or resisted.

Question 5b: Ask yourself, do I measure sin? Will I extend love to anyone despite where they live, what they did, what they look like, or their financial state (James 2:16, James 4:16-17, and, 1 Tim. 5:8)?

_____

_____

_____

Question 6: Lord how can I use my painful event to help someone come through a storm(Isa. 58:10, Matt. 25:44-45, and, John 21:17)?

_____

_____

_____

CHAPTER III

A NEW BEGINNING

The Knight

In September 1986, I divorced my husband. Even though it was the right thing to do, no one wants to fail at anything. I chose to focus on my wonderful partnership with the Lord and getting a college education. The Lord eradicated my conceit, but there was not a thing wrong with my self-esteem. In my secret place, I whispered to the Lord that I did want Him to provide me with a husband someday. With thoughts of this possibly occurring years down the road, it became a figment of my imagination. In the fall of 1986, I planned to exit the military in 1987, move to Atlanta, Georgia, and pursue my college education at Emory University. God had other plans.

Most of my friends in Hawaii lived in military housing. My new townhouse was not a military home and was far away from them. Some weekends, I would stay at their homes. During a visit with one of my friends, we were reminiscing and singing old music. As we continued to reminisce, she said, I know someone who has a lot of old music. Let us see if we can borrow some of his albums. I agreed. The person she was referencing lived across the street from her. We went casually to his home. She knocked on the door for a couple of minutes without a response. As soon as we started to leave, he opened the door. There stood this athletically built guy with pearly white teeth and beautiful legs named Larry. Yes, he was and is eye candy to me. He surpassed the gorgeous guy's physical chemistry barometer check considerably. On the surface, it may seem like my interest in men was driven by physical attributes. Things are not always what they seem. Physical beauty was not the driving force in my selections; however, it is certainly a plus. My friend and I listened to music at Larry's home for three hours. Aside from listening to music with him, there was interesting dialogue. His perspective on various subjects was quite interesting. The night was passing away and, covertly I did not want it to end. Larry and I were on the same sheet of music. He wanted my friend to leave but not me. He presented his position in a charming diplomatic way. My friend left and we continued our conversation.

Fast forwarding the storyline, Larry got down on one knee and proposed to me two weeks from the day we met. My head was spinning so fast. I told him that it was too soon. We decided to marry six weeks from the day we met. It was love at first sight for both of us! Although we knew it was love, neither one of us wanted to say the three-word phrase; I Love You, first. My mother was not thrilled. She could not believe that I was recently divorced and getting married so quickly. I was not a wounded and weak vessel. I loved him, he loved me, and we knew what we were doing. We planned a discrete ceremony with the two of us. However, my girlfriends figured out our plans and insisted on being present and having a quaint reception. The minister arrived at the chapel wearing flaming red pants. The notion of a minister marrying me in red pants did not leave me with the impression that it was going to be a marriage made in heaven so, I asked him to change them, and he did. We were married on November 7, 1986.

Shortly thereafter, Larry shared that he prayed to God for a wife, and I conveyed what I prayed as well (Prov. 18:22). God answered both of our prayers. I had no idea that the figment of my imagination would be transformed into a shining knight and appear within days of my prayer. Look at God! I departed the military in April 1987 and my new beginning sprung forth. Larry was a senior Non-Commissioned Officer and his tour in Hawaii had not ended. Because we were not departing until 1988, I started college in Hawaii. Larry's new assignment was being contemplated.

I asked God to send us anywhere but Fort Campbell, Kentucky. Initially, he received orders for Colorado, and, I was elated. Much to my chagrin, his orders were changed. Guess where God sent us? He sent us to Fort Campbell, Kentucky. Out of all the bases that Larry could have been assigned, this was the last place I wanted to go. Undoubtedly, God knew something that we did not. He would not be God if this were not true (Rom. 11:33-34). God's plans for us were greater than my mind could comprehend. Have you ever wondered why God does not show His full hand to us immediately? Sometimes, it can be too much for our carnal minds to grasp or a difficult pill to swallow.

God's decision was not questioned. His plans for us would unveil in due time (Isa. 14:24 and, Eph. 1:11). Besides, I was married to an incredible man that hung the moon. His undying commitment to me has made my life easier for the last thirty-five years. I do not have to get in and out of the rain without him. After a brief stint in an apartment, we purchased our first home. This home is the symbolism of our new beginning and our movement forward with the Lord (2 Cor. 6:14). We are equally yoked in our love for

Jesus which enables the Lord to operate freely in our home (2 Cor. 3:17). At this time, the Lord was teaching me the Biblical significance of numbers. As I continued to mature in my Christian faith, understanding the presence of these numbers helped me to see God's movement, His wisdom, and my direction as His warrior. The number eight represents a new beginning. Larry, our son David-James (DJ) and I moved into our home on August 8, 1988 (8/8/88). Our address was 3401 Candy Drive. God recently pointed out the address. Our telephone number for our home was 886-8818. Look at the pattern of eights.

Before the Lord consecrated the home as ours, He let us know that we needed to fully clean all areas of the home (2 Tim. 2:20-21). God led me to an attic that was outside over our garage port. Something was up there that was not of God. What could it possibly be? Brawn was needed to climb into the attic which I did not have. This meant that Larry had to climb up there and explore its' contents. With astonishment on his face, Larry came down from the attic with a brand new Weegie board in his hand. Oh, my Lord! **Undeniably, my spirit detected unclean spirits that were attached to the board.** Frantically, I said Larry, throw that thing straight in the garbage. He immediately discarded it in the outside trash can. The Lord needed us to know of the unwanted spirits' existence.

The Lord also knew that once we discovered the board, the purge would soon follow. God wanted us to have a fresh clean start and a new home free of ungodly spirits. God gave us a sweet gift symbolizing a new beginning on our horizon. The number five (God's grace and anointing) and seven (it is finished or completed) have followed us throughout our marriage[1]. The magnitude of God's giving cannot be overstated. Nevertheless, the Lord does expect us to appropriately use what He offers. This includes the wisdom He imparts. It would not have been wise to keep that Weegie board and allow evil forces to run rampant in our home (Prov. 2:11-12). The intrigue of something new may lure someone to open the box and release demons. Believe what the Holy Spirit is saying and respond sensibly.

The Shake-Up

My top two priorities after arriving in Kentucky were finding a church home and getting into college. The church that we selected in the latter part of 1988 was a traditional Baptist church. There was no way of knowing what traditionalism meant at this church before we attended. It turned out that our mere presence agitated several members. Some of them did not desire pepper to be added with their salt. The Biblical correlation of salt is not indicative of who they were. The Lord unraveled what was taking place and wanted me to become unmovable (1 Cor. 15:58 and, Ps. 46:5, [KJV]). The Lord intended to shine the light on what was in the hearts of some of the saints at that church. The light was also cast on some leaders (1 Cor. 14:25).

As I understand it, there were some heated discussions concerning diversity in the church that led to some members seeking fellowship elsewhere. We came every Sunday and praised the Lord knowing that some members did not want us. You could tell those who were struggling with the issue. When the time came to meet and greet each other at the beginning of service, they would turn their heads away from us quickly or abruptly move to another aisle to avoid interacting with us. I always smiled. The pastor had a heart of gold and embraced anyone who entered the church doors. He pulled me aside one Sunday and said Sabrina when this church gets to the point where you and your family are not accepted, I am going to leave. A few years later, he did leave. God put on his heart to start a new church in 1997 with a new vision and mission.

Meeting The Needs

A considerable time before the pastor's departure, the Lord convicted me of not addressing the needs of the urban community. He used Larry to deliver the message. In the book of John, God asks Peter three times if he loved Him. After Peter's reply each time, the Lord said to him feed my lambs, shepherd my sheep and feed my sheep (John 21:15-17). Why do you think Jesus repeated His words? My belief and experience with the Lord are that He wanted to emphasize the need to care for His people out of love for Him. Jesus was not just speaking of giving them food. Note that He told him to also shepherd His sheep. Jesus wanted Peter and all of us to understand that we should meet the needs of the people. To understand what the needs are and to determine how God can use you, you have to get involved in a meaningful way. Each one of us is expected to be a doer and not a spectator.

At God's direction, we left the traditional Baptist church in the mid-nineties and joined Means Avenue Baptist Church located in the projects. Larry became a trustee, leader of the bus ministry, and sports. I introduced and facilitated the Evangelism Explosion and other outreach programs. The pastor of Means Avenue was new. This meant a new church (although the same building) was being planted. Larry and I partnered with God and the pastor through the reconstruction and well beyond. Soon, I was an EE trainer of trainers and an adult Sunday school teacher. The EE program and outreach ministries that the Lord used me to activate were flourishing by leaps and bounds.

Everything that happens in the natural that we experience as Christians happen in the spirit realm first. The Bible tells us about the enormous crowds in need of assistance which sparked the scripture; the harvest is plentiful, but the workers are few (Matt. 9:37). The Means Avenue Church community exemplified this scripture. The workers were so scant that one time, I single-handedly prepared food for 700 people for a special event and functioned in multiple capacities at the same event. We simply did not have willing vessels. There was a lengthy line of people desiring to eat, but there was no one in line to help cook or clean up. This was not an isolated scenario. This is a chief reason why the Lord wants to use us as His partner in expanding His kingdom and feeding His sheep.

As a result of the EE program, most of the houses in the projects were visited and, incredible needs surfaced that God so graciously met through the church. God also used me to combat some fears that others had about walking and witnessing in the projects. The Lord placed His stamp of approval on the new church which was evidenced by a huge growth spurt. Both believers and non-believers from all walks of life in the community and surrounding areas were joining the church and unleashing their gifts and talents. The new members were a sight for sore eyes, and, in my case, they were a sight for a sore back, sore legs, and arms too! Thank you, Lord, for the timely rescue.

The Woman In the Street

Meanwhile, I was accepted to Austin Peay State University (APSU) in 1989 in the Medical Technology Program. Of course, I was excited. A goal that I put on the back burner was now in motion. In 1991, I was elected the class president. My grades were stellar and, I had the end in mind, my degree. As a non-traditional student,

I often brought my lunch with me. From time to time, I wanted something different. There was a restaurant across the street from the university that made some juicy homemade burgers. The aroma from the burgers and onions was luring me. One day for lunch, I decided that I had to have one.

As I started to cross the street to the burger place, several horns were honking. The honking would stop abruptly and start up again. I decided to walk toward the noise. Well, you know how nosy I am. Low and behold, I discovered the root of the honking. In the middle of the street was a very frail woman. She had a hunch back larger than the Hunch Back of Notre Dame (no kidding). In addition to her hunch back, she had a sloping forehead that extended near her eyes impairing her vision. The passing cars were honking because she was in the middle of the street and, they had to maneuver around her. Without a second thought, I ran to help her cross the street safely. I held on to her hand and shoulder and briskly guided her to the sidewalk across the street. Thanks to the Lord, she was not harmed. Once she safely cross the street, she turned to me and said verbatim, get away from me you filthy African slut. Instantaneously, I communicated to the Lord and said, forgive her Lord for she knows not what she does (Luke 23:34).

In a state of bewilderment, I said to myself wait a minute, did those words just come out of my mouth. I turned around really thinking that there must be someone behind me who is responsible for saying these words. No, the words came from my mouth, Trust me, these are not the words that Sabrina would say after that humiliating outburst. The flesh does what is contrary to or against the spirit (Gal. 5:17). Not this time. My flesh was placed in submission (1 Cor. 9:27). The realization of the Holy Spirit's intervention hit me. My spirit was crying out for this woman and uttered those words in prayer to the Lord. My flesh did not win! My new beginning was unfolding and, my transformation was ever before me.

The lady in the street may have been frail, but she was not crazy. She waited until she was safe before making the negative remarks. Before this event, I had never seen this lady. God says in His Word if we do not love then, we don't know Him for He is love (1 John 4:7-8). Knowing our God, He showed her how to love all people at one point in her life. Perhaps, God also used me to aid in softening her heart.

Reshaping Character

Larry went to war in Saudi Arabia in October 1990. Because of his senior position, he was a member of the advance party. There is an understanding of a soldier's role yet, you pray that war will never come. DJ and I were glued to the news every night. When the balloon went up which is the signal for war, I lost it. DJ who was only eight years old came over to me and rubbed my shoulders to comfort me.

In March of 1991, Larry called to let me know he was coming home in early May 1991. I leaped with joy! Within a month, I was pregnant with our son. Unfortunately, I went into early labor at five months and our son Anthony was not able to thrive outside of the womb. I moaned so loud and so often that Larry asked if I needed any professional help. I laid prostrate on the floor day and night, beseeching God for His rationale and begging Him for an answer. Because God is my friend, I fussed at Him for planting the seed and then uprooting it. Why Lord? He did not answer (Job 30:20).

There was nothing in this world that I wanted more than a child. My God knew my desire. For a brief period, I thought I was being punished for something, but I was not. As time progressed, my prayers focused on divine healing from the mental anguish that I could not shake (Jer. 6:24). God's love and mercy eventually healed the anguish and pain. Little did I know that this thorn would produce fruit in my life for many years and be instrumental in reshaping my character. My love for the Lord did not waiver even when I was angry and deeply wounded (Ps. 26:1 and, Heb. 10:23).

After my physical healing from the loss of my baby, my witnessing recommenced. Sometimes a tragedy in your life becomes a rainbow in the life of someone else (Gen. 9:13 and, Ezek. 1:28). About a year after my tragedy, I remember visiting a home of a woman roughly in her thirties who seemed to be very meek. God gave me the signal to proceed with the gospel presentation. An element of the presentation illustrates the loving character of God (John 3:16 and, 1 John 4:16). In a blink of an eye, her pleasant demeanor swiftly changed to rage. I was caught off guard.

The woman communicated that God was not a God of love and she resented Him. She explained that a loving God would not permit her baby to die. She was mourning the recent loss of her baby, blamed God for the outcome, and had a hardened heart (John 12:40). Then, she stated that no one could understand her pain. I looked her straight in her eyes and said, I can and began to share my testimony. Reliving my traumatic experience was tough. This was the first time I shared my testimony after the death of my child. My testimony offered her the empathy she frantically wanted and, it created a window of opportunity to demonstrate how God's love healed my pain (Eph. 2:4).

God's love and comfort to her through me was meek and tender. God showed me her fragility and equipped me with the discernment to know that soft conversational tones, warm embraces, and mild strokes of acceptance were warranted. Before I knew it, we were humbly before the throne of grace. With our knees on the carpet and our heads bowed on the couch, she cried out to God for forgiveness, a resolution for her despair and her feeling of disgrace that imprisoned her. Glory to God He saved her soul and set the captive free (Isa. 61:1 and, John 8:36).

At the same time, God was reshaping my mind to be sensitive to the unique needs of each individual. To know that my testimony helped someone who understood my pain on a personal level was a liberating experience for me. This component of my testimony continues to be a tool for women and couples experiencing similar life-altering events (John 1:7, and, Luke 8:39). Trials are to be counted as all joy (James 1:2). You could have changed my name to joy based on the trials I was going to face in the years to come.

D-Day

The day my mother was waiting for was finally here. I graduated from college with honors in the spring of 1993. My parents were ecstatic. My oldest sister Cecilia along with my parents traveled to partake in the celebration. My husband threw a celebratory bash and gave me the broom back during the celebration. While I was pursuing my degree, he took over the domestic work. This is what a man that hung the moon will do. Now, it was time for me to land a job. I interviewed with both the private and Federal sectors. After learning that the mission of the Veterans' Health Administration (VHA) was to assist those who had borne the battle, I did not want to work anywhere else, but there was a problem. I accepted a private-sector position beforehand. A Human Resource (HR) professional in VHA helped with that entanglement. She wrote a nice letter on my behalf to the private sector hospital rescinding the acceptance with a detailed explanation as to why.

That letter ultimately aided in increasing my starting VHA salary as well. You and I know that everything good and perfect comes from the Lord (James 1:17). Was the HR person a gift from the Lord also? I like to think that the Lord was using her to assist me. Thus, she was a gift from the Lord. I was hired in June 1993 for a daytime Medical Technology position. Generally, new hires start on the evening or night shift which tends to be the least desired. In my heart, I wanted a daytime position but thought it would be a remote possibility. I asked the Lord for a daytime position and, it was given to me (Matt. 7:7). To whom much is given, much is required. (Luke 12:48). The Lord created a good launch for my new career. As His children, the Lord expects that we yield ongoing returns. What will be my returns on the Lord's investment in the days ahead?

When Your Work Gets In the Way of The Lord's Work

In the 1990s, Medical Technologists had to also function as phlebotomists at the hospital where I worked. As Christians, we take Jesus with us wherever we go, or we should. On a morning routine in the year 1994 or 1995, I went to a male patient's room to draw his blood. We developed a quick rapport and our conversation progressed to questions regarding his salvation. He told me that he did terrible things in his life and, he knew that he was going to go straight to hell. He believed that hell was exactly what he deserved. Satan had a comfortable place in his life. I politely shared with him that God will forgive him and, he wept at his bedside (Luke 5:24). After drawing his blood, I needed to collect specimens from other patients and then take them to the laboratory for processing. Therefore, I told him that I would be back. Except, I never came back that day to see him.

I got busy with work and simply forgot to follow up with the prospect God provided (Eph. 2:10). A day later, I went to his room with hopes of sharing the gospel of Jesus Christ with him. His bed was empty. A nurse entered his room with a blank look on her face. **Regrettably, he was dead and, I left his room with his blood dripping from my hands!** I sobbed all day and repented, over and over again. His death was a sting to my soul for a long time. It was my prayer that God did save him before he departed the earth. His death stung because I failed on two levels. I let God down and, I did not honor my word with the patient. It was a terrible feeling that forever changed my life and my character. God's work has to take precedence over all things. Secondly, I have to honor my word (Matt. 5:33 and, Deut. 23:21). Hope is instilled in others when someone gives a commitment or their word.

A man or woman who is a listener of the word and not an implementer of the Word is like a man who looks in the mirror and forgets who he or she looks like. We are to do what the Word says (James 1:22-23). The image in the mirror is to be reflective of the Lord. In this situation, I should have shared the gospel (Mark 16:15). Instead, I focused on temporal things and work I deemed more important than the Lord's work. In the book of John, it is written that we are not to work for food that spoils, but for food that endures to eternal life, which the Son of Man will give you. For on Him God the Father has placed His seal of approval (John 6:26). The point of the scripture is all things of this world are temporal. Odd as it seems, my busyness, selfish ambition, and work were a form of idolatry. Our God is a loving and jealous God who detests idolatry in any form (Exod. 34:14 and, Gal. 5:20). Idolatry is anything you put before the Lord. Evaluate what you place before the work of the kingdom especially when the Lord's will is directing you elsewhere.

He Opened Her Eyes

My commute from my home in Hopkinsville, Kentucky to work in Nashville, Tennessee was eighty miles one way. Some people thought I was crazy for driving that far for a job. If you recall, it was the mission of the organization that captured me and by no means were miles going to derail the Lord's will and my desire to serve Veterans. Two years after I started working in Nashville, I became aware of a commuting van. This van would transport employees from Clarksville, Tennessee to Nashville for a reasonable price which became free a few years later. The van's pick-up point was about forty miles from my home. Considering that I would save money on gas, potentially relax or sleep for the additional forty miles, I signed my name on the dotted line to be a bona fide commuter on this van.

The commuters worked at various locations and were dropped off accordingly. I was surprised to see the number of commuters from my hospital. When you spend time with people for five days a week on a van, you get to see their character in some form. In a few months, I found out that there was a young lady who lived in Hopkinsville near me. We decided that it would be prudent to drive together from Hopkinsville to Clarksville to board the commuter van. Besides, we like one another.

Every week, we alternated driving. This reduced additional wear and tear on our cars and further reduced fuel costs for both of us. We met each morning in the local Kroger parking lot at 5:15 am. She and I enjoyed the conversation en route to the van. We learned that we had a lot of interests in common. Our families became frequent fun conversations. She was a newlywed who recently married someone she met at work, but he was not an employee. As she put it, he swept her off her feet with his knowledge of the Bible and charm. One evening, the Lord spoke to me about sharing the gospel of Jesus Christ with her.

The next morning thoughts of her salvation weighed heavily on my mind. I arrived at Kroger's parking lot a little earlier than usual. Do you know what, she did also? Look at God. It was still winter, pitch-black outside and this darkness filled the parking lot. Because it was her week to drive, I shared with her that I wanted to talk to her for a few minutes before we left. She agreed. After we got settled in the car, the Holy Spirit went to work. Her responses left no questions regarding her salvation. She did not believe that she was going to heaven and was never converted. After the Lord used me to share His plan of salvation, her acceptance of Jesus Christ as her Lord and redeemer came swiftly. I wished her Happy Birthday and, handed her a small book of Saint John to read that evening. She smiled the rest of the morning with no knowledge of the mysteries and deep issues that the Holy Spirit was going to unravel and expose for her (1 Cor. 2:10).

On the night of her new birth, we conversed on the telephone and, I encouraged her to ask God to guide her to additional scriptures to read. The following day, she let me know that she was going to call me later in the evening and, she did. Before she called, the good Lord informed me of the scriptures he led her to read. With a smile on my face, I voiced the scriptures that she read before she did. She was floored with amazement. Without hesitation, I let her know that the Lord made me aware of the scriptures so that we could discuss what she believed they meant and the relevance they had in her life.

When we are unbelievers, we are blind to the things of the Lord and what exists in our midst. Once He saves us, the Lord opens our eyes and turns us away from darkness to light, and from the power of Satan to God, so that we may receive forgiveness of sins and a place among those who are sanctified by faith in the Lord (Acts 26:18). Once the Lord saved my friend, He opened her eyes at the same time and, she was enlightened by the Lord's truths and instructions (New Living Translation [NLT], Ps. 119:18). From the inception of her new birth, the Lord used the scriptures to warn her. She was led to read scriptures concerning imposters masquerading as apostles of Christ, wolves in sheep clothing, and taking heed to prophets who fill her with false hopes and visions of their own minds and not the Lord's mind. (2 Cor. 11:13-14, Matt. 7:15 and, Jer. 23:16). These are powerful scriptures for a baby in Christ to drink, but they became living water for her. At first, she believed that these warning scriptures were given to protect her from things to come. Little did she know that she was drowning in a world of deep-seated darkness. The Lord continually nourished her soul and transformed the meaning of His words before her very eyes. I bared witness to what God revealed to her and, it was shocking (Acts 13:10)!

By all accounts, the newlywed couple was enjoying life. She moved into his dwelling place. However, she shared that when she attended her husband's church something did not seem right about the church, but she could not put her finger on it. She explained that her son would also have uncontrollable outbursts when he attended that church. When my friend attended the church after she received Jesus as Lord, her spirit let her know that what was being said and practiced did not line up with the Word of God. It got to the point that she could no longer tolerate the church and needed a way out without upsetting her husband. Based on what she described to me and what my spirit discerned, this place was a building that housed a cult and, the Lord was absent. The rituals and other practices of the cult glorified Satan (2 Thess. 2:9). However, this building was the least of her worries.

A New Beginning

The Means Avenue Church was hosting a friend and family day celebration during the same week that she communicated her issue of concern. I invited her and her family to attend. Her husband was an official at his church and did not want to come to my church so, she came along with her toddler. Her son was in my Sunday school class. My friend enjoyed the worship service, remarked that she felt a sense of peace at Means Avenue and wanted to return. At her husband's insistence, she returned to the cult the next Sunday, but the Holy Spirit would not let her remain in the building. She told me that she felt ill and, her son yelled in the building as loud as he could that he wanted to go back to the "good" church. Wow! Out of the mouth of a babe, the truth is spoken (Luke 10:21, Matt. 11:25, and, Matt. 21:6). Her son's use of the word "good" correlated to the presence of the Lord at the Means Avenue Church. The toddler also correlated the presence of demonic forces at the building with the occult activity as "bad."

If the Holy Spirit told you to leave, would you leave or would you remain with your loved one? Your answer to the question supports who you are serving (Josh. 24:15). As for me, I would be out of that place faster than a cheetah. She left abruptly without her husband's consent and showed up at Means Avenue for worship. She conveyed her apprehensions to her spouse who did not concur with her sentiment. Why would he? Her husband was a long-standing member of that so-called church. Nevertheless, she as well as her son fellowshipped at Means Avenue until she departed Hopkinsville. My friend started feeling quite uneasy about her husband's behavior. What he professed to be words of the Lord; she did not believe. Her husband spoke of her being in rebellion because she disliked his church. When she questioned him as to where to find the corresponding scripture, he could never point her to it. He could not show her something that did not exist. Nor could she find it on her own. Her husband belongs to the devil and when he speaks lies, he is speaking his native language (John 8:44).

Her spirit concluded that he made up the quotations. Her uneasiness around her husband in conjunction with the false doctrine he was trying to fill her mind with daily, made her ponder: Who is this man I am married to really? Soon, the Lord answered her question. The Bible tells us that God reveals the truth to us through the Holy Spirit. The Spirit searches all things, even the deep things of God (1 Cor. 2:9).

My friend indicated that she told her husband about our friendship, how great my church was and, she wanted me to meet him. We planned a Saturday afternoon visit. I think that she wanted my opinion regarding her husband's spirit. The blinded eyes of a non-believer were no more. Her new sight and new senses through the Holy Spirit perceived an unclean heavyweight that the Lord planned to address (Ps. 146:8). When I arrived, her husband was not home yet. We chatted for about thirty minutes before he arrived. The house was purchased by her spouse long before they were married. It was a cold, lifeless place that was still dark inside although the light from the sun was at its highest. No one would mistake this house for a home. My friend offered me a seat on the couch in the family room. Her husband joined me. He sat in a chair near the couch and started the dialogue. My friend was not present because she was still finalizing the lunch that she was preparing for us. My eyes pierced my friend's husband's brown eyes like a laser. Within an instant, my spirit tested his spirit and knew that he was born of darkness (1 John 4:1 and, Matt. 6:23). The light from my spirit and the spirit of his wife shattered his darkness and the true being that dwelt in him came forth (2 Cor. 4:6).

While we were relaxing and awaiting lunch, her husband's eyes changed to a pale gray, he then said to me with a frog-like

voice, We know who you are, and I said to it with a steadfast look, I know who you are. The "we" that he was speaking of was Beelzebul who owned his soul and was now speaking through him. In seconds, he returned to normal as if he were unaware of what just transpired. I prayed and rebuked the devil in the name of Jesus on the spot. His spirit was powerless against God's spirit thus, he retreated (James 4:7). I remained silent about what I witnessed until I departed their house. We enjoyed lunch together and exchanged kind words. After chatting for an hour after lunch, I departed. On my way out of the door, I signaled to my friend to call me. It was important that I not startle her. It was also important that the devil did not think that he was successful in creating fear.

When she called me, I told her everything that I witnessed. She became petrified. His ungodliness had a whole new meaning to her. Truly, the Lord opened her eyes. With her eyes wide open, she was now faced with the fact that her husband was demonic and, her marriage was built on pretenses. The spiritual order of the household is with God being the supreme head overall all mankind and Christ is beneath God. The husband is the head of his household beneath the Lord and leads the family under the Lord's guidance (Eph. 5:23 and, 1 Cor. 11:3). Most assuredly, her husband was not getting any direction from God or the Lord. Her husband's direction and teachings can only be ungodly because Satan owned his soul. Imagine what the young child's life would be under his teachings and direction. The Bible tells us that my friend and her son would acquire the mindset of the devil. In the latter part of Matthew 10:25, the scripture says if the head of the house has been called Beelzebul, how much more the members of his household!

My friend and I prayed until our knees received carpet burns. She asked God for a way out. Her feeling that her husband may potentially harm her and or her son cemented her decision to leave him. She planned her exit strategy and, the Lord protected her throughout the process. On the chosen exit day, her husband was either out of town or working. I came over to help her pack her things and load them in a U-Haul that she had waiting. We embraced and, I hugged her son. She got in the U-Haul and, away she went. Her exit led by the Lord can be viewed as the great escape (2 Tim. 2:26)! When she got settled in another state, she successfully annulled her marriage. Close your eyes for a minute and visualize what the Lord did. The Lord took her to a spacious place and rescued her. Out of pure joy for her repenting heart, the Lord tenderly nestled and protected her under His wings (Ps. 18:19, Ps. 57:1, and, Ps. 27:5). That spacious place was the Kroger's parking lot and, His wings were the Holy scriptures. Glory!

If she had never given her life to the Lord, she would have remained in darkness and tormented to death. Like Lot in the Bible, our God rescued her from torment (2 Pet. 2: 7-9). You and I are among demonic forces that often appear docile every day, but these forces are on a mission to destroy your soul for all eternity. Stay in tune with the Holy Spirit. Assess your surroundings, assess the people you are among, and the items entering your home. Satan will attempt to fool Christians as well as unbelievers if it is possible (Mark 13:12). Thank you, Lord, for opening her eyes and using me to be a part of her enlightenment.

The Christmas Surprise

Teaching Sunday school for fifth and sixth graders at the Means Avenue Church was near and dear to my heart. My class size varied every Sunday. Most of the time, I had at least ten children. Two of the children were brother and sister. Their eagerness to learn and their gentle spirits would always capture my attention. They were well-behaved kids and followed the instructions. On one particular Sunday, I told the little girl to put on her shoes. She was walking on the back of them and, as she walked, they would make an annoying flip-flopping sound. I assumed that she would put the shoes on her feet correctly after I brought the issue to her attention the first time. About fifteen minutes later, I noticed that the shoes were dangling from her feet when she was seated. I shared with her again, please put your shoes on your feet, and continued to teach.

At the end of the class, she still did not have her shoes on her feet correctly. I asked her why she had not put her shoes on her feet. She looked at me and said: Ms. Hughes I have a lot of shoes, but none of them fit my feet. They are all too small. Wow! Again, things are not always as they seem. Shoes were purchased for her immediately. In a few months, we sponsored a weekend youth festival out of town. The little girl and her brother attended. All of the children's clothing was washed before we returned home to reduce the parents' burden. Two members of our church that were responsible for washing the clothing made inappropriate comments about the little girl's undergarments and her mother. The undergarments were ragged and heavily soiled, giving the appearance that they were worn for a long period. One member stated that the girl's mother sent her with these tattered garments as a ploy to get new things from the church.

I rebuked the church member and reminded everyone of our roles as leaders and that the Lord has allowed us to meet a need. Undergarments were purchased when we returned from the trip. I had an opportunity to spend some time with the mother and was able to determine that the needs of the family were great. The Lord is clear on our role and responsibilities as it relates to the poor and those with a need. If anyone has material possessions and sees a brother or sister in need but has no pity on them, how can the love of God be in that person (1 John 3:17)? Our money is also a material possession that should be used to show compassion.

Christmas was approaching. In November 1995, names from the angel tree at work were circulating. Our department always chipped in as a unit to purchase gifts for a couple of children on the angel tree. This particular year, I said that I was not going to participate in the angel tree gift giving. My peers were disappointed and asked why. I shared that I have two angels in my church who would be blessed by my family's giving. They must have felt the sincerity of my heart because my colleagues rallied around my interest! They decided to provide gifts to the brother and sister duo in my Sunday school class instead of selecting angels from work. I was moved to tears and cried all day with joy. Their attitudes and approach to giving to my students got better. We decided to go shopping for them as a team after work! We purchased bicycles, toys, games, and clothing for them. Considering that we planned to shop at a few stores and then have dinner, I planned an overnight stay with one of my colleagues. The children or their parents had no idea of what was transpiring.

Larry came to my workplace and picked up everything. Because of my giddiness, you would have thought the gifts were for me. Two days before Christmas, Larry and I headed to the children's home. The mother thought that we were just stopping by to see how she was doing since I had been to her home a few times. When I told her about the purpose of our visit, she screamed. Once she returned to earth, she calmly communicated that she did not see any way that her children would have any gifts for Christmas and, she was saddened by that thought. Hearing the joy from the mother and gratitude from the kids was worth all of the effort. This was a double surprise. I was surprised at the generosity of my colleagues and, the chosen family received a Christmas surprise that they will never forget. This still ranks as my best Christmas present ever. The Lord made all of this happen for a beautiful and deserving family. I believe that the mother prayed for a blessing and, the Lord answered her cry far above her imagination (Ps. 40:1).

Building on His Foundation

The Lord's work through Means Avenue Church continued to prosper. When the church was on solid ground, the Lord moved me to New Work Fellowship at the beginning of 1998. There, the Lord further refined my character, continued to bless and use me. New Work Fellowship was recently formed with services being held in a small area in a stadium. Like the onset of the Means Avenue Church, the workers were scant. Yet, all of the members of the New Work Fellowship rolled up their sleeves.

A heart for the elderly population arose in my spirit. God inspired me to devise a broad ministry for the elderly that the pastor embraced. In passing one day, the pastor asked me how was the elderly ministry coming along? I looked at him with my glasses pulled down over my nose and said that no one has done a thing with the document I prepared for the ministry. With a puzzled look on his face, he indicated that when God gives you the vision you have a responsibility to see that it prospers. Since I wrote the plan, I thought that someone else would take it to the next step. I was wrong and, he was correct.

Tactfully, he also chastised the way I looked at him and more than likely the way I looked at others. He indicated that I purposely positioned my glasses on my face to create a stern look. He shared that when I did that, he simply did the same thing. His observation and comment could not be disputed. I corrected that aspect of my character rapidly. The elderly ministry was launched through the nursing homes first and, other aspects evolved at a later time with several members being active participants. Through us, the Lord continued to demonstrate His love and compassion for the elderly. Some received salvation. Others had a void filled in their lives with new Christian companionship. When my focus is on meeting the needs of others, the impact of my struggles seems to diminish or be of no effect. Yet, the Lord never forgets the matters of our hearts. He will never forsake us (Deut. 31:6). His timing is always perfect regardless of the waiting period.

An Answer After A Gut-Wrenching Event

Larry and I decided to delay having children. We waited seven years from the time our son Anthony passed away to have another baby. I thought that this timing delay would heal all wounds. During the waiting period, God did not provide us with an answer to the mystery concerning my early labor that resulted in our son's death. Once we planned to try again in 1998, the pregnancy occurred in two weeks. I had this lightheadedness again and took a pregnancy test at work. I could not wait until Larry got home to share the wonderful news. I brought the positive test home and placed it in his favorite chair. We were tickled pink and, our families and friends were also. My physician took additional steps to secure the pregnancy that gave me some temporary peace.

At four months of gestation, my doctor placed me on bed rest with a plan to deliver our baby at thirty-six weeks because of ongoing complications. I had a rigorous supervisory role at this time that required a lot of spontaneous actions that I was unable to ignore as a professional. My job greatly contributed to these complications. While I was home, my boss kept me apprised of significant work activities to keep me engaged which I enjoyed. Every book that I was able to get my hands on concerning pregnancy was read. My reading coupled with what I was experiencing during my prescribed bed rest sparked several questions and concerns. My doctor was on speed dial and the recipient of my inquiries. In a dream, I was rushed to the hospital and our baby died. My doctor felt that I was paranoid and became weary of my frequent calls. Thus, she said Sabrina you need to put your books away. Did she forget I was bedridden? Reading occupied my time.

When my pregnancy term was five and a half months, I woke up in the middle of the night with sharp labor pains. Larry rushed me to Vanderbilt hospital where our nightmare commenced! Tests were performed that determined that the baby was in distress. Amid intense labor pains that were pounding every three to five minutes, premature birth and probable death were knocking at my hospital room door. A few hours later, I delivered a stillborn baby girl named Aniiya in June 1998. This was not a dream, but a revelation that I wished did not come true! **I became an instant basket case destined for a straitjacket.** This was a gut-wrenching experience that mummified me. Losing one child was a lot to bear. Losing two babies was an unfathomable crushing blow to my soul. Lord, how am I going to survive this pain and grief? Despite being helpless and grief-stricken, another battle confronted me head-on immediately following the delivery. My blood loss was substantial and, my laboratory results went haywire after the delivery causing a prolonged hospital stay. My uncle's wife was in the hospital in another state at the same time. My clinical stats were worse than hers. She died and, I survived.

The recuperation period ended and, it was time to return to work. The expression of sympathy from many colleagues was appreciated. However, every hug received and, every question asked expanded the size of my gaping wound. My pain was indescribable, but the naked eye saw a façade of happiness. Only God had the power to help me in this situation (Ps. 147:3). What was the point of creating an atmosphere of sadness for others? One day in the latter part of the summer, I went to the break room to relax during lunch. There was no one present except me. When I sat down at a table, there was a tiny book open to two significant pages. The book was the size of a matchbook so, it is fascinating that the book remained open to these particular pages. Because you know how curious I am, you know what happened next. I picked up the book to read what was inside.

As I started to read the passages, my jaw dropped. The pages contained a story about a woman who struggled for years to have a child and finally had a baby at the point of her death. God had this story predestined for me! With a sorrowful look of surprise, I began to play back my reproductive history in my mind. **Then, God spoke to me sweetly and said: "Sabrina, how long do you want me to continue to honor the wishes and desires of your heart"? As God spoke, it felt like He was cradling me in His arms (Mark 10:16). God was letting me know that the next birth will cause my death.** That specific door of my life closed permanently, but hallelujah I am alive by His grace! God loves me and has more in store for me. Soon the Lord fully answered the question that I posed to Him seven years ago when Larry and I suffered the loss of our son.

New Work Fellowship implemented a new witnessing strategy. Those interested in the program had to attend a week-long seminar in Franklin, Tennessee. My time off was approved and, I headed to the seminar. Members from several churches attended. The training and the dialogue were inspiring. Have you ever noticed that there is always one person present that gives you the feeling that you have known him or her for years yet, you just met the person? This seminar was no different. This identified person and I started having lunch and dinner together to get to know each other better and discuss the training.

One of these times, the subject of our children surfaced. She disclosed that she lost two babies consecutively within two years during childbirth. Crocodile tears were running down her face as she shared: I should have waited a longer period before having another child. If I had waited, at least one of them would be alive. God who is this lady? What are the chances of me meeting someone who had the same gut-wrenching experience? I moved a little closer to her and said softly, I know what you are going through, my husband and I suffered the loss of two babies consecutively as well. The difference between you and me is the timing. I thought that time would heal all wounds so, we waited seven years before trying to conceive again. The outcomes were the same each time.

We stared at each other for a minute in silence realizing that our meeting was a divine appointment. Collectively, we concluded that time was not a factor. Having babies was not in God's plan for us. This did not mean we could not be parents. Following the end of the seminar, we embraced exchanged information, and departed to our homes. God fully answered the question I posed seven years ago in detail. Recapping it all, God loved me and honored my request to conceive and carry a child twice. Out of His love for me, He made me aware of the death consequence that I would face if, I pursued childbirth again. He was quite aware of my physical barrier. However, I did not discover the physical impediment and root cause until I decided to permanently terminate reproduction.

His answers provided the relief and peace that I desperately needed. Lord thank you for loving both of us! He used us to exhort one another and accelerate our healing (Heb. 3:13). We were blessed by all that He did during that October seminar and divine appointment. God's response seven years later symbolizes completion. The gap in my understanding was complete. The Lord's timing does not always coincide with ours. We have to patiently wait on the Lord for His purposeful action and response. My strength was renewed based on the manner and timeframe that the Lord responded (Isa. 40:31).

If the Lord shared with me the ultimate outcomes at an earlier time, the chances of me receiving and accepting it would be zero. My heart and mind were very fractured and unable to withstand the inevitable. My newfound ally's heart and mind were likely in the same state as mine. With gentleness and kindness, the Lord knitted our hearts together through our circumstances (Col. 2:2). There was a time in my life when I would not have shared the struggles, I experienced with anyone outside of my circle. Where the spirit of the Lord is, there is freedom and protection (2 Cor. 3:17). We were both liberated by our spoken truths. Someone is waiting to be liberated by your testimony.

A Visitor from the Past

The Bible tells us that when we know to do something good and we do not do it, that is a sin (James 4:17). It has already been established that the God in us wills us to do that which is considered good. As a child of the King, Veteran, and leader in VHA, I served as a facilitator for Operation Stand-Down (OPSD) in Nashville, Tennessee as a way of giving back to the community. This is an outreach program designed to assist and support Homeless Veterans in the surrounding communities through several clinical and administrative services. Before I became a facilitator, I led laboratory operations. As a facilitator, my chief role was to partner with a wide array of organizations to provide needed services during and after the scheduled weekend program. When OPSD was in session, it was a busy time for me.

A New Beginning

It was unusual for me to be in one specific building for a long time unless there was a problem. Ongoing assessments and interventions were needed around the clock to maintain an effective operation and address any gaps. As I was making my rounds one Saturday afternoon in 1999, I heard someone calling my name. After the third time, I turned around. This extremely disheveled, thin man was moving toward me and continuing to call my name to get my attention. He was so puny that his clothes were hanging off of his body. As he walked, he had to adjust his apparel. I stopped and looked at him still not recognizing the face or the voice. This man was not only remarkably disheveled, but he was in dire need of a bath and nourishment too.

Then, the man said his name. You are not going to guess in a million years who it was? Oh my God, It was none other than Mr. Gorgeous. Remember the guy that I shared with you was a fine specimen of a man and turned my head at Fort Bragg, well, he was now a far cry from that man. The change was so drastic that it was troubling. Mr. Gorgeous became a homeless man. The first thing he said to me was why in the world are you here? I explained my role and my hospital position. I observed him looking at my wedding rings and, I shared my happiness. Nashville was his home which was something I did not recall.

We sat down at a nearby table to chat. You know I was dying to hear what happened. He shared his unpleasant crime-ridden story and blamed his mate for not doing something with all the money he made. He was recently released from prison and seeking a way to thrive which led him to OPSD. You could see and hear the deep-seated hurt regarding his current state. At the same time, I sensed that his heart was ripe for God's intervention (Ps. 34:18 and, Ps. 40:17). He was very concerned that he had no job, no money, and no place to live. I recommended organizations that may be able to address his needs. Before his departure, I ministered to him and escorted him to the chapel on site which was his desire after our conversation. Although I do not know if he gave his life to the Lord in the chapel or his outcome, my prayers of restoration were with him.

What a chance encounter. God used me to encourage a new beginning with him and the Lord. This chance meeting has a profound parallel regarding the impact of our choices. Often our outcomes whether they are positive, or negative are not a result of something God did or as a result of Satan's involvement. It is often the result of a choice we made. Sometimes our choices are driven by our flesh which we should never put confidence in at any point (Phil. 3:3 and, 2 Tim. 3:4). We must look at that person in the mirror to make that determination as hard as it may be. I made a conscious decision to discontinue a relationship with the guy who became homeless. He selected a life of crime driven by an impulse to make large sums of money through ill-gotten gain (1 Tim. 6:9 and, 2 Tim. 3:2). Assessing the outcome, I made a wise decision. His choice led to his incarceration.

Despite our choices and mistakes, God will forgive us and direct us if we ask. God restores those with a contrite (remorseful) and lowly (humble) spirit (Isa. 57:15). The Lord used me to speak to his heart because I still had a place in it. Catastrophic events are never welcomed. No one knows how a person's life may be altered by one. Such an event can happen to you and me at any time. We are who we are because of God's grace (1 Cor. 15:10). We are urged to live in harmony with those who may be poor or adversely impacted. To live in harmony, we must be willing to accept and love the current state of the human being. Conceit and arrogance are not characteristics that God can use (Rom. 12:16).

Reflections and Movement Forward (Chapter III)

Question 1: Lord show me if my sorrow or pain is overshadowing your light (1 Thess. 3:2-5, Matt. 6:16 and, Ps. 30:11).

_____

_____

_____

Question 2: Lord what area of my spiritual life and or work-life do I need to press through so your will may be done through me (Matt. 6:33 and, 1 Thess. 5:16-18).

_____

_____

_____

Question 3: Lord am I consulting you before making a decision that impacts my life or the life of someone else? How can I bring you nearer (Jer. 33:3 and, Rev. 3:20)?

_____

_____

_____

Question 4: Lord, identify how I may be causing someone to stumble and fall (Rom. 14:13, 1 Pet. 2:1-2 and, Jer. 50:32).

_____

_____

_____

Question 5: How can you use your testimony to express the goodness of the Lord and use it to help someone through a challenging time (Isa. 63:7 and, Acts 26:22)?

_____

_____

_____

CHAPTER IV

MOVING WITH THE MASTER

The Lord calls us to be the light and salt wherever we go. This includes your place of employment. One of my struggles as a new supervisor in VHA was blending my beliefs and actions in such a way that they were not misunderstood as overbearing. The Lord gave me a Christmas gift in December 1996. I was promoted to my first leadership position in VHA as a manager and served in that capacity until the year 2000. The operations of the department I inherited were dysfunctional with a rebellious bunch operating it. The service line chief who was the selecting official stated that he needed a strong leader to take over the operation. He remarked that he was spending too much time resolving problems in that unit. I accepted the position with my eyes wide open. It would have been nice to know that I was entering a lion's den (Jer. 51:38 and, Dan. 6:16)! There was much to do, yet I was anxious to take on the challenge and redesign the department that was in desperate need of an overhaul. The Lord disclosed that it was love that the staff needed the most.

The majority of my staff were single women with children. Each of them, like me, was struggling with some aspect of their lives.

Counseling became a key component of my role. I had an open-door policy and, the door revolved like the doors in a bank. The women would come to my office and deposit their hearts on my lap without any form of prying on my part. An interesting article surrounding abortion appeared in the prior evening's newspaper. I brought the paper to work hoping to read the rest of the article at lunch. Inadvertently, I left it on a table used by all staff.

Before the end of the day, one of my staff members wanted to speak with me. As always, I said sure. She asked if the newspaper belonged to me. I said yes. With hesitation, she articulated that she read the article concerning abortion and wanted to know how did I know she was pregnant and thinking of an abortion. Her remarks were startling because I did not know about her pregnancy or her contemplation. At that moment, God nudged me to say more. I shared with her that I did not know her issues, but God knows all about them. She explained that she had a one-night stand and got pregnant.

She threw her hands up in the air while shaking her head indicating that she did not know what to do. Embarrassment and disgrace were embossed on her face. At the time, she had two toddlers. Having an additional mouth to feed on an existing tight budget further complicated her impasse. This young lady knew the Lord and stumbled, but the Lord was there to hear her repenting heart, forgive her and give her the love she needed (James 3:2 and, Hosea 14:4). We prayed together in my office and petitioned God to direct her path (Prov. 3:5-6). She ultimately elected to not have an abortion. She delivered a beautiful healthy baby that I was able to hold a few days after her delivery. Praise the Lord!

The newspaper article written by a God-fearing priest was a practical instrument that God used to speak to the young lady's spirit and, it convicted her (2 Tim. 3:16). I was available and waiting for the Master to move. The Lord used me as a carrier of the instrument and a guide to the throne through prayer. My beliefs were not thrust upon her nor was my opinion solicited. God exerted all of the efforts through the Holy Spirit and the article.

The Lord also permitted me to see another employee's scars that were formed from the child abuse that was inflicted upon her. What the Lord did not give was permission to discuss the issues surrounding it at the time of the vision. The clarity I needed from God came six months later. Unknowingly, both of us went outside to take a break at the same location. She appeared sad that day and, I asked her if everything was okay. She shared the current domestic issues that she was having with her spouse and son.

The Lord made His move and pricked me yet again. Through me, God illustrated how past abuse has a way of interfering with current relationships and a living environment. That statement stimulated her testimony about her abusive past as a child. The vision and words that the Lord revealed to me about her in the past were shared. Once she heard what the Lord told me, she wept profusely. I prayed with her for divine healing and, I know the Lord healed her because this was the plan that He composed to begin her healing process (Jer.17:14). The Lord's interventions in this department were bountiful and amazing.

When my staff were not revolving in my office door, the union representatives were. This was an administratively challenging group that required several management techniques to influence a change in their behavior. My management tool kit had to be replenished frequently. Within the unit, there were long-standing tyrants that other leaders feared throughout the hospital. They implemented every trick they had up their sleeves to make my life at work difficult. Because of my actions, the union representatives made frequent visits that I welcomed. The union vice president visited so much that we became friends over time. The stabilization of the department took a taxing two years. Once the tyrants were uprooted from the unit, the department was running like a well-oiled machine, and, I became bored. In 1999, it was time to move to higher ground. Some of my peers said you are on an easy street. Now that you have everything operating as it should go to your office and sleep. Complacency is not a part of my fabric.

Once God provides me with the wisdom to move, my actions soon follow. God has established a certain pattern when He is preparing to move me to higher ground. A precursor to the movement is to rid my office of documents I no longer need in preparation for the new person. Then, He leads me to tie up loose ends. Lastly, He points me in the direction He wants me to go. One day in 2000, God pointed me to the hospital bulletin that I read electronically. In it was a recruitment announcement for a Graduate Health Administration Training Program (GHATP) trainee.

My professional interest shifted to hospital administration. This program was exactly what I needed to make the transition. The program highly recommended the selection of students with a graduate degree. At the time, I did not have one. After discussing the program with my husband, I applied anyway. When the Lord opens a door of opportunity, you should walk through it despite how hard the door appears to open. If faith will move a mountain, it most assuredly will open a door (Matt. 21:21 and, Matt. 17:20).

Once I applied, I found out that the Associate Director of the hospital; Dr. Robert Ratliff was the selecting official. This posed a problem for me. Because I proposed and implemented substantial disciplinary actions in my unit, some of the grievances filed rose to his level for review. Therefore, I had to meet with him to discuss the issues and my actions. He appeared to have a close relationship with the union president that I thought formed a bias against managers. Being the person that I am, I shared what I felt with him.

Since I shared my frank opinions with him in the past, I thought he would throw my application in the trash without considering its' merit. My blessings rained down yet again, and, I was chosen. The selecting official stated that one of the reasons that he selected me was because of my moral stance. His statement affirmed that it is okay to be me. You are fearfully and wonderfully made (Ps. 139:14). Do not be afraid to be the person that God designed you to be. There are no flaws in God's designs (Ps. 119:73 and, Ps.139:15).

Despite my joy in being selected, it created misery and vindictiveness for someone else. The chief of the service who was Satan's twin brother had a hissy fit. He went to the presiding Chief Executive Officer (CEO) and told him that my place was with him while demanding that my selection be rescinded. He never knew that his actions were disclosed to me. Having me as the leader in a department that was once riddled with significant issues, eliminated his nightmares. He no longer had to spend his time resolving problems in my department. Now that he could relax, he spent time openly evaluating his investment portfolio and counting his investment earnings. If he was not swiveling in his big leather chair and looking at his investment portfolio, he was in his office sleeping. I have startled and awakened him from his sleep on a few occasions.

My new appointment meant a disruption of his relaxed environment and the potential reemergence of his nightmares. When he realized that his efforts were fruitless, he gave me a grueling assignment as a form of punishment. To be released from his service by my desired date, I had to complete this assignment. The hospital has two campuses about forty miles apart from one another. He assigned me to redesign the operations of two units with a department at the other campus and provide him with a formal written proposal. This assignment required research, ongoing travel, and an assessment of huge data sets. Given the daunting task and the time constraints, my boss more than likely thought that I would not achieve my goal. He was dead wrong.

My will to complete this task was unrelenting. In the final week of my assessment, I got ill. Every joint in my body ached. Despite my pain, I pressed my way through the process and completed the report. After submitting the report, I went home and collapsed with fever, chills, and sweats. My sweating was so copious that I thought I had malaria. I remained in bed with the full-blown influenza virus for a week. Once, I nursed myself back to health, I returned to work to finalize all incomplete assignments before transitioning to my new role. My preference would have been to avoid the chief. Unfortunately, some of my unfinished business required his approval. Thus, there was no way to skirt around him.

Daily, staff at all levels of the organization were subjected to the chief's flamboyant offensive racial and gender slurs that included inappropriate jokes. Everything he did was intentionally malicious. At a meeting, a male supervisor came into the room to join the team. The chief greeted him while sniggering at the same time and said: Welcome to the women's suffrage group. Behind his back, he was considered to be a cantankerous old man. The chief's inappropriate outbursts were common in all settings without any repercussions for the emotional scars he caused for others. The employees at large were prey for his iron fist and the bondage he felt empowered to inflict upon them. One thing he ignored was the Lord's omniscience. The Lord was closely watching everything that was transpiring and executed a plan to address his behavior and free the captives forever (Luke 4:18).

My new role as a trainee was one that the Lord ordained. No matter what the chief tried, he could not outwit the arm of the Lord

(Num. 11:23 and, Isa. 59:1). My departure from my prior position took place as planned at the end of November 2000. The entire service line showered me with thoughtful gifts. My staff gave me a card that I have cherished for over twenty-one years. The card is quite moving and denotes how one person can make a difference in the world. To my surprise, some of them thanked me for the structure and discipline. I was humbly gratified that God used me to make a difference in their lives and, I was thankful for everyone's kindness. We should never forget that the glory goes to the Lord who wills us to do good.

My training exposed me to a new world, the world of health care administration, and, operations from both a macro and micro level. The more education I received the more I wanted. My selection did come with a promise that I would obtain my graduate degree. My dear husband got the broom back in 2001. My GHATP training and graduate studies were completed at an accelerated pace. This pace was a personal goal that I established. Before I completed my training, my eyes were on another prize; a position with the CEO named Roland Moore. This particular position functioned as the right hand of the CEO.

He needed me except he did not know it or believe it. When I gave him my pitch for the job, he told me that he did not think I was ready. Furthermore, I did not meet the eligibility requirements for the grade level. Getting this dream job seemed to be out of my reach. Do you know what? I made him a believer. I was out of town on travel related to my training when the job was posted. When I returned, Roland said to me, Have you looked at the job board? I think that there is a job you may like. Low and behold, my dream job was posted. It was posted with a targeted grade level which allowed me to apply. The rest is history. I got the job. The Lord used the CEO to groom me over the next two years. His mentorship and investment in my career are immeasurable and paved the way for opportunities at a higher level. Our working relationship grew into an everlasting friendship.

The Lady with the Alabaster Glow

Shortly after my promotion, the person who selected me for the training position got a CEO position at another hospital. A new Associate Director named Michelle Blakely arrived on the scene on June 30, 2001. I remember that actual day she arrived because it was her birthday. Although I reported to Roland, she was the next person in command. Like Roland, Michelle insisted that I called her Michelle and not Ms. Blakely. The informality was not comfortable for me. It took a while before I was comfortable enough to call either of them by their first name. Michelle was attempting to befriend me. Her chummy personality was initially a turn-off to me. I said to my inner being, what is her agenda? What does she want? I bet she is another lethargic leader trying to get her work accomplished through me. Our hospital was filled with crafty leaders of this caliber. Their inaction often created more work for me. Although new to her role, Michelle came to us as a highly credentialed leader.

To be honest, the issues I had with informalities and potentially befriending Michelle was internal to me. Remaining formal was a way of guarding my heart. My experience with women caused me to form a stereotype against them. Based on my experiences, most women did have a hidden agenda. They wanted to get close enough to know your innermost secrets and then blast your private life to anyone with an ear. Considering that I am a woman, I bet this seems odd to you. Yet, this was my prior belief. Our experiences do shape our belief systems and our actions soon follow. There was something different about Michelle. She had this captivating beaming light on her face. In passing, Michelle invited me to lunch one afternoon and, I joined her. This was a good icebreaker that casts a seed of doubt regarding my prior belief concerning women. Perhaps she was not like most women? It turns out she was not and, the Lord was about to show me why.

Our shuttle bus ride to our other campus was the second time we had a one-on-one chat. Once we were firmly in our seats, the Lord started to speak to me. The Lord said: Sabrina, she is just like you. The Lord paused for a minute. During His pause, I am attempting to discern what the Lord means. The Lord subsequently stated: She is barren just like you. I am theoretically scratching my head thinking that this thought is far-fetched. Was my brain in a scramble mode? Did I hear God correctly? Yes, God's words were true and, my brain was not in scramble mode. Michelle experienced cervical cancer in her early twenties which resulted in her inability to have children. When Michelle shared her truth, I was mystified. Why was there a need for God to share that level of Michelle's private life with me? He disclosed this truth to carve a pathway to my heart for Michelle. God knows my heart and understands that I had no interest in letting her into my life.

In time, our hearts became tightly woven together. Our hearts were sewn so intricately, it was as though I could see inside of her soul. In the spirit realm, I have seen her at the foot of Jesus pouring her heart out for someone else's cause. This caused me to author a poem for her called the Lady with the Alabaster glow. I am not sure if I ever told her how the poem evolved. When God wanted me to speak a word into her spirit, the light that I noticed in her face would sometimes appear on or near the issue of concern. Flashing back, Michelle had a picture in her office that reflected a beam of light whenever I went by it or approached her office. God gave me a message to share with her concerning the person in the picture that may have been a hard pill for her to swallow. God has allowed me to see and hear things that others cannot (Luke 10:23-24).

The insights that the Lord gave me concerning Michelle continue to be unveiled with each passing day (2 Cor. 3:18). The words from the Lord to her from me were multiplying rapidly at work. It got to a point that she said, I wished you would stop reading me. You need to know that I was following the Lord's footsteps (Ps. 17:5 and, Matt. 16:24). If I failed to share His words with her, I would be guilty of defying the Lord (Exod. 23:21). I did not need another spanking from the Lord. One day out of the blue, God told me that Michelle was in Ohio. I called Michelle and asked: why are you in Ohio? She was astonished and replied, how in the world did you know I was in Ohio? My response was that the Lord told me. She admits that her choice to go to Ohio was not a good decision. Deeper insights from the Lord concerning Michelle continued to mount.

Only God can see in the future. Still, He prepares us for the unavoidable in due time. God uses me as a warning light and exhorter in her life. As such, I deliver both the bitter and the sweet. Periodically, the Lord places a heaviness in my heart when turbulence is headed in Michelle's direction, accompanied by a word linked to the reason for the heavyweight. Never does God in part any form of fear. I have encouraged her to call specific family members and friends based on God's inspiration. In some cases, death was looming and other times, she needed to serve as a personal source of inspiration for someone else.

Timing is crucial when delivering God's word. Delivering a prophetic word before God gives the green light is moving in the flesh (Rom. 8:9). If the timing is not sanctioned by God, the person will not receive the intended message, the messenger may be misunderstood and, a conflict may erupt. Follow God's lead. Move in the discrete direction of the Master (Phil. 3:3 and, Rom.13:14). Girls will be girls. In addition to enjoying our spiritual connection, we have shopped until we dropped more times than I can count over the last twenty years. Michelle remained in Nashville for a year. She indicates this is the shortest assignment that she ever had in her career. If you ask her today, why did she come to Nashville, she will tell you that she believes it was to meet me. Michelle left in 2002 shortly after her birthday.

The point that God is illustrating here is that he uses us everywhere. If you are willing, He will use you to speak life into anyone regardless of their background or status. The Lord will also equip you with the courage you need to fully operate in the gifts He loans you (Phil. 1:20). The Lord connected us in a work environment knowing that His ultimate plan was to connect our spiritual gifts to expand His kingdom and, heal the oppressed (Rom. 12:5-7). Watch how the Lord moves and how his plan is magnified on the road ahead.

A Purposeful Delay

My role with the CEO; Roland Moore fueled a desire to expand my career outside of Nashville. The work that I performed under his leadership and the exposure it afforded me, increased my desire to influence change at a higher level. In the summer of 2002, much of my time after work was spent on the computer searching for an ideal opportunity. The roles that got my attention were those that shaped strategic direction at a national level. I got several first and second-level interviews but not the job offer. My level of frustration was on ten. The notion of always being the bride's maid and never the bride gave me the blues. In October 2002, I went to visit Michelle in Chicago over a long holiday weekend.

When I got to the designated airport gate in Nashville, a big ray of light appeared like the light you see coming from the high beams on your car. This long and narrow ray of light started from where I was standing and stopped in the face of a man sitting in a chair in the boarding area. The beam of light formed a direct path to him only. Since it was the light, my spirit knew it came from the Lord (John 8:12 and, Ps. 4:6). My steps were being ordered to move near this man and, I did. I sat next to him and, he began to prophesize about my life. The only way he could have known the particular things he shared about me was through the Holy Spirit (Luke 2:26 and, Eph. 3:5).

He was a minister in Nashville. God used him to inform me that he loved me, saw me as a peacemaker, and linked my behavior to Jesus' character. These words warmed my heart greatly. I expressed to him how tiring it is working for the Lord. Quickly, the Lord used this man to rebuke my statement of "working for the Lord." The Lord said that He did not need me to work "for" Him but wanted me to work "with" Him. I will never forget these words.

In closing, the man communicated that God said He was guiding my movement (Ps. 37:23). Right after he concluded, it was time to line up to board the aircraft. Unexpectedly, the Lord had more words of wisdom to share with me through this man. Remarkably, this guy's seat was next to mine! You know that the Lord planned this from the start. Our dialogue continued. I exited the airplane awe-struck. However, the connection between my frustration in not attaining a role of interest and God's saying that my movement was guided by Him went over my head. My light did not come on until I fellowshipped at Michelle's church during the planned weekend visit.

Michelle was in the process of purchasing a home. Her excitement in showing her home matched my interest in seeing it. **As we approached the top step before entering her home, the Holy Spirit hit me with a ton of bricks square in the center of my chest. As I was gasping for air, my movement ceased. My spirit detected that something was living in Michelle's new house that was not of God. Immediately, I told Michelle that something demonic was in her home.** We went through the front door praying and seeking the source.

In the basement was a Weegie board that appeared to have been used by someone at some point in time. Do you recall the time that Larry found an unopen Weegie board in our outside attic in our first home? Now, fourteen years later another one surfaces in Michelle's home. Take note of the pattern of seven. Lucifer's effort to claim territory in God's house failed again (Job 18:18 and, Matt. 10:8). God completely derailed his plan. As surreal as it is, it happened. After Michelle discarded it, we anointed that house from top to bottom (Mark 1:39 and, Mark 16:17). It was critical to free her home of the demonic spirits that were attached to the object of witchcraft and released before she occupied it.

I remember the days when I could liberally eat strawberries. Strawberry ice cream used to be my favorite late-night snack. One day, I brought a mixture of strawberries and bananas to work for lunch. That night, my body reacted to something. I had hives all over my body. I thought I had poison ivy or something like that. I never thought I was reacting to something I ate until my body responded the second time. The next time I ate a strawberry, I could not breathe. To this day, I cannot even tolerate the smell of them.

When you are allergic to something that you eat, your body remembers. You may not have a violent reaction the first time, but the second time you are exposed, your body may go into a tailspin and violently oppose whatever you ingested. Our spirits will react to demonic forces in the same way. I became sensitized to a demonic force (a Weegie board) back in 1988. When the exposure came the second time at Michelle's house, my spiritual response was radical. It had me gasping for air. Demonic forces are poisonous to our souls like allergens are to our bodies. Such forces may be connected to a person, place, or thing. As children of the king, we must stay on guard and be prepared for battle. Demonic spirits are stronger than any weapon man may arm himself with for war, except the King of Glory. Who is this King of Glory? The Lord strong and mighty, the Lord mighty in battle (Ps. 24:8, Luke 13:32, and, Rev. 12:9). This is who we had leading us then and now. Who is fighting your battles these days?

On Sunday, we went to church to praise the Lord and be fed manna from heaven via the gospel. The pastor of the church was not preaching that day. Instead, a rather petite young woman was chosen to deliver the message. She was a darling little lady who preached without her shoes on her feet. No one ever knows what the king's next move will be. The minister introduced herself and revealed the title of her sermon. The sermon title was none other than Moving with the Master. I almost fell out of my chair in amazement.

The Lord whose love for me is exceedingly great wanted to finish what He started at the airport. I was a pawn in His hands as my eyes and ears were fixated on every word she voiced. The content of her message accentuated the prophetic words of the man at the airport. To sum up her sermon, the Lord orders every step of a Christian who is walking in the plan that God has willed. If your work seems to be at a stalemate, your work is probably not finished. This sermon was definitely for me (Ps. 37:23, [KJV]). Our weekend was wonderful although being ghostbusters was not in our plans!

Once I returned backed to Nashville, moving forward in my career remained a focus. I enhanced some interviewing techniques with hopes of a different outcome. The result was the same. Thoughts of the sermon in Chicago reverberated from the time I left Chicago until the end of March 2003. My mind was rewinding and reassessing every aspect of my life that may have an element of incompletion. Nothing appeared in my spirit or mind.

Despite the interest in advancing my career, my work ethic and spirit of excellence on the job in Nashville never declined. While completing a report in my office, a senior leader came to see me. We had an established relationship with mutual respect. She asked if I had some time to talk. I nodded my head yes. I stopped what I was doing to listen to what she had to say. She closed the door and sat down. She explained that my prior boss made some derogatory statements about me in a meeting that offended some leaders. She indicated that she wanted me to be aware of the statements and wanted to know if there were any actions that I wanted to pursue.

Those that were offended knew me well. However, she begged them to not divulge to me what occurred. She was appointed to address the matter from an executive level. They complied with her request and did not share anything with me surrounding the issue. The tyrant who made derogatory statements against me was angry that I was performing an assignment as intended. The assignment meant that I had to assess areas that he was responsible for managing and, he did not like it. His statements attacked my race, gender, and physical attributes. I am told that he placed an exclamation point at the end of his statements signified by a hearty laugh.

Smoke may have been coming from the top of my head because I was fuming. Rash decisions are generally not wise ones. Thus, I told the senior leader that I needed to take a few days before determining what direction I desired to pursue. God never forgot the evil deeds of this service chief who purposefully oppressed, degraded, and emotionally scarred a countless number of people. God gave me the ability to store and recall enormous amounts of information. This capability did not favor this service chief. I went to the senior leader's office who was appointed to investigate the matter to inform her of my decision. My decision was a recommendation to terminate the physician from his role in the hospital.

The supporting evidence was a litany of horrid events and outcomes that he caused for approximately ten years. God empowered me to mentally recall and transcribe the events in writing formally. Presented with this evidence, the new CEO wanted to speak with me. He was flabbergasted at the evidence and the behavior of the service chief. Furthermore, he could not understand why he treated me in this manner considering the way I turned around his underperforming department.

A dilemma arose regarding my desired outcome. Who does Sabrina think she is? He is a doctor. I reiterated my position to the relevant executives. I closed my remarks by stating that if this action did not occur, I planned to pursue the matter at the highest level in the Veterans Administration. Fearing that his demise was near, the service chief stopped me in the hall to speak with me. I did not honor his request. The Lord had spoken and, His position was clear.

This man was going to move permanently. The rumor mill indicates that he was given an option to retire. The exit strategy was immaterial to me. The result was that he was gone! He was my unfinished business! His departure was celebrated throughout the hospital. You should have seen the number of smiling faces and joyous tears. God set so many people free (Job 3:18-19).

My journey to advancement was never denied. God had a purposeful delay that was aligned with His glory and will. Two months after the Lord completed His work, my assignment was finished and, my window of opportunity opened wide. When I landed in North Carolina for my interview in January, I said this place looks like Canaan land to me! On February 14, 2003, I was offered an opportunity of a lifetime. I accepted the new role and launched my thinking toward my movement forward. God has plans to prosper us and to give us hope without harm (Jer. 29:11). God's will and His work take precedence. Patience is a virtue that requires humility (Ps. 27:14). This is something that I had to learn. Waiting on the Lord's direction is always the right move despite our circumstances or feelings. The servant is not greater than the Master (John 13:16). Thank you, Lord, for your wisdom!

We lived in our home on Candy Drive for fifteen glorious years. The fond memories and lessons learned will be with us forever. While I was away on a business trip in California, Larry was busy discarding our home of unwanted goods in preparation for our move to North Carolina. It was tough saying goodbye to my dear friend and neighbor, Ms. Norma. My new journey began on March 31, 2003. There are a few times we moved to other states because of Larry's positions. The roles reversed in 2003. Larry started traveling with me because of my new roles and, he was happy to do it. The Lord anchored His seal of approval regarding our move with an offer on our home within twenty-four hours from the time the sign was placed in the front yard.

Based on the job description and conversations with my new boss, I envisioned my new position to be full of excitement and challenges which were welcomed. Do you remember how getting something new makes you feel? You cannot wait to get home to try on that new outfit although you tried it on in the store. On Christmas you get a gift and, you hurriedly rip the wrapping paper and the box wide open to see what is inside. Getting something new seems to always be complemented by euphoria. Getting this new position was no different. I was leaping with joy. My joy was so tremendous that it surpassed the highest leap you could ever imagine on a trampoline. Larry drove the entire trip without complaining which allowed me to snore at will and partake of the scenery.

This was the first position that included executive privilege for us. This meant that the government would provide us with temporary housing at their expense while we looked for a permanent residence. We selected an apartment a month before we arrived in North Carolina. It was fully furnished with all of the desired amenities including linen and dishes. The apartment was less than two miles from my workplace. The new surroundings and the well-adorned apartment afforded us a sense of peace and a calming atmosphere. A move with the Master is always great (Phil. 4:19, 2 Cor. 9:8, and, Ps. 23:1). We are humbly grateful for all the blessings that were coming forth.

Abounding Grace

The first day of my new position was full of excitement. My day started with a quaint orientation from my new boss who was a physician by trade. The night before my first day on the job, I prepared a document of what I planned to accomplish within the first ninety days. The contents were shared with my new boss. He laughed and remarked that my plans were a bit aggressive. Like a sponge, I absorbed as much as possible day and night about my new role and the organization. I needed to study to determine the needs of my organization (2 Tim. 2:15). Although I was located in North Carolina, our principal office was in Washington D.C. Within two weeks of my appointment, I visited the D.C. office and met the full team. After making some assessments, a business plan was created that I presented to my boss with zeal. He embraced it with open arms and gave me a card blanch to fully execute the plan about four months after my arrival. Sabrina was walking on cloud nine. At last, I landed a position with a boss that valued me and my skill set. What a welcome change and a great feeling.

The launch of my business plan was delayed. A first cousin that I grew up with me in Delaware died suddenly. There was never a thought in my mind of not attending his homegoing services. My residence in North Carolina was only six hours from Delaware. The timing of the funeral along with the short distance meant that I only needed to request a few days off from work. My boss graciously honored my request.

Larry and DJ remained in the nest and, I flew home on a Saturday evening. Once I got cozy in my seat and the plane was airborne, the good Lord began to speak. He said, Sabrina, you need to see your sister Carmen when you land. His voice was well understood and, His command became my number one priority. Carmen is my youngest sister and, she was barely six months pregnant. Cecilia picked me up from the Philadelphia airport with plans to make some stops before reaching our parents' home. Emphatically, I stated that we must see Carmen first. I explained that the Lord gave me my marching orders. Have you noticed the pattern between God and me on the airplanes? The Lord and I became close friends.

Carmen was surprised to see us so soon, but she gave us warm embraces as we entered through the door. When someone is in pain, their discomfort will sometimes be reflected in their movements and facial expressions. Carmen's eyes were dim, her forehead was wrinkled with lines and her movements were very sluggish. This was not Carmen at all. She was simply a gorgeous vivacious woman. Her eyes were always bright and wide, her skin was smooth and emollient and, she walked with a quickness. Because of these changes, I knew something was not right. I asked her what was wrong and, she stated that she was having labor pains. My antenna went up with alarm.

My recollections of the two stillbirths that I had at five months permeated my mind. Certainly, I did not want her to experience what I did. I urged her to let us take her to the hospital. Carmen said she recently went to the hospital for the same reason and, it was a false alarm. Therefore, she did not feel the need to go again. The more I observed her, the more discomfort I could see in her body. Her labor pains got sharper and closer together. My spirit knew that this particular experience was unlike the one Carmen previously encountered. Sensing the possible demise of the baby, I begged Carmen to go to the hospital. I was not going to take no for an answer. She conceded. Cecilia drove her to the hospital and, I accompanied them praying all the way.

The hospital was nearby but not a preference. The medical team did an assessment and determined that she was in active labor. She was given medication to stop her labor and we were informed that she needed to go to another hospital equipped with a neonatal unit.

Transferring Carmen to another hospital gave us comfort that she would receive the proper level of care. She arrived at the new hospital by ambulance after we got there. We kissed her and, she was immediately admitted, taken to a room, and assessed. Fear had no place in her hospital room. We prayed with faith (James 1:6 and, James 5:15). If the throne of grace could be worn out by insurmountable prayers, it surely would have occurred on the night of August 2, 2003. Every place we went in the hospital we prayed. All the prayer warriors and people we knew were summoned and on bended knees.

When Cecilia and I were allowed to come into the room, Carmen's mate was present and holding her hand. Aside from his presence, several doctors were in the room including Carmen's actual obstetrician. An instrument was connected to Carmen to show the timing and severity of her labor and contractions. The readings suggested that Carmen's baby was going to be born. She was given doses of medication to speed up the development of the baby's lungs as well as medicine to stop her contractions. **At Carmen's bedside, the obstetrician openly shared that we do not want the baby to be born now. She said the baby has a gaping hole in her esophagus that was identified on a previous ultrasound. The doctor reiterated that she would not survive if she were born today.** I asked the doctor if the defect could be corrected in utero and, she said no, the baby will require surgery after birth. Before the doctor could finalize her statements, Carmen had a big contraction. Simultaneously, God used me to lay hands on her belly and pray out aloud amid a substantial size medical team (Acts 28:8). My spirit cried out to God in both my prayer and natural English language. Carmen's labor and contractions subsided. She had a tough night and needed some rest.

Cecilia and I needed some rest also. We departed the hospital around 4:00 am on the morning of August 3, 2003, with Carmen in stable condition and free of contractions. Because of the time we departed, I decided to stay the night with Cecilia as opposed to going to our parents' home. We finally got in bed around 5:00 am. Before our bodies could make an impression in the bed, the telephone rang. It was the hospital. The baby had turned in the birth canal and was going to be born. We sprung up like bunny rabbits and rushed to the hospital. **Shalondamae (Shalonda) Marie was born within minutes of our arrival and, she was perfect! The hole in her esophagus that the doctors visualized on the ultrasound was not there.** God healed her and every organ in her body was functioning well! (Matt. 9:22 and, Matt. 15:28). She was just a teensy baby. Truly God's grace and mercy prevailed that morning (2 John 1:3 and, Heb. 4:16)!

God orchestrated a plan to miraculously heal Shalondamae and used me as well as Cecilia to fulfill His plan. He did this because of His undying love and so that others might believe in His glorious name and be saved (John 2:22-24, John 4:48, and, John 11:45). If you could see me at this moment, you would see a woman shouting for joy and praising the Lord as I relive this event. Glory to God in the highest! You and I may never know whose heart was knitted with God's heart as a result of this miracle. Was it someone at the bedside or was it someone else who heard of the healing? I do not know. Surely, I would have liked to be a fly on the wall inside the doctors' lounge as they discussed this miracle.

Did I ever make it to my cousin's funeral? I certainly did. My cousin's services took place a day after Shalonda was born. This was the first cousin who died in our family. Helping my family members cope with the loss was one of the chief reasons for my visit. After the funeral services, Cecilia and I visited Carmen and her miracle baby named Shalondamae. This truth gets better. Shalonda's premature birth required that she remain in the hospital in an incubator for a few months. I had multiple chances to touch her through an opening in her incubator. A pacifier was inside of her incubator and, it seemed enormously large for her tiny mouth. Gently, I tried to insert the pacifier into her mouth, but I was having a challenging time. My struggle was the sheer size of the pacifier in comparison to her mouth. From the naked eye, it appeared as though inserting it into her mouth could cause an injury. Unbelievably, Shalonda removed the pacifier from my hand and inserted it in her mouth. She was only a day old! From that moment, I called her Grace.

She continued to defy odds and perform miraculously. On the third day of her existence, my sister Crystal was leaving her room and told Grace goodbye. You are not going to believe what Grace did. She waved goodbye to Crystal. My sister and I were dumbfounded. Who does this at three days old? A child anointed by God; a child called Grace. As Grace grew, we marveled at the skills and the level of intelligence that God endowed her with at an early age. She was also featured in a magazine because of her miraculous outcomes. We must always put our hope in the Lord and not man (1 Pet. 1:21 and, Ps. 119:114).

Is the Grass Really Greener on the Other Side?

After witnessing the Lord's miraculous healing, power, and grace, I returned to North Carolina floating on a cloud bigger than the one I was on before I left. Larry was given the unadulterated details of what God did during my visit to Delaware. Coming home always brings about peace. There is nothing like a hug and a kiss from your husband and sleeping in your bed. Before going to bed, my brain switched gears and went into business mode. I was returning to work the very next day, so launching the delayed business plan was at the forefront of my mind. To be successful, I needed buy-in from the department heads. Over the next few weeks,

I acquired the necessary buy-in without a hitch. The execution of the plan was smooth as silk.

My successful execution scored a lot of brownie points with my boss. His trust in me became apparent with the number of leadership projects I was asked to oversee or manage. Oh, my life was grand. I got a promotion and several monetary awards in two years. My life was further sweetened by a short commute to work. My work life could not get any better, or could it? In the meantime, a transition was being planned in D.C. at the end of 2004. My boss's supervisor who was a part of my upper echelon was retiring and, the baton was being handed to a female physician who was coming from another Federal agency.

Soon after her appointment in 2005, she visited my office in North Carolina to meet everyone. Although she was pleasant, something did not sit well with me concerning her. In time, my eerie feelings about her became transparent. On a subsequent visit, she informed me that I needed to train a colleague. Her position was he should know everything that I know and while I was at it, teach him how to lead as well. My boss was not in agreement with her strategy and pushed back quite a bit. His pushback resulted in him losing his leadership role within that organization, but he landed on his feet. At the same time, she worked hard to discredit me from attaining higher roles inside and outside of the VA.

On one of her visits to my office, she pretended to be interested in me and my work. The moment she saw me she hugged me and became very talkative. From the outside looking in, one would have thought that we had a good relationship. In front of my staff, colleagues, and boss, she echoed some accolades about the caliber of my work that she heard about from others. Her behavior was conspicuously artificial to the point of nausea.

This leader acted as though she was thrilled about my devised business plan and asked to see how I came to my conclusions. I became giddy and metaphorically skipped to my office to retrieve the necessary documents. She sat in an unoccupied office next to mine and just skimmed through the documents. I could see what she was doing from my office window. After her brief review, she dumped all of my work on the floor and summoned me to pick up everything. Being the person that I am, I took pictures and sought resolutions on a grander scale. Although I was livid, a calm composure was maintained. No one saw my sweat or anger. If a ruler's anger rises against you, do not leave your post; calmness can lay great offenses to rest (Eccles. 10:4).

Stevie Wonder could see that she was seeking to get me angry enough to have an outburst. Stevie could also see that this leader wanted to ensure that the colleague that she was fond of went to the top of the line for my boss's position. At the same time, she was contriving devious plots to ensure that Sabrina would not have a chance to be considered. To ensure that her plan flourished, she promoted this guy to a higher grade level without merit to seal his fate. Before his promotion, we were at the same level. Her beguiling tactic worked. Unfortunately, this colleague was promoted to a position of incompetence. He had no earthly idea what to do. He played nice with me in the sandbox to accomplish his work. This colleague became my boss. God requires that we work in the spirit of excellence despite our leadership or circumstances. This is confirmed in the Bible which tells us that we are to work willingly at whatever we do, as though we are working for the Lord rather than for people (Col. 3:23, [NLT]). I did just that.

Nevertheless, the upper echelon kept undue pressure and heat on me. It is said that if you are unable to stand the heat, get out of the kitchen. With that being said, gainful employment outside of the department was pursued constantly. The positions I competed for and were offered were at a high level. One would think that the new leader would be ecstatic that I was getting job offers elsewhere. With me getting a new position outside of her regime, I would be out of the way and her chosen employee would have the freedom to lead without me being an inferred threat. She got wind of my complaints about her unethical behavior and created background noise.

The noise was so loud that my job offers were rescinded. When I discovered what she had done, I became enraged. My anger exceeded a boiling point and from that point, I was consumed with revenge. The thought of this new position being Canaan land disintegrated and my new reality was a knockout punch. In reality, there was no prosperity for me here and the grass was not green at all. In fact, there was no grass. What appeared to be grass was actually sinking sand and, I was being swallowed in the depths of it. I began to internalize everything that was happening around me as a personal attack whether it was or not. My fixation with revenge muted the voice of the Lord. I did not want to read the Bible and, I was a bump on a log at church. Instead, my concentration was on mounting a legal defense at full speed. Before mounting a legal defense, Larry was not made aware of what I was dealing with at work. I did all I could to protect the sanctity of my family.

My internal agony took a toll on my body. Stress will not show up on an x-ray, but it will let you know that is present. This ordeal caused my blood pressure and glucose levels to soar. This was never an issue for me in the past. My mind became clouded with everything that was happening to me and in my periphery. If God were speaking to me, I could not hear Him. Why was I feeling so alone and so rejected? I had a great marriage and a great life. Why was this leader attacking me? I did nothing wrong. This agonizing ordeal took place for two years. I left misery to gain agony. I was feeling like a person that fled from a lion only to meet a bear, and when I returned home and rested my hand on the wall, I was bitten by a snake (Amos 5:19). What a tradeoff!

Proverbs 17:22 tells us that a cheerful heart is good medicine, but a crushed spirit dries up the bones. What should you glean from this scripture? I read an article recently that dissects this scripture well, thus I am sharing it with you. A segment of the article says the following: "There is a mysterious power that mood has over physical health. When one has a "crushed spirit" it cannot but help hurting the body. Unlike Platonic heresies that separate the body from the soul, the Christian is a created soul and body by God. Life is holistic and the body and soul are interlinked. Indeed, even in the New Heavens and Earth at the end of the age, our physical bodies will rise and be transformed into a new body that is spiritual, but also physical."[2]. How powerful and truthful this passage is. The emotional upheavals of this particular trial zapped my spirit and altered my physical wellness at the same time.

In the middle of 2005, which was the eye of my storm, the co-pastor of our church spoke life into my soul through scripture. She quoted Jeremiah 33:3 which says in the King James Version to Call unto me, and I will answer thee, and show thee great and mighty things, which thou knowest not. What penetrated my soul the most was the word "call." You know, I was not calling on the Lord much. Sabrina was working through the storm on her strength. Then, I began to dissect the entire passage. The notion that the Lord wanted to show me great and mighty things was something I needed to investigate.

Our guest room was the place where I often read my word in our home in Apex. A day or so after the pastor spoke to me, I started reading the old testament again. In particular, I read some passages in the books of Chronicles, Deuteronomy, and Jeremiah.

After reading, I turned out the pole lamp that I used for reading and went into another room. Well, when I headed back down the hallway where the guest room was located, I noticed that the lamp I turned off was well lit and, I know I turned it off. The light drew me back into the room. When I got there, I knew that the Lord wanted to speak to me through the scriptures. I continued to read the same books. Some of the words within the passages seem to be raised from the pages to ensure that I noticed them and would read them. Each passage centered on battles with God's enemies and being in the wilderness as a child of God.

The next morning when I was in the kitchen, the Lord spoke to me and said that I was His battle-ax and my fear of man-caused this delay. I walked away understanding that I am in a war. Yet, I was not understanding the Lord's connotation regarding fear. What did the Lord mean that my fear of man caused this delay? There was no one on the planet that I was fearful of in my mind. The fact is that I missed the big picture altogether.

My understanding came when I read with a sincere intent to receive from God. What God revealed and what I learned were incredible. Let me sum it up in a nutshell. Sabrina was in a season of spiritual trials and testing characterized by the unwarranted attacks, isolation, rejection, and loneliness. The faith of King David, Apostle Paul, Moses, Job, Peter, and many others in the Bible was also tested. A test is very painful but necessary for your spiritual walk and maturation as a Christian. Our faith must be tested and strengthened. That which is sewn in our hearts must be revealed and sometimes expunged. You always gain insight and learn from the Lord's revelations.

I was compelled to read about the wilderness because God tested His people for forty years. Like the Israelites, I found myself in the wilderness being tested. Is being in the wilderness purposeful? God did this to humble them, to see the depths of their hearts, and determine if they would follow His commands (Deut. 8:2). Remember that the Lord told me in the kitchen that I was his battle-ax? The scripture that I read that references this is: You are my battle-ax and weapons of war: For with you I will break the nation in pieces; With you, I will destroy kingdoms (Jer. 51:20, [KJV]). How can the Lord use me if, He is unable to trust me or if I do not trust Him? Like the Israelites, humility was a struggle for me. Choosing to resolve issues in my strength instead of seeking the Lord's guidance demonstrates my inability to humble myself (Prov. 18:12).

Similarly, if I am fearful in any aspect of my life, my faith is not as strong as it should be. Potentially losing my job emerged as a deep-seated fear and a snare for me. God's Word tells us that fear of man will prove to be a snare (Prov. 29:25). This meant I believed man's power was greater than the Lord's power. What happened to the scripture if God is for you who could be against you? I know this scripture by heart (Rom. 8:31). Why did it not spring up? It did not spring up because it was not ingrained in my soul. The knowledge was in my head but did not make its way to my heart. Knowledge without action is useless (James 2:20 and, James 2:26). The Lord will continue to strengthen us through our weaknesses.

Our godly inheritance is kept in heaven for us. Through faith, we are shielded by God's power until salvation. In all of this, we greatly rejoice, though now for a little while, we may have had to suffer grief in all kinds of trials. These have come so that the proven genuineness of our faith of greater worth than gold, which perishes even though refined by fire may result in praise, glory, and honor when Jesus Christ is revealed (1 Pet. 1:5-8). My friends, the Lord is unequivocally stating that tests are inevitable for a Christian seeking to walk with God, a necessity to move to higher ground and gain a stronger partnership with Him to complete His splendid work.

Earlier in my Christian faith, I learned an acronym for fear. It is coined as false evidence appearing real. This is the exact opposite of faith. For faith is the substance of things hoped for and the evidence of things not seen (Heb. 11:1).

A Way Out of No Way

If you are in a weakened state or have a broken spirit, you are still useful to the Lord. Our reliance on the Lord tends to increase when we are fragile (2 Cor. 12:9-10). In a trial or when your back is against the wall, who you are in Christ Jesus will emerge. While I was knee-deep in my storm, I received a call at work from a Christian whom I mentored. Not only was I her mentor, but she was also my employee for a few years. From the moment I answered the telephone, she poured her heart out. On a scale of one to ten, her voice, anger, and emotional stress were on twenty. Yet, her faith was not apparent. She was in the middle of a quandary and needed some spiritual guidance.

She applied for nursing school and was being offered an incredible opportunity. The specific program would pay her tuition and current salary while she was a full-time student. What a Godsend! There was one caveat. Her leadership needed to agree to the terms of the program and approve her application. She waited and waited for a response from her leadership without success. Finally, she got an answer from her direct line supervisor. He disapproved her application which crushed her spirit (Prov. 18:14). I envisioned her walking in circles, throwing her hands up in the air, and fuming in disgust.

I knew her direct line supervisor well and, he was not a friend of the Lord. His actions for several years illuminated his alignment with Satan (Titus 1:16, Prov. 30:12, and, Eph. 5:6). The time to submit her application was ticking away and was due in twenty-four hours on the day she called me. What she had in her favor was her perseverance. She was unwilling to take no for an answer. Nevertheless, no options were remaining that she could think of at the time. Oh! There was an option she did not consider. She forgot about the good Lord. I quelled her anger by asking her if she believed that God could do all things but fail? God's love never fails. He never deserts His children (Ps. 136:1 and, Heb. 13:5).

After she acknowledged God's greatness and power, she reiterated that she only had twenty-four hours to submit her package. I said: Where is your faith? Her fear of being rejected and not getting into the nursing program was consuming her soul and body. (Prov. 29:25 and, Ps. 55:5). I was walking in her shoes, but she did not know it. With a tone of endearment, I said girl, twenty-four hours are nothing for God. He can move a mountain in a blink of an eye (Job 9:5). Through our faith, we have been given the same power to move a mountain. You must believe that you can. With a morsel of faith, what you pray for, or decree will materialize providing your request is aligned with God's will and plan for your life (Matt. 17:5). Do you believe you can move a mountain? I know I can.

Even when we are in the midst of a storm, the Lord calls His people to render guidance and assistance to those in need (Prov. 3:27, Rom. 12:13, and, Rom. 15:1-2). Our guidance must be godly. Despite the titles we hold, we must go to the throne of grace to ensure that we hear from the Lord and give advice pleasing to Him. We prayed on the telephone for over thirty minutes; asking the Lord to move that mountain named disapproval and make her enemy (her supervisor) her footstool (Ps.110:1 and, Heb. 1:13). We resumed our praying partnership in the evening hours.

We thanked the Lord in advance for the blessing we entrusted Him to give. Sometimes, we have not because we ask not. The Lord does want us to have an abundant life (James 4:2 and, John 10:10). Thank God for the Holy Spirit because our carnal minds do not know what to pray. Did you know that the Holy Spirit that dwells in us intercedes on our behalf because we do not know what to pray? (Rom. 8:26). The Bible also tells us that the prayers of the righteous are powerful and effective (James 5:16). As a reminder, our righteousness is only attained through Christ as a Born-Again Christian. Where do you stand?

After prayer, I recommended that she seek approval from her supervisor's boss the next morning. She was a little wary of potential friction from her supervisor for going over his head. I reminded her that she had nothing to fear. The Lord would keep her safe (Jer.15:21 and, Ps. 20:1). Our call ended with an understanding that her priority for the next day was meeting with the higher-level manager in the morning.

The infamous day arrived and what a difference it made! Her application had to be submitted by the end of the day. Before Noon, she was contacted by her upper management and informed that her disapproved application was overturned and approved. The leader apologized to her for the delay in getting her application approved, thanked her for her leadership and commitment to healthcare. She also communicated that the leader stated that he was in support of her career aspirations.

You and I know what happened. Late in the midnight hour, God moved that mountain, touched that leader's heart, and placed her enemy at her feet in less than twenty-four hours. Look at the All-Mighty God! When she called me to give her praise report, her emotion and spirit were aligned and on a blistering twenty on a joy scale of one to ten. The young lady's faith was tested and strengthened. Remember the scripture Jeremiah 33:3? She called on the Lord and, He showed her great and mighty things that she did not know. What a miracle and testament of faith in action.

God used me to exhort her, serve as a counselor, and be a prayer warrior to influence an increase in her faith.

During this time, my current trial had no sting or effect. Did the trial evaporate? No, it did not. The difference was my focus. Throughout my mentee's trial, my focus was completely on God and His Word. At no time did I focus on my situation. Through her test, I was taught a valuable lesson. Never focus on the situation or surroundings, focus on the Lord. Only the Lord has the power to move a mountain and destroy both body and soul (Matt. 10:28). There is another point that the Lord is reemphasizing here. Do you know what it is? If the additional point is foggy, let me clear it up for you. The Lord can use you for His glory even when you are broken, being mended, or going through the firing process (a trial). By the way, she graduated from college with honors and is still working at the same hospital as a Registered Nurse with specialized skills. She continues to give the Lord honor and praise for her victory and blessings through her turbulent time (Ps. 50:15).

Beyond The Green Grass, Living In The Green Zone

Based on the valuable lessons, I repented and snapped out of the fog that encapsulated me in August of 2006. I apologized to the church leadership for my dormancy and became re-engaged in my outreach work as though the storm and test did not occur. When I did this, I could feel the Lord's love even more. The next weekend, the church planned a barbeque and a back-to-school supply giveaway at a local park. I joined the team with elation. The Lord prearranged some divine appointments. Throughout the day, someone was always sitting on a bench alone but not for long. God used me to develop a rapport with each prospect and to share the gospel of Jesus Christ with them. Every time, someone appeared on a bench, the Lord made me aware of their presence and, the need to act. On that day, the Lord saved several people who were both young and old. Hallelujah! I do not know who was smiling the most; me or the Lord.

Remember, all of God's actions are purposeful. He wants to use you to the fullest extent possible and further develop you at the same time. Moving to a higher level with the Lord means a constant shedding of yourself. God will provide the needed revelations and instruct you. Think about any test you have encountered. While you are thinking, do not forget to include the tests taken in a school of any kind, an interview, as well as a spiritual trial. Every aspect of a test can be tough and painful. Your mental and physical stamina must be aligned with the ultimate goal of passing the test. Once the test is completed, we tend to forget about the pain. Recollecting what caused your discomfort or struggle will serve you well in the future. There is a strong likelihood that you will repeat the test if you fail to apply what you have learned. The Lord does want us to examine and test our faith. The Bible states to examine yourselves to test whether you are in the faith; test yourselves. Do you not realize that Christ Jesus is in you unless you fail the test (2 Cor. 13:5)?

How do you think I scored during my storm? My assessment may differ from yours and that is okay. At the beginning of the test, I believed I scored high. My composure was maintained and, I work diligently, focusing on God and not man during repeated persecution. My score dropped significantly during the period of isolation. God could not use me when my mind was cluttered, nor did I utilize any of the spiritual gifts He loaned me. A bump on a log in church (or on the couch at home) is a lukewarm Christian and useless in God's eyes (Rev. 3:15-16). Through God's words and His instruction, I recovered and bounced back with a rehabilitated sense of purpose and a deeper appreciation of God's love.

This experience promoted a profound interest in monitoring the way that I apply lessons learned and their impact. This shift moved me to the green zone. Do you want to know what is the green zone? A green zone is a place of everlasting growth. Learning something new is good, applying what you learn is great. Monitoring the impact of it all is outstanding and is how you achieve growth. I will be forever green.

In 2007, a truce took place. I accepted a leadership position in Alabama. My family and I left North Carolina in September 2007. Before we departed, our church had a sending-off ceremony. Other saints were moving, and they were also a part of the ceremony. Like gut-wrenching experiences, you never forget the super feel-good events either. The sending-off ceremony was euphoric and followed the close of the morning worship service. It was a little odd standing in front of the congregation. The Lord swiftly took that awkwardness away when He began to speak through the pastor.

The pastor came to each person standing and shared what the Lord downloaded in his spirit. I will never forget the words. When he came to my husband Larry, he said that God said that he is a great man of God! He then went to another person and shared God's word. He went back to Larry and reiterated boldly that God said that he is a great man of God. Hearing these words from God was music to my ears. What I know about my husband was now being proclaimed by the Lord. Larry's joy overflowed as well as mine.

When the pastor came to me, he said that God said that I will share the gospel at any cost, and together Larry and I are kingdom builders. Wow, it does not get any better than that. These words translated into well done for me. This event felt so good, that I probably pinched myself to see if I was still in the land of the living. God's words through the pastor were gifts that raised our level of thanksgiving and praise. Reflecting on my entire life from 1979 until 2007, the trials of my faith were plentiful. What reflections do you see in your life from the past and now?

Reflections and Movement Forward (Chapters IV)

Question 1: Lord show me if there are any lukewarm areas in my life (Matt. 23:28, Rev. 3:16, and, James 1:23).

_____

_____

_____

Question 2: Lord what aspect of my trials or test do I continue to fail? Show me how to pass this test so that I may come out of the wilderness (Heb. 12:1-2, 2 Cor. 13:5, 9, and, James 1:23).

_____

_____

_____

Question 3: What hidden fear do I have of people or their actions that are delaying my spiritual growth and receiving all that you have planned for me (Prov. 29:25, Luke 12:4, and, Matt. 10:28)?

_____

_____

_____

Question 4: Lord do I possess the boldness to pray and share your name among men so your miracles and powers may be manifested (Luke 12:8 and, Luke 18 1:14)? If I do not have this Lord, I welcome the Holy Spirit's power to spring up in my soul (Acts 4:31).

_____

_____

_____

Question 5: Lord show me indiscretions or secrets that I need to take to the throne of grace (Luke 8:17 and, James 5:16)?

_____

_____

_____

Question 6: Lord am I guilty of judging (Matt. 7:1, Rom. 2:1-2, Phil. 2:30 and, James 2:13)?

_____

_____

_____

CHAPTER V

A PLACE CALLED WETUMPKA

Before embarking on our new journey, we had to sell our home in Apex. The real estate market had changed dramatically and houses were selling at a snail's pace. God then stepped in and provided us with another gift. We were afforded an option to allow the government to purchase our home. Our real estate agent did not know that we were contemplating this. God took care of us! We accepted the buyout offer in record time and at the brink of the real estate market collapse. When you are in God's will, things will align despite the trials you may face.

Moving with the Master has straightened my walk with the Lord. Despite understanding God's will and purpose for your life, no one knows what He has in store during the journey. The thought that was promenading in my mind was what does the Lord have planned in Alabama? The circle of life is peculiar. My old mentor, Robert Ratliff, was going to be my new boss in Alabama. This was not foreseen. He had tried to recruit me to this location on a few occasions, but the previous offers had not been enticing. Why the change in desire now? I wanted to attend a Christian law school and help those who were disenfranchised.

My fervent prayer availed much. God sent me to a book that was shelved in my bedroom closet. It was a book of law schools around the country. The Lord then led me to a page with a Christian law college in Montgomery, Alabama. Their mission resonated with my calling. Once this school was identified and the new job offer emerged, a match made in heaven materialized in my mind.

The Hughes family began our journey to Alabama during Labor Day Weekend in 2007. We were moving to a destination that was further south and approximately 486 miles from our prior home in Apex. We were granted executive privilege yet again. Thus, we had a prearranged furnished apartment awaiting our arrival. Except for stopping for food and gas, Larry drove non-stop to Montgomery, Alabama. Knowing the God we serve, we expected an apartment that had a pleasant aroma and was well-appointed. We were very satisfied. This allowed us to kick our shoes off and rest immediately on a soft fluffy couch. Working with the Lord does have rewards, but the kingdom of heaven must be sought first before our earthy wishes are granted (Matt. 6:33).

My new position started the day after Labor Day. The CEO and I had a well-established relationship. He did not waste any time sharing the challenges of the organization and what he needed me to do as a priority. I was stunned when I walked around the building. My mentor had pictures of me, and my career path plastered on the wall. He was showcasing the success of his mentoring relationships and had these pictures mounted at least a year before my arrival. While walking in the halls, I would see people looking at the wall, then gaze at me and burst out and say, "Oh, that is you!" Perhaps I should have been flattered, but I was embarrassed. Seeing my pictures on the wall seemed less than humble and very self-serving. I told Robert about the impression that I felt the pictures were sending since I was now on board, and the pictures were eventually removed.

On the weekends, our real estate agent would pick us up to go house hunting. Within six weeks, we looked at fifty homes before we found one that met both of our requirements. Larry was interested in having land and, I wanted to make sure that the chosen house could accommodate the furniture we had in storage. When we were not looking for a home, I was studying for my law entrance exam. I began studying while I was in Apex. After preparing for an additional six weeks, I was ready for the exam. The exam was tough and, I must admit that some anxiety flared regarding how well I performed. Have you ever participated in self-talk? This was a self-talking moment for me. I told myself that I studied hard to show myself approved so why did I have this anxiety (2 Tim. 2:15). With that, I had peace, and the anxiety rapidly diminished.

In a few weeks, I got my results in the mail and, I screamed because I scored well. The door to getting my law degree was wide open and the next step was in reach. My application was submitted for the Christian law school night program shortly after I received my exam results. A letter came from the college within a month of submitting my application. Larry handed me the letter and it was like a Christmas gift to me! I ripped the letter open in a hurry to read its' contents.

The contents were not what I expected. The night program was closing. What a bummer. The college accepted me as a full-time student, but this was not going to work for me. I could not quit my full-time position. Needless to say, this open door slammed shut. Disappointment surfaced briefly. The circulating thought in my mind was Lord what are you up to? It was the Lord who pointed me to this law school in the first place. Why the closed door? The Lord certainly knew that I wanted to be a lawyer and that I needed to be employed. In time, the Lord revealed His hand, and His revelations blew my mind.

In the meantime, we continued to look for a home. At last, we selected a brand-new home in Wetumpka, Alabama. The setting was very rural and beautiful. Have you ever heard of a place called Wetumpka, Alabama? This city was news to us. The house we selected was not quite finished and an address number for the house did not exist. The house was completed in mid-October 2007 and, we gained custody of it on October 31st. All of the houses on our street had addresses in the twenties and thirties.

One would have thought that our new address would follow the established numbering pattern. It did not. You will be shocked to know what our address became. Well, it was just the number seven. This house number did not fit in with the sequence surrounding us. We gained insight from the Holy Spirit as to why. The Holy Spirit reminded us of the spiritual correlation between the number seven and completion or something being finished. Our house address was a sign and a reminder that God's children are not designed to fit in with the world system (John 15:19). Thus, our address was considered a misfit in man's established numbering pattern, but it was a perfect fit in God's plan. Larry and I knew that the Lord chose this home for us. The Holy Spirit's message alone quickened my spirit to know that we were on the brink of beholding and being a part of God's majesty. Watch God in the days and years ahead (Ps. 46:10).

A new chapter in our lives should invoke reflections from past chapters. Some questions that surfaced in my mind when we got to Alabama were: What worked well at other locations? I wonder if I will be able to infuse lessons learned and strategies acquired into my new work environment? What are the things that blind-sided or ensnared me in the past? When I reassessed all of the outcomes associated with my past, there was one specific lesson I learned that

I must be prepared for as a Christian: A trial and persecution await. In every trial, the outcomes or ending yielded fruit and positive impact but oh my goodness, why did I have to endure physical and mental anguish, sickness, ostracism, isolation, and rejection in the process. I am not complaining Lord. Who am I but a servant of the Lord? The servant is not greater than the Master (John 15:20). The suffering I experienced during my trials cannot hold a candle to the suffering and persecution of the Lord, Jesus Christ (1 Pet. 4:1, 1 Pet. 3:18, and, 1 Pet. 2:21).

The Apostle Paul said that his power given by the grace of God is perfected in his weakness therefore he will boast all the more in his weaknesses, so that the power of Christ may rest on him. That is why, for the sake of Christ, I delight in weakness, insults, hardships, persecutions, and difficulties. For when I am weak, I am strong (2 Cor. 12:9-10). Because I am covered by the Lord's grace and I desire to grow in Christ, I say to you bring on the battle! No one knows for sure what trial is awaiting or when it will begin. Since the enemy is prowling, it is essential to equip yourself every day with God's full armor in preparation for spiritual warfare (Eph. 6:11-18). Adopting this principle as a habitual routine is easier said than done, but necessary.

I was appointed as an administrative leader providing oversite and support of clinical programs. Our regional office mandated specific performance requirements that some of the clinical programs were challenged to achieve. Developing a rapport with people fairly quickly was another gift the Lord allowed me to use. Building these relationships with the respective leaders allowed me to earn their trust and candidly speak about areas that needed improvement. In partnership with many leaders, we made some notable improvements in less than three months that my upper echelon attributed to me. I attribute the success to the Lord. He wanted me to have some easy and early wins because the road ahead was going to be rocky except, I was oblivious.

Who Will Stand For Me?

One of my roles was to identify and mitigate risks for the good of the patients and the organization. Every rock I turned over, exposed some serious problems and generated heat. Once all the rocks and covers were turned over, we had a blazing fire that had to be extinguished. However, several clinicians were hoping that I would turn my head to what was exposed and ignore the blazing fire. Because I would not have a blinded eye, the true colors of the leaders I supported in the clinical realm were paraded before me. Their colors resonated with darkness and deceit. Their displays were aimed directly at me and, they were venomous. Here I go again, back in battle. Little did the enemies of the Lord know that the Lord gave me a discerning spirit to see the battle brewing beforehand. Therefore, I was spiritually armed (Prov. 16:21 and, Hosea 14:9).

The fire started to blaze when I was asked to lead an investigation regarding an adverse outcome and uncovered some atrocities. My investigative team was comprised of well-respected physicians who were severely wounded and saddened by the findings. There were patients tied to the negative outcomes who could not defend or speak for themselves. Who was going to stand in the gap for them? Who was going to speak for them and fight their battles (Prov. 31:9, and, Isa. 1:17)?

Throughout the process, the CEO was kept in the loop regarding significant findings. When my team and I finished the investigation, we formally presented the report to the executive team. After the team members left the room, I remained to further discuss the findings and actions that should take precedence from my perspective.

A look of anguish covered the face of one executive leader who professed to be a devout Christian. I thought the executive was troubled by the gravity of the outcomes. This was not the source of the anger. The reality that the report contained proven facts, pointed to particular culprits, circulated to the other executives meant that action was ultimately required for this individual.

If looks could kill, I would be dead. This executive snarled at me with hatred and yelled in the presence of the CEO, "You better not tell nobody about this report!" Did this person think that I was going to become a shrinking violet at his voice? I must have been mistaken for someone else. My Lord did not give me the spirit of fear (Rom. 8:15). Not everyone who professes to be a Christian will receive the Lord's inheritance. The fruit that one produces which equates to a person's actions and outcomes is measured by God (Matt.7:21). This person's fruit was rotten to the core. Prayerfully, his heart and the quality of his fruit have changed with time. As heirs of the royal priesthood, we are expected to pray for and love our enemies (Matt. 5:44). I promise that your knees will not wear out. Mine are still intact!

Every step we take and every place the Lord sends us is in preparation for the next assignment. Remember the time in North Carolina when the Lord told me that I was His battle-ax and weapon of war? The Lord planned to put this ax in motion in Alabama. The Lord Himself would be the one raising and throwing the ax (Isa. 10:15). With the Lord as my guide and friend, I stood firmly and sought justice for the weak, afflicted, and those who could no longer speak (Eph. 6:13 and, Isa. 1:17).

The CEO that I respected was appointed at another hospital. After this CEO left, all actions to address the findings went to the waste side. The new CEO united with those desiring to sweep everything under the rug. This was unacceptable! As a Christian, I stood my ground and sounded the alarm far and wide. The new CEO was informed that I planned to share the report with his boss at the regional level and, I kept my word. Sounding the alarm at a higher level promoted appropriate action and needed follow-up that remediated the outcomes to the extent possible, but I was hated all the more for it (Luke 21:17). It did not matter. The Lord was on a mission and, I was in His service despite the enemies' whispers of hate and plots to harm me (Ps. 41:7).

I cried out to the Lord many nights on behalf of the afflicted. In time, the Lord's enemies came tumbling down. Those whom the Lord annihilated were responsible for inaction and the perpetrators of wrongdoings. Like the walls of Jericho, this dynasty collapsed for all to see. The Lord demolished their weapons and strongholds (Heb. 11:30 and, 2 Cor. 10:4-5). There are times in our lives that we have to stand against unjust behavior in our environments. Are you willing to speak and fight for those who are unable to fight for themselves? The saints of the Lord are expected to protect, stand in the gap and fight for those who are unable (Ps. 82:3). With this aspect of my assignment being completed, the Lord had reconstruction on His mind and, I was the unanticipated carpenter chosen to remodel a department by His design (Isa. 41:7 [KJV]).

Reconstruction Period

Before the CEO that I admired departed in 2008, an opening developed in a department with high visibility and responsibility. The problem with the department was that it was written off as completely inept. The prior leader was ineffective in revitalizing the unit. The department as a whole was a well-known laughingstock throughout the hospital. The staff and the work they produced were not respected. However, the work that they were supposed to perform was of vital importance to the hospital's oversite of performance and, it was the kind of work that I was passionate about. This CEO asked if I would take the helm and, it was an opportunity that I could not refuse. After having a dialogue with each staff member individually, it was apparent that they were in a daze regarding their roles and what skills they needed to be proficient or better.

Not only was I assessing my working environment, living in the state of Alabama was under critical observation. To be honest, I felt like I went back in time at least twenty years. The technology and thought processes of businesses and colleagues appeared to be out of touch with the current trends. It bothered me so much that I started looking for gainful employment again. Every night after work, I got on the computer to seek a new job. This persisted for six months until the Lord became disturbed with my behavior. He regurgitated my words back to me and said: Sabrina you said that you wanted to help the disenfranchised, the poor, and the weak. "Quit your complaining because you are here." The Lord despises complaining and murmuring. The Bible tells us that His anger burns when someone complains (Num. 11:1 and, Jude 1:16).

The Lord made me see that looking for a new job was spiritual adultery. He ordered my steps to Alabama and gave me the Holy Spirit as an engagement ring. Oh, but what did I do? I turned my back on the Lord and decided His will was not going to be mine. The mere fact that I was looking for jobs was an act of spiritual adultery. I kidded with the Lord after my repentance and said, Lord, you spanked me. The Lord answered and said, "I did not spank you. I cut you" and, it was deep. Thankfully, the Lord had mercy on me and did not change me into a Leppard like he did Miriam for her complaining nor did the Lord have me killed by the destroying angel (Num. 12:9-10 and, 1 Cor.10:10).

My mind was appropriately recentered and reconstructed to keep my concentration on His will. With my eyes on the prize, the blueprints for the reconstruction of my new department were created. I found that the staff in the department had the aptitude to accomplish the work. They needed education, training, and support. No one cared enough to invest in the staff. In two years, this department was noted as top-notch. The work was not easy, but love and patience made it possible (1 Cor. 13:4). When we had our grand triannual inspection, the inspectors informed everyone at the exit presentation that our department was either number one or number two in the country. Some regional leaders were present as well. My staff and I were flooded with congratulatory words and handshakes. How I wish that you could see the proud faces of my staff on that day. The cascade of good news skyrocketed our workload and requests for consultation. My intervention was needed to prioritize work. What a beautiful problem to have! You know who is always lurking and hoping to destroy the Lord's victories.

Not everyone at the regional office was elated with our success. The fact that I informed the regional executive leaders of clinical issues was never forgotten. Secretly, one person, in particular, formed a vendetta against me. This person was hoping that the investigators would find some deficiencies during their review to take some action against me. Hearing that there were none, this person became infuriated. Privately, one of the investigators told me that this regional person came to their team and said: "You mean to tell me that you cannot find anything wrong in her department? We are never going to be able to get her." Because of this person's clout, there was an element of certainty that the investigative team would arbitrarily create a false deficiency. Can you believe it? They did not fall prey to the wicked scheme. You need to understand that I had no idea that someone was trying to destroy me at the regional level. The Lord will expose the evil schemes of your enemies (Eph. 5:13). All I can say at this point is: God's will is the only place to be. If we remain in His will, no weapons formed against us will ever prosper (Isa. 54:17).

Throughout this trial, God as Jehovah Jireh (the provider) prevailed in my life more times than I can count (Gen. 22:14). My family and I still had a void that needed to be filled. It was now the summer of 2009 and a church home for us was still not secured. Finding a church that feels like home is like finding a good hairdresser. You will try many before you find the right fit. Praising the Lord at home and visiting churches is okay, yet a void remains until you are in ongoing fellowship with other saints. Such an assembly is needed to teach and exhort one another (Heb. 10:25). The Lord is aware of every thought you have. In due time, He answers, or in my case, He will provide a sign (Isa. 38:7).

Father's Day

On the Saturday before Father's day in June 2009, DJ and I were on our way to Walgreens. While I was driving, a big sign on the right side of the road caught my attention. My curiosity lured me to drive to where the sign was located. When we got out of the car, it was a sign in a grassy area near a sidewalk with the name of the church, the time of the service, and arrows pointing to the church. We followed the path of the arrows to a storefront church located in a small strip mall. I peeped in the window through the windowpane to see if there was any activity inside and, there was none. I rattled the door a little to see if it was locked and it was.

It was Saturday and, I did not expect the church to be open. The storefront church did fit the bill. At this point in our lives, Larry and I acknowledged that the Lord's will for us is to be a part of church planting. For several years, He was sending us to churches that were either reconstructing or just beginning. Most of all, I was smiling and laughing with God. He gave me an actual sign to the church He selected for us. As you can see, our God has a profound sense of humor! I told DJ that we were going to visit the church on the next day which was Father's Day. Larry was scheduled to work.

DJ and I arose with excitement. Because the Lord made the provision, I knew that this particular church was the one. The Lord does not make any mistakes, nor will He ever lie (Heb. 6:18 and, Num. 23:19). The church was less than two miles from our home and was named Fresh Anointing House of Worship (FAHOW). When we entered the church, we were greeted by the pastor and his wife. DJ and I sat down in the center of the church. The praise team consisted of the pastor who was the singer and his son who was the drummer. Approximately ten people were in the congregation including me and my son. Most of the congregation was the pastor's family. His commitment to instruct his family is faith in action and gives honor to God. If we are faithful with little, the Lord's blessing will shower us (Gen.18:19, Deut. 11:19, Prov. 22:6, and, Matt. 25:21).

Praise and worship commenced with prayer. You are going to be impressed by the Lord's next step. The Lord said through the pastor: "We have an evangelist in the house, I wonder if she would pray for us." My eyes roamed discretely to see who he was talking about. All of a sudden, he came to where I was sitting and handed me the microphone! Immediately I knew I was home. After quickly regrouping from a stunning debut, I prayed out loud with the microphone. This pastor never met me before nor did he know of my passion for evangelism. The Lord had him on speed dial and told him all about me. I was overwhelmed with joy and surprise. God's love for me just warmed my heart immensely. My Heavenly Father anchored His undying love for me and a sense of belonging on Father's Day in a place called Wetumpka. How great and loving He is (1 John 3:1).

I chatted with the pastor after church for a few minutes. Intrigued by his statement about having an evangelist in the house, I asked him how did he know that. Mind you, I knew the answer. I wanted confirmation. The pastor indicated that the Lord told him. DJ and I went home and, I called everyone I knew to tell them what the Lord did. Consider this thought. The Lord wanted me to tell everyone. Why? My proclamation offers further proof of God's power, His miracles, and His wonders so that others may believe in Him (Luke 8:39, Mark 5:19-20, and, Ps. 66:16). From Father's Day forward, my walk with the Lord was never the same. The Lord and I were already close, yet I wanted Him closer and, He came closer. No longer were we walking parallel on different streets. Now, we were walking side by side. Every day, the Lord would wake me up, lead me to some specific scriptures, and minister to my soul. Thinking back, it was in Wetumpka when the Lord started calling me His friend. The Lord would often awaken me and identify me as a friend instead of calling me Sabrina. At other times, an angel of the Lord would sing to me and say He calls you friend. Each time the word friend was spoken, it was an endearing moment.

How do you know if the Lord views you as His friend? There is a scripture that explains it very crisply. We are the Lord's friend when we do what He commands us to do. A mere servant does not know what His Master is doing. Everything that the Lord learned from His Heavenly Father, He makes known to His friends (John 15:14-15). Building my friendship with the Lord started long ago. My instructions from the Lord on airplanes, through visions and the Holy Spirits' touches, are some events that formed our friendship. It is never too late to build a friendship with the Lord. Seek Him and you will find Him (Jer. 29:13).

My time with the Lord was either at the kitchen table or in my bathroom. The bathroom was my secret place/prayer closet. The Lord loved to speak to me in the bathroom and, there was nothing in this room to muffle His voice. I planned to attend FAHOW on the following Sunday after Father's Day. The Saturday before, the Lord was busy. He was giving me scripture after scripture to absorb. It was enough to make you scratch your head in wonderment.

Sunday arrived and, we went to church again. Guess what happened this time? Once the praise and worship portion of the service concluded, the pastor was slated to preach. He got off the pulpit and came to my pew again. He handed me the microphone and said that God wanted to speak to the church through me. I leaned back in my seat unprepared for this moment. At least, I thought I was unprepared. The scriptures that the Lord poured into my spirit on Saturday discharged from my soul. From my seat in the pew, I shared all that the Lord instilled in me to say. This was the Lord's plan and, He blew my mind! When I went home and had my devotions to the Lord, I asked Him about the Sunday on-the-spot mini-sermon. Do you know what the Lord said? "Do you think I gave you all of that information for nothing"? I could actually feel the Lord laughing at the same time. The Lord is as much fun as He is sincere.

Our community was untapped from a Christian perspective. There were fewer people available to work in the mission field than the scant workers at the Means Avenue Church in Kentucky, but you did not know it. The pastor and first lady were the hardest working people I knew. It was nothing for them to perform multiple jobs with a smile. The Lord wanted me to see this model for some reason. We joined the church and became very active. My heart for evangelism was still blazing hot and, the Lord was planning to take this passion for evangelism to another level (1 Cor. 2:9).

What Happens When The Kingdom Takes Precedence?

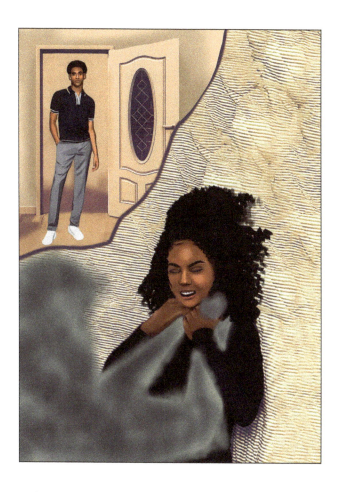

We often think about the mission field as being outside of our home. What about our families? I told the Lord that I was going after the souls of my family members and His guidance was needed. My sister Cecilia's youngest son named Jereld visited us in Alabama on a few occasions. His charisma and fun-loving spirit granted him an open invitation to our home. Larry and Jereld were very close. They had a unique big brother/little brother bond that was sharpened by their mutual military careers. Whenever Jereld was in town, I had to make my homemade spaghetti and meatball dish and prepare an additional batch for him to take with him when he departed. He fellowshipped with us at church in addition to celebrating some holidays when he could. Jereld planned a one-week visit with us during the fall of 2009. Usually, he only stays a couple of days. This time, I was going to make it my priority to be about my Heavenly Father's business during Jereld's week-long visit. Before he came to see us, he spent some time with his daughter's grandparents in a remote city in Alabama. We picked him up and headed back to Wetumpka.

Five days of his seven-day visit flew by and, I had not shared the gospel with him. My slothfulness made me very angry with myself. I went into my prayer closet and did a lot of self-talk. I said why in the world am I procrastinating? Jereld's eternal life may be at stake. There is absolutely no way I can allow him to go home without sharing the gospel! Memories of the time that I failed to share the gospel with a patient in Tennessee who died, erupted like a volcano. Exasperated by my failure, I dragged myself to bed and went to sleep. Something startled me and, I arose. My eyes went to the entrance of my bedroom door and a neatly dressed young man was walking through it. Oh, my goodness, an intruder just entered our home! I yelled at this man; how in the world did you get into our home? Who are you? Not a single alarm in the house went off! This stranger did not say a single word. I attempted to get out of bed to call the police. **All of a sudden, that man transformed into a spirit and leaped on my chest with great force. In a split second, the demon began choking the daylights out of me and, the Holy Spirit took control. I mustered enough air to tell this demonic force with authority that God did not give me the spirit of fear but of power, and of love, and of a sound mind (2 Tim. 1:7 [KJV]).** I rebuked

Satan in the name of Jesus and said you do not live here! flee! The demonic spirit vanished in front of my eyes (Zech. 3:2, James 4:7, and, Acts 16:18). **This was not a dream nor was it a vision. It was happening in living color in my bedroom and, I was fully awake!**

Why did this demon appear? Satan appeared because I was serious about the Lord saving my nephew's soul. He also knew that through the Lord, and His divine power, I can do all things (2 Pet. 1:2 and, 1 Thess. 1:5). The very thought of a soul being saved or delivered from an ungodly force enrages Satan. These attacks are subject to occur to Christians when we seek to expand the kingdom of heaven. I am commissioned to share the gospel in full (1 Col. 1:25). A vow to the Lord is sacred. Therefore, when you make a commitment to the Lord you are required to fulfill it (Num. 30:2 and, Eccles. 5:4).

Only the Lord can read your mind and know what is in your heart (1Kings 8:39, John 6:64, John 2:25, and, Matt. 9:4). Satan is a prowler. Thus, he listens to our conversations and watches our actions to plan his attacks and suffering (1 Pet. 5:8-9). Undeniably, Satan watches me often. Every soul that I lead to the throne of grace causes his blood to boil. Hearing the sincerity of my self-talk concerning my nephew's salvation was his tipping point, and, he wanted me dead. I can picture Satan being so riled that he told his cronies, I will take care of Sabrina myself! Our Lord wanted me alive! Greater is He that is in me than he that is in the world (1 John 4:4).

It was now day six of Jereld's visit and what happened to me the night before was going to be under wraps until Jereld left. I did not see Jereld much on day six. He was with Larry most of the day and night looking for a rental car. My anxiety flared and, I could see that Jereld was physically and mentally exhausted. No gospel was going to be shared on day six. Was I going to get a chance to share the gospel? I pleaded to the Lord to make a way. In the end, Jereld was not going to get a rental car. Because of his age and because he was only going one way, none of the businesses would rent him a car regardless of our signatures. Larry had to work and could not take Jereld to his destination. Jereld's rural and remote target was well beyond my navigation skills. Therefore, it was out of the question for me to drive. Instead of one problem, I am now faced with two; the gospel has not been shared and, Jereld did not have a way to travel. The Lord put the name of a friend and old mentee named Marcus Oliver in my spirit.

    I asked Larry if it was okay if I asked Marcus to drive Jereld to his destination in one of our cars. I also asked Larry if Marcus said yes, could we give him some money for doing this favor for us. My darling husband said yes to both. I called Marcus early in the morning on the seventh day. He answered the telephone immediately and said yes to my request. The seventh day was the final day of Jereld's visit and the only chance I had left to share the gospel. Anticipating that the Lord planned to save Jereld, I prepared a new believer's packet for him. Jereld and I got in the car. As soon as I hit the main highway, the Holy Spirit took the driver's seat. Jereld openly confessed, wept, and said yes to Jesus Christ as his Lord and Savior (Rom. 10:9-10) Hallelujah! With the utmost glee, I shouted Happy Birthday to my nephew and gave him his new believers' packet.

    Marcus and I agreed to meet where Larry and I worked. Since Marcus was going to use my car to transport Jereld, Larry was going to bring me his car to go home and would get mine when Marcus returned. Marcus called me after he settled in from the trip. I probably thanked him a thousand times. Marcus said: "Sabrina you think that I blessed you? Well, you blessed me." He said that he woke up in the morning with bills that needed to be paid and no money to pay them. He told the Lord, you have to make a way, and then, I called. Would you look at God! The Bible says to seek first the kingdom of heaven and its righteousness, and all these things shall be added (Matt. 6:33 [KJV]).

The priority was Jereld's salvation. He was added to the kingdom of heaven and became righteous when he accepted Jesus Christ as his Lord and Savior! What does the Lord mean when he said in the latter part of the scripture that all these things will be added? I am glad you asked. Because Jereld's salvation was the focus and the prize, our earthly desires were met. The Lord added transportation for Jereld's destination via Marcus and, He added money to pay Marcus' bills via Larry. Lastly, He gave me the peace that I needed regarding my nephew's soul. **This is what happens when you put the kingdom of heaven first!** Jereld's faith in the Lord grew and, he shared the Word of God with his mother Cecilia often. We do not know the day or the hour of our loved ones' transitions. If you are uncomfortable sharing the gospel, ask the Lord to lead your loved one to someone who can share the word without reservation. Either way, you will be used by the Lord to save a soul. Make today count. Someone's eternal life is awaiting your direction.

And Then The Ordination

All of the leaders at my job in Alabama were required to take Covey training. My graduate studies included a course in Covey principles. Taking another course did not make sense to me. Despite my graduate-level knowledge, I could not dodge the requirement. Because I had to attend the course in the summer of 2010, I adopted the mindset that I was going to learn something new in this particular course. During a break, I relaxed outside on a bench and chatted with one of my colleagues whom I never met before this training. He repositioned his body to look straight into my eyes.

Then, he stated: "You are an evangelist, aren't you?" I asked him what makes him think that and, he responded, I can feel it.

His eyes and hand gestures let me know how sincere his words were. My passion is evangelism and, I performed the work of one for many years. Perhaps, this is why he had these feelings. However, at no time did I ever coin myself as an evangelist nor was I ordained. There is only one way he could have known this. The Lord revealed it to him through the Holy Spirit (1 Cor. 2:10). His expression came across as a form of praise. This stranger was exhorting me (Prov. 27:2). Lord, are you using this guy to affirm in my mind who I am? The more I live the more I learn. Innovative ideas were gained from the Covey class. Nevertheless, my biggest lesson and affirmation was that God may equip believers whether he or she is a stranger or not to discern the spirit and gifts of another believer. You and I have already established that the Lord will reveal His plan to His friends. When will His plan be disclosed?

The Lord was not hiding His hand. A few days after being exhorted by the colleague in class, the Lord informed me in my prayer closet that I was going to be ordained. The prior interaction with the colleague popped into my head and, I knew it was an ordination relating to evangelism. Although I heard and believed what the Lord said, I did not know how this ordination was going to materialize until I went to church. After church one Sunday, my pastor asked to speak with me. I joined him in his office to honor his request. The pastor said: Do you have your papers? Puzzled by his statement I replied, papers? He responded: your evangelism papers. I informed him that I completed advanced EE training and similar seminars. He said no, I am asking if you are ordained. I said that I am not, but the Lord spoke to me about it recently. He said I know because He talked to me also.

For many years, I shared the gospel of Jesus Christ across the country and abroad because I love doing it. Above it being my love, I knew it was a life-changing step and the most significant step that anyone could take. The thought of being ordained never crossed my mind nor was it a desire. The Lord shared "first the demonstration and then, the ordination." At this time, I had over twenty years of demonstration. The ordination was planned for October 10, 2010 (10/10/10). Did you notice the multiples of five which symbolize His anointing and grace? Being ordained as an evangelist also meant being ordained as a minister. As the time for the ordination drew near, I got a little apprehensive.

All of my flaws were resounding in my head and, I did not feel worthy of this office or calling. A week before the ordination, I got down on my knees on the throne (my toilet with the lid closed of course) and earnestly cried out to the Lord. I told the Lord that I was not happy with my flaws. I even told Him that there were things I did not like about myself. I waited for an answer from the Lord. He answered the day of the ordination that was being held at the parent FAHOW church in Montgomery, Alabama. Before the ordination service began, everyone who was being ordained was asked to go to a specific room for prayer. I quietly prayed with the minister leading the prayer service. When she got to me, she said that God said that your old self is gone! Her words left no room for misunderstanding. My God heard and answered my prayers.

A few others were ordained before me. It seemed like heaven opened wide when it was my turn. I climbed on the stage used as the altar, knelt before the Lord, and closed my eyes to concentrate on the Holy Spirit. The apostle of the church said the Lord said: "You are receiving a golden anointing today and sister we are going to really mess up your hair." He was letting me know that he was going to soak my hair with oil (Exod. 29:7). He told me that the

Lord said I have a spirit of a bear. He stopped for a minute and said that God prompted him to look at the clock. We all turned and, it was 5:55 pm and 55 seconds on the clock! Surely, the Lord wanted me to see that numbering pattern during my ordination. The Lord chose me and ordained me to bear fruit that would last (John 15:16 [KJV]). My ordination was a part of His divine appointment and, the Lord conducted the service. The apostle of the church explained the role of every office. He stated that the role of an evangelist is itinerated. Promptly, the Lord pinged my soul to let me know that this characterization is me. The Lord has moved Larry and me from place to place and, I knew that more travel was on our horizon. My family and friends that attended the service felt the Lord's power and presence as much as I did. This is an evening that I will cherish.

The Lord showed FAHOW in Wetumpka great favor. He ushered in members with incredible talent that formed the fivefold ministry (Eph. 4:11 and, 1 Cor. 12:28). My spirit was well in tune with evangelism opportunities. Hence, I examined all of our programs for potential gaps. One gap that the Lord shared with me was our altar call. Initially, accepting Jesus as Lord was not being offered during this time. I brought the concern to the pastor's attention and, it was changed the next Sunday. The day the change was made, fruit was produced and, it was produced perpetually. In a year, the church was bursting at the seams. We needed more space and were able to acquire more adjacent to our building. The Lord fully unleashed my creativity through witnessing, outreach, teaching, and writing. These are gifts that the Lord still allows me to use for His glory.

As a minister of the gospel, I did not see myself as a preacher. Some of you may chuckle, but I just did not. One time, our church fellowshipped with another church. All of the ministers including me were on the pulpit. At the end of the church service, the host pastor asked all of the preachers to come down from the pulpit and greet the guests. I remained seated since he asked for all the preachers to come down. I said to myself, I am not a preacher. My pastor waved his hand for me to come down. His hand movement was the way you signal your children when they are somewhere they should not be. It was funny. On our way home, I told my pastor why I remained seated and, he laughed so hard until he cried. The office of a pastor and that of an evangelist are different. My comfort zone was ministering at a personal one-on-one level and, I loved it.

Soon, I was preaching from the FAHOW pulpit. This was outside the scope of my imagination. Our pastor requested that I preach and, I gave him a squeaky yes. The Lord gave me the text and storyline for every sermon. However, my delivery did not seem natural to me. From my point of view, my script became a crutch to the point that it handicapped my delivery. Because the script was on paper, it needed to rest on the podium which confined my movement to that particular spot. This limited my interaction with the audience to some degree. Was the script responsible for my confinement or was it my thinking? If you thought that it was my thinking, I concur. The thought that I needed the script to preach created a yoke of slavery (Gal. 5:1).

The Lord told me that I needed to lighten up and relax. He meant that I needed to add some humor to my script. How was I going to achieve humor? I am a terrible joke-teller. No one ever seems to get my punch line but me. What is the fun in that? Being the God that He is, I was led to a Christian website that housed jokes and humor. The Lord also steered me to some jokes to use to make my search easier. Telling a joke that coincided with the Lord's message did help to put the congregation at ease. Never underestimate the extent to which the Lord will help you through your difficulties. Preaching from the pulpit was awkward and did not appear to be the place where I belonged. Yet, my awkwardness was never noticed by others. Nevertheless, I continued to preach many sermons as an evangelist. Is your comfort zone a place of complacency? What is the Lord's position in this regard? In time, the Lord answered and rendered a solution. In a little while, you will see how the Lord set me free and enriched me with the power to preach with liberty.

Like Hezekiah

Over time, the Lord afforded me countless opportunities to share the gospel with family members. It was a blessing to be a part of my dad's conversion. In the summer of 2010, we went on a family trip to Ocean City Maryland for a long weekend. We rented a beautiful place that sufficiently accommodated eleven of us. Our parents participated in all festivities including the planned family competitions. Our dad was a fairly tall guy who was in tip-top shape. He may even be called a spring chicken. Off and on, my dad was stricken with inflation of his hands. Periodically, the inflammation moved to other locations of his body.

In the middle of 2011, my mother called to share that my dad was diagnosed with cancer and his prognosis looked grim. Larry and I went to Delaware and had to hold back our tears. My dad was as thin as a matchstick and wasting away. How could a man as fit as he was, dwindle to almost nothing in such a brief period? My dad would not eat or drink anything. After repeated insistence, he would eat a morsel or two. The disease invaded his body and took ownership of it.

His condition was so grave that the surgeon did not want to operate and, the oncologist did not want to do chemotherapy or radiation. Neither physician was feeling that their intervention would work in my dad's case. After consultation and an evaluation of the pros and cons of the proposed medical interventions, my parents decided that surgery was the best option. Before the surgery, he needed to get a battery of tests at the hospital. Since dad was incapacitated, Larry had to pick him up, place him in the car, and put the seat belt on him. We were very thankful that the Lord allowed us to come home. My mother needed help. Dad's body was in shambles, but his mind was well intact. During the hospital visits, the Lord gave him frequent visions that he shared with us. In one of the visions, he saw several doors. One door led to death and the other to life. He explained that in his vision, he was heading for the door of death and was detoured to the door of life (Acts 2:17).

As a family, we held a praying vigil at my parents' home. We anointed my dad's head with oil, prayed over him, and cited scriptures like you would not believe (James 5:13-15). In the name of Jesus, we decreed his healing. We know that God was listening because the heavens opened wide. Amid our persistent prayers during the evening hours, the thunder, the lightning, and the rains were rocking the house. All eyes were flooded with tears. My church family in Wetumpka, Alabama was also praying up a storm.

Much of my time was spent praying (Luke 18:1). On one of the days that my dad had to go for an exam, I went to the hospital chapel to pray. The chapel was empty. I told my dear friend; the Lord that you gave Hezekiah more time on earth when he requested it. Lord, I know you remember when he was about to die and, he petitioned you for more time. If you can give Hezekiah more time to live, surely you can give my dad additional time (2 Kings 20:1-3). If anyone was listening to my prayer from afar, my plea probably translated to a demand. I was not disrespectful to my Lord; the heaviness of my heart was speaking. I left my burden on the altar believing that the Lord was going to heal my dad. Without saying the words, my dad's physicians thought that he was a hopeless case. Nonetheless, you and I serve a God that will turn hopelessness into joy (Rom. 15:13).

On the second day after my plea to God, he answered me in a dream. The Lord appeared as my grandfather (Big Daddy) wearing a suit and his pocket watch. The Lord knew that I would listen and remember what he had to say through Big Daddy. The Lord said this: **"I said ten more years!"** The Lord was telling me that He granted my dad ten more years! Like Hezekiah, God granted my dad more time on earth (2 Kings 20:4-6). The next morning, I ran to my dad's side like a little kid chasing an ice cream truck to tell him what the Lord said. He lit up like a Christmas tree and told all the family and his friends the news. After a while, he was telling this truth as though the Lord told it to him directly. I got tickled every time he would share the Lord's words.

The surgery was scheduled for the late summer of 2011. The waiting room was filled with nervous family members. Throughout the day, friends, church folks, and missionaries visited. The surgery was a grueling ten hours. The Lord let me know that he was the surgeon in the room. Every room that my dad went into was registered on an electronic board that we could see. I watched the length of time he stayed in each room as well as the assigned room number. Every room including the operating room had patterns of five and seven! This was my sign that the Lord was healing my dad (2 Kings 20:7-11). The Lord was present and, He was the Master surgeon delicately operating on and healing my dad. After the surgery was completed, we were escorted to another location.

The surgeon and the oncologist entered the room. All eyes were on them. We were so quiet that the tiniest whisper would sound like a fire alarm. The oncologist spoke first and said: "He is lucid and extubated"! I translated for my family and said: He is talking and breathing on his own! Glory to God in the heavens! The surgeon said that he was so amazed at how well everything went. The physicians collectively thought that dad was going to be a vegetable after the surgery. Hearing the physicians' amazement, **I asked: Is this a miracle? The oncologist smiled and said: "If it is not a miracle it is dog on fabulous"! The Lord performed another miracle in my life and, it was my dad!** My family danced and, I left the room and danced in the hallways. I was on such a spiritual high, I wanted to climb on the top of the hospital's roof and magnify the name of the Lord to the world as loud as possible (Ps. 34:3 and, Luke 1:46)! This would not have been a wise thing to do. Someone would have thought that I was crazy and recommend that I be admitted to a psychiatric ward.

During a period of idleness at the hospital, The Lord used me to share the gospel with my dad's sister and, she accepted Jesus as Lord. God continued to perform miracles in my dad's life. The day after the surgery, he removed all of his intravenous lines (he should not have) and walked freely on the unit as though he did not have major surgery the previous day. This is another testament to his healing. I could hear the Lord saying take up thy bed and walk (John 5:8). The nurses were amazed and troubled at the same time. As for me, I marveled at the Lord's wonder. In a few months, we watched God expand my dad's body. His hearty appetite returned and, that matchstick of a man was no more. He reached his ideal weight in record time. His weight was not the only thing that returned. His energy and activity levels resumed to normal very quickly and astonished everyone. Three months after his surgery, we went on a seven-day family cruise to celebrate. Watching him have fun on the cruise fostered more praise and worship to the Lord.

How did the Lord use me during this time? I believe that my role was to anoint my dad's body, initiate the laying on of hands and prayer (Rom. 12:12 and, Eph. 6:18). God also used me as a witness to testify about the miracles he performed so others may believe in Him (John 1:7). Our God is still in the healing business. His power, wonders, and miracles are everlasting. What miracle will I see the Lord perform next? I cannot wait. Can you?

What Are You Doing With Your Overflow?

Larry, DJ, and I left Delaware with dad in excellent condition and my mother full of happiness. My pastor was informed of dad's progress and the miracles that the Lord performed while I was in Delaware. However, I could not wait to tell my church family in Alabama all about the vision linked to Hezekiah and the other miracles I witnessed through my dad. My testimony was also shared with other Christians when I returned to work.

Twice a year, I do a deep fall and spring cleaning. Nooks and crannies that are often overlooked during the year get my love and attention at these intervals. I remember being in a closet one day in our Wetumpka home and, **the Lord began to speak to me. He said: What are you doing with your overflow?** His words put me in motion. I started going through every room, the pantry, the patio, and the garage to determine what was in good condition but not being used. Our overflow was bountiful. We had clothes, furniture, appliances, and more that were piled high and not being used.

Looking at the overflow made me thank God more for His abundant blessings. After the thanksgiving to the Lord, I thought if we are not using this stuff, it is just a waste. Someone else may need the things in my home that were overflowing (2 Cor. 8:14-15 and, Acts 4:34). We donate to charities every year and still have an abundance remaining in our home. The Lord knows that. He wanted me to look at this uniquely. Every year when we donate goods to charity, we make sure that the items are donated by December 31st.

What is the true aim, meeting the needs of others or getting the tax write-off? Determine for yourselves what your motivating factor is?

The Lord put on my heart to sponsor a harvest festival. He wanted me to devise a plan like no other. He intended to meet the needs of the community at every level. The Lord wanted FAHOW to display their love for Him by feeding and shepherding His sheep in every possible way (John 21:15-17). I planned to have a two-day event. I presented my idea to the pastor and the other officers of the church followed by the congregation. I was touched by everyone's willingness to serve. Our church did not have many resources, but what we had was the Source! Donations of every kind overflowed. Members, family, friends, and businesses donated brand-new items or items in pristine condition. We had clothes, computers, furniture, appliances, and much more donated to our church. We previously established a food pantry. It too was heavily stocked in anticipation of a large crowd. You cannot beat or measure the Lord's giving (Luke 6:38). Areas of the church had to be rearranged to accommodate the bountiful giving. When we finished with the arrangement, it looked like a department store! The large furniture items and toys were moved outside before the festival launched.

The sanctuary was going to remain open for prayer and witnessing opportunities. The pastor and another minister volunteered to operate that component. Signage was placed strategically around the community to invite and welcome anyone with an interest. The event started early on a Saturday morning with prayer and hot coffee. Diverse groups came in droves. Surprisingly, many arrived as family units. The husband and his wife were accompanied by their children. All races and ages came with needs that were fulfilled. Most of the activity was outside. I toggled between the outside and the sanctuary. In addition to gifts for the home, we offered food and fun games outdoors. Our festival was designed to be a gift to the community, but each person offered us money for the items they desired. It was hard for people to believe that everything was free. Not a penny was accepted. I reiterated that everything they desired was a free gift. The Lord added additional words for me to say. He said: This is a free gift just like heaven is a free gift (Rom. 6:23). This was the spur for a deeper conversation and movement to the sanctuary.

I noticed some elderly ladies crying as they left the sanctuary. The pastor told me that they had no food. The subsidy that they were given by the government was depleted. They went to the sanctuary to thank the Lord for His provisions through FAHOW (Ps. 81:16 and, Hosea 11:4). Some people gave their lives to the Lord. The elderly ladies were not the only ones shedding tears. My pastor was gazing in the sky and weeping out of pure joy. His cup as well as mine was running over in thanksgiving (Num. 14:8 and, Prov. 3:9-10). Saturday night, we held a church service and, many from the community came to worship with us. The praise and worship on Saturday were as good as Sundays. Having the festival was a great idea for multiple reasons. Many of the people who participated in the festival communicated that they had never heard of our church. This festival expanded our recognition and knowledge of our location! The celebration concluded on Sunday and, we praised the Lord with great jubilation.

The Bible includes countless scriptures about giving to the poor and the afflicted. Have you ever wondered why some people with financial wealth are miserable? Despite their wealth, a huge hole or void exists in their lives. In the end, they have nothing. Others acquire wealth that vanishes without a clue of how it went up in smoke. The opposite of this is also true. You can have very little money and be gifted with all the riches you could ever want or need. (Eccles. 6:2, Prov. 13:7 and, Hag. 1:5-7). If you give freely of yourselves from the heart, every need you have will be met (2 Cor. 9:6 and, Prov. 11:24).

During a visit with my sister Cecilia, she popped her trunk after one of our shopping sprees and, I noticed all of these sneakers. They were her sons' old sneakers, in good condition, but her sons no longer wanted them. I asked, what are you planning to do with them? She told me that she takes the shoes to places where homeless people tend to congregate or sleep and simply drops them off. She would also go under bridges and deposit shoes. She did this quietly and from her heart. Kindness to the poor is a loan to the Lord and He will repay the lender (Prov. 19:17). To this day, she lacks for nothing. Giving is far more than money. Assess how you are using your time, talent, and spiritual gifts to advance the kingdom and help those in need. While you are conducting your assessment, determine if a potential for waste exists in your home. Dare to be different. **Start a festival for someone today. Such a festival could start with a pair of shoes.**

Not By Chance

Once you understand the nature of God, you also recognize that everything that He does is calculated and predestined (Isa.14:24 and, Rom. 8:30). Therefore, our steps are not by chance. They are ordered. When I think about faith as it relates to the Lord ordering my steps and the people placed in my path, I am reminded of a plaque given to me by a dear friend who has transitioned. On this plaque, the inscription states: "Every experience God gives us, every person He puts into our lives, is the perfect preparation for a future only He can see."[3] When I was in Alabama, I met a male Christian leader named Richard who received a promotion and was going to Illinois. We interacted on occasion. Since he was moving to Illinois and, this was new territory for him, I thought it would be a good idea for Richard to connect with Michelle. Illinois is her home and, she would be able to help him navigate the area. I also felt that it would be mutually gratifying for them to get to know one another and exchange ideas as Christian health care executives.

I connected the two of them via email. They bonded very well and became good friends. As time progressed, their ministries took center stage. Michelle's heart and ministry are to influence a positive change in the lives of girls and young women. It turned out that Richard has similar compassion and ministry for boys and young men. Their ministries were flourishing through their friendship. The Lord placed Michelle in my path several years before meeting Richard. We knew then and now, that meeting each other was not by chance. The Lord used me to connect them for His divine purpose.

My evangelism and outreach programs continued to expand based on identified needs. The Lord inspired me to plan weekend seminars and workshops at FAHOW focused on Michelle's and Richard's ministries. I just had to get them to agree! Michelle and Richard embraced the idea, planned accordingly, and stayed with me and my family for the weekend. In the summer of 2011, they came equipped to teach through the art of storytelling and the use of tools that they created. Through them, the Holy Spirit ministered to many. On day one, they held a seminar for the entire audience. Members were accompanied by family and friends. Using a tag-team approach, Michelle and Richard set the stage and expectations for the workshops.

The two sessions were held in separate locations within the church. I attended Michelle's workshop for girls and women and, it was powerful. Every stronghold you could think of came forth and was broken through spiritual teaching, storytelling, prayer, and God's love (2 Cor. 10:4-5)! You could feel and see years of self-imposed torture and bondage being released from the participants' hearts and minds as they openly spoke of their mental anguish, abuse, fear, shame, and addictions. The Lord also used this workshop to bring some family members closer together. As I understand it from the pastor and Richard, the workshop for the boys and men was a tearjerker and, as enriching as Michelle's session. Look at how the Lord linked and wove together three distinct ministries. This was prearranged by the Lord before I met Michelle in 2001 and was manifested ten years after we met! Have you ever wondered why someone is in your life?

The Race to the Finish Line

My quest to share the gospel of Jesus Christ with my family never waned. I entered an ongoing spiritual relay race starting with my family nucleus and branched outward. My immediate family, parents, siblings, and their offspring are my family nucleus. My parents' siblings and their offspring are my branches. Other branches grew as time progressed (John 15:5, Rom. 11:24, and, Song of Sol. 4:13). Do you remember being taught that we must share the gospel with a sense of urgency? I did not receive that level of instruction in my youth or as an adult. It was the Lord who placed the sense of urgency in my spirit. I do understand why it is an urgent matter.

A human being's departure from this world and the return of the Lord is unknown. A person's age is not a predictor of death. Like many of you, I have experienced the death of the young and the old in my family. Therefore, sharing the gospel with someone when the Holy Spirit offers an opportunity is critical. One of God's amazing attributes is His ability to create modern-day parables and examples in our lives that enhance our understanding and offer realism. The use of a spiritual relay race is a modern-day parable for me (Matt. 4:2).

In both an earthly and spiritual relay race, there are four sprinters. In a spiritual race, the Holy Spirit runs the first leg. The Holy Spirit hands me the baton by pricking me to share the gospel (Acts 1:8). Remember, the Holy Spirit is the one delivering the Word of God. The baton is then passed to the family member or unbeliever who decides to accept Jesus as Lord and Savior. Hearing the word yes, Jesus gets the baton from the new convert and hands it to the last runner, our Heavenly Father. As the anchorman, He proudly seals our loved one's name in the book of life for all eternity which is the golden reward (Heb. 6:19 and, Rev. 3:5). The Lord put me on a course to run a race like no other.

Unlike the temporary reward of a typical relay race, the prize gained in a spiritual relay will last throughout eternity (1 Cor. 9:25). Earthly and spiritual relay races have some additional commonalities. In the two relays, timing is crucial, and all team members must run. In an earthy relay, failing to synchronize the run and baton hand-off results in team disqualification. The team walks away with no prize and perhaps a wounded ego. However, timing failures in a spiritual race are detrimental to the soul. If a person does not accept Jesus Christ as Lord and Savior before death, eternal damnation is the final result. Jesus is the only ticket to heaven (John 3:3, John 14:6, 2 Thess. 1:9, and, Rev. 21:8). This is why we must run and, run with a purpose (1 Cor. 9:26-27)! At the appropriate time, God will let you know who will run the second leg (the unbeliever). In every instance, God predestines a divine appointment. Sometimes, you may be fortunate to be a part of multiple conversions during one divine appointment.

By nature, I am a structured and task-oriented person. Because I am this way, I create lists and establish priorities from them. As

I complete tasks, they get crossed off my list. Our Lord has a way of re-prioritizing your list. After I had an opportunity to share the gospel with my dad in 2010, a divine appointment with an uncle came to light. In my mind, he was not a priority because he was not listed as a member of my family nucleus. God detoured my path. I called him on the telephone and, we talked for a few hours. This was the first time I had a conversation with him for that long. He had some unanswered Biblical questions. Of course, the Lord rendered scriptures to answer his questions. In the end, he said yes to Jesus. Within a year, he went home to be with the Lord. Thank you, Lord, for saving my uncle and directing my path (Prov. 3:3-5). Always allow the Lord to direct you.

One evening in the spring of 2012, Crystal called and informed me that she spoke with one of our cousins who said that her brother was dying. My heart was grieving for the family so, I called another cousin who was also the sibling of the cousin who talked to Crystal. He informed me that his brother was dying and, he did not know how long he had left on earth. Considering that I lived in the same state that my cousin lived in, I wanted to pray for him and anoint his head with oil (James 5:14). Most importantly, I wanted to determine his salvation. To get to his home which was a few hours away, I had to overcome a huge hurdle; a big bridge. This bridge is so big that it seems as though the peak of it enters the gates of heaven. My determination erased the anxiety that was forming. DJ and I tackled the bridge with the help of the Lord and some good gospel music. We arrived safely at our hotel, checked in, and headed off to my cousin's house.

After greeting my family, I had a brief chat with the cousin that conversed with Crystal. My cousin asked how did I find out about her brother. I shared with her what Crystal told me. She got that deer in the headlight look and said: I never talked to Crystal about that. **The Holy Spirit that dwells in Crystal told her all about the situation because it was real.** I spent some personal time with my cousin who was ill. Since we have not seen each other in several years, I asked him if he knew who I was. With teary eyes, he said yes. My family was aware of my plans to have a prayer service and anoint his head before I arrived. Before any of that commenced, I was able to determine that he knew the Lord as his Savior. We joined hands, bowed our heads, and I led the prayer. The room was cold as ice. The coldness had nothing to do with the temperature in the room. It was the absence of the Lord in the lives of several relatives present that created the coldness. The Lord gave me some specific scriptures to share with my ailing cousin before anointing his head. After the ceremony, we did what we always do when we unite. We ate! I left my cousin's house for the evening knowing that my mission for tomorrow was going to be different.

When DJ and I returned to the hotel, I prayed to the Lord to keep me on the straight and narrow pathway (Matt. 7:13-14). I did not want any distractions or stumbling blocks to get in my way of sharing the gospel with my family (Matt. 16:23 and, Luke 17:10). My spirit was restless and, I did not sleep as well as I would have liked. My cousin that was ill was the vehicle to get me to his home. The Lord was not sending me forth for him, He sent me for the souls of those who were not saved. The next day, twelve of us gathered to pray. The Holy Spirit led the prayer and, the gospel of Jesus Christ was shared. In closing, I let everyone know that if they gave their lives to the Lord to let me know. Several of them did. Two of my cousins indicated to me that they were already Christians.

The Lord saved several of my family members during one divine appointment! Through this act of mercy and kindness, the Lord multiplied my blessings! On the evening of the second day of my visit, I returned to our hotel room praising Him all the way. Sunday morning which was the following day was going to be the last day that I fellowshipped with them. I planned to leave after prayer.

We arrived on Sunday morning and gathered in our prayer circle after chatting for a while. This time, the prayer was different and, the coldness that my spirit sensed two days ago was gone. The spirit of the Lord was freely moving in that house on Sunday! DJ and I left in the early afternoon in the middle of a terrible rainstorm. I called Michelle to testify about the goodness of the Lord. I was basking in the glory of the Lord and, He just glided us over that intimidating bridge! Michelle and I continued to praise the Lord on the telephone until I returned home safe and sound in Wetumpka. After relaxing for a bit, I called all of my immediate family to share the good news! My cousin that was ill, went home to be with the Lord one day after I departed. My quest for the souls of my family to be saved is one that will continue until I transition from the earth. The Lord used Crystal to start this spiritual relay race. He is looking for more runners to participate in His relay races for their families and all nations. Will you join the Lord?

The Dress of Chiffon Floating in the Wind

The Lord continued to shower me with revelations and blessings at home, through the church, and work in Wetumpka. Have you noticed how every revelation from the Lord has a domino effect? Each revelation that I receive leads to action. Our God will never cease to be a God of action. Because we are made in His image, we are called to be the same and be prepared to act at all times (James 2:22-26 and, Acts 7:22). Idleness is the devil's workshop (Prov. 31:27 and, 1 Tim. 5:1). The devil will use this idleness in Christians' lives against them if he is allowed.

King David led a well-functioning regime. He sent his entire army to war, but he remained in Jerusalem. By remaining in Jerusalem, King David removed himself from the action. He got super comfortable being away from God and had a lot of idle time on his hands. What happened to King David when he had too much time on his hands and removed his mindset from the things of God? He climbed on the palace rooftop and became smitten by a beautiful woman bathing. He enticed this woman into an extramarital affair and, she conceived. His wickedness, deceit, and trickery spiraled out of control and, King David ordered the death of her husband in battle (1 Sam. 11:2-16). His action supported that he denied God (Titus 1:16). This series of events in David's life evolved because he removed his mind and actions away from God during a period of idleness. The Lord does want us to have fun, celebrate and rest. The Bible is full of events that support this. Be mindful that God still judges our actions during these times (Ezek. 36:19). Failing to act is also an action.

During the spring and summer of 2012, the trials of my faith at work in Alabama were minimal. Nevertheless, I was fully equipped with my armor every day and ready for action at a moment's notice. The reconstruction of my department paid off handsomely. My staff was comfortable and competent in their roles. My need to intervene in their work reduced tremendously and, the time I had to strategically plan increased. This also afforded me occasions to relax and breathe some fresh air.

One day, I was in my office enjoying a break. My telephone rang and, it was a young lady who wanted to learn some fundamentals of health care quality. She recently changed her career path and job location. Her prior career was in finance in the state of Florida. She went back to school to become a Registered Nurse and decided to move home to Alabama. We arranged a meeting in my office for the following week. When she arrived, we exchanged pleasantries and sat at my table. She said that she was in my office at another time and felt the greatest sense of peace (Luke 10:16 and, 2 Cor. 13:11). I have no recollection of her prior visit nor was her face memorable. She must have been accompanied by my staff in the past.

I went into my teaching stance and started explaining why and how health care quality was connected to organizational performance and patient outcomes. At some point in my explanation, I triggered something in her brain and, there was a diversion in our conversation. I am unaware of what I said that triggered her mind. What I do remember vividly is this: She said that if she died tonight, she was not sure that she was going to heaven. Her heartfelt sentiment catapulted the Holy Spirit into gear. The full gospel of Jesus Christ was shared with her and, she accepted Him as her Lord and Savior! I opened my desk drawer and pulled out a new believers' packet and a small book containing the scriptures of Saint John. I always keep these tools handy. We embraced after I told her Happy Birthday and, we sat down again. Her conversation diverted once more. This time, she was voicing her dismay with the church she attends. She was unhappy with the church because women could not have a leadership role. This made her feel devalued.

I shared some scriptures with her that support how the Lord used women throughout the Bible and how he uses me. This was the church that her husband and his family attended. She did not want to leave the church but did not know what to do about the situation. I offered prayer, we bowed our heads and petitioned the Lord. I also recommended that she seek the Lord further for His direction. The Lord needed to direct her, not me. Before I knew it, her conversation diverted yet again. This time, she shared a truth with me about her sister. She said that if anyone was destined to go to hell it was her sister who lived in Florida where she used to live. She indicated that her sister did unspeakable things.

One day her sister went on a journey to change her life. Her change was quite noticeable. The sister that she detested was now preaching the gospel and displaying love in every way that she could (2 Tim. 2:21). She further explained that her sister kept saying that she was getting married, but her fiancé's name or face was never seen. Her sister also described the dress that she was going to wear at her wedding. Her family thought that she was becoming deranged. Yet, her sister's ministering kept elevating. She did not let a day pass without ministering to someone in her family (Joel 2:17 and, Heb. 6:10).

Her sister talked about heaven so much that she asked her: Are you dying? She told her no, but she did die. She died on July 7, 2007 (07/07/07). It took some time before the mortuary could locate her to inform her of her sister's death. Before she arrived, the mortuary would not let anyone see her sister's body. I am told that they guarded her body like the tomb of Jesus(Matt. 27:66). She described that her sister's body glowed for days. The radiance of her body moved the mortuary staff emotionally. They believed that she was special and was touched by the Lord. When she went to her sister's home, she found her journal. In it was a dress that she drew to meet the Bridegroom! She took the drawing of her sister's dress from her journal and had a replica made for her sister's homegoing service! This young lady's words were such a sweet melody.

Instantly, the Lord gave me a vision of the most beautiful white chiffon with a mother pearl effect blowing in the wind. With that visual, He added the sound of delicate chimes ringing at the same time. I sprung up from my seat, lifted my hands high, and praised the Lord! I said in the young lady's presence, God are you taking me home now because what you have allowed me to hear and see about your child is the most beautiful thing I ever experienced? Before she exited my office, she said: You know, I came to your office to just learn about quality. I said to her, Oh! you did get quality.

Let us dissect what happened. The Lord planned a divine appointment in my office and saved the young lady's soul. I believe that the Lord used her sister to prepare her heart before she died. The visual and auditory sounds that the Lord gave me about the woman who died were a gift to me from the Lord for sharing the gospel. Working with the Lord has advantages. Although we work with the Lord because we love Him and expect nothing, He generously blesses us in the process. In my spirit, I know that the woman who died brought many to the feet of Jesus for eternal life before her transition. She knew she was going to be with the Lord for all eternity and did not see her departure as death. This is why she told her sister that she was not dying. Truly, she was spiritually minded. Her radiance after her natural death also brought people to the Lord. Who are we to ever call detestable whom the Lord called His beloved (Acts 10:15, 29, 34, and, Song of Sol. 1:14-15)? This truth prompted me to write a sermon in the days ahead and the wedding dress became a gift in my future.

Unexpected Elevation and Anointing

After returning from my cousin's home, I was asked to serve as a consultant in a Louisiana hospital for six weeks in the early summer of 2012. The CEO identified several gaps in organizational performance. She realized that the incumbent responsible for the oversite did not have the requisite skills to lead the organization in the desired direction. I came on board to mentor the incumbent and develop some tools that would be helpful with their oversite efforts. The executive team and the clinical leaders were pleased with our results. They were so pleased that I was urged to stay. Some of the clinical leaders dangled a few carrots, but I had no interest in working there. Except, I had this odd spiritual attraction whenever I entered the hospital or roamed in the community. The majority of the time, I worked twelve hours a day. My mind and my body were dog-tired and, I was ready to go home to my family, sleep in my own bed, and fellowship at my church. It took a few days to unwind. The saying that there is no place like home is an absolute truth.

After my mind and body returned to normal, my routine resumed. FAHOW invited a guest minister to teach on a Wednesday evening. Everyone was excited about his visit because he was going to share some elements of a recent book he authored. My pastor gave formal introductions to the visiting minister and, he delivered some very good messages with practical application. Have you ever got a feeling that someone was looking at you strangely? This minister gave me that kind of look. At the time, I had no idea why.

While I was passing through a bathroom in my home designated as my secret place, the Lord spoke with great power. He said I am going to ordain you as a pastor. What did He say? Did I hear the Lord correctly? My ears were not clogged, those were the Lord's words. This was a big surprise! In 2010, I was ordained as an evangelist. Even though I never desired this ordination in my heart, it is a fit for me. If being ordained as an evangelist did not make it to my bucket list, certainly being ordained as a pastor would not. Never in my wildest dreams would I envision being called to an office of a pastor. The thought of being a pastor simmered in my spirit for two days before I shared it with Larry. Like me, he was stunned. Laughing to myself, I know Larry was thinking; what will be my role in this?

After I told my husband, I informed my pastor about what the Lord said. He already knew! My pastor then shared, remember that minister who taught at the church? I said yes. Thinking to myself, I said: This is the guy who was looking at me strangely. The pastor communicated that he had a chance to speak with him in passing. The minister told him: Do you know that evangelist at your church? "She is walking in a pastor's anointing." He told the pastor that he wanted to say something, but he decided against it. Hearing these words, secured the affirmation of my new elevation in my mind. Why do you think he did not share what his spirit discerned on that Wednesday night? I believe he did not share it because the Lord wanted to tell me first. What are your thoughts?

This time, the ordination was going to be held at our church in Wetumpka, Alabama. This is what I wanted, but another location would have been fine. Whenever functions are held at our church, I have some roles. Because it was my ordination, no one wanted me to lift a finger. I did not agree and insisted on cooking a few dishes. Our church was small with big appetites! Plus, I was humbly honored that God chose to ordain me as a pastor. Cooking for others is an act of servitude and was the least that I could do for the blessings I received. With this blessing came another surprise.

That spiritual attraction I was sensing in Louisiana got stronger. The Lord let me know that what I was sensing in my spirit was due to a genuine need for the gospel in that area and, He was sending me there (Rom. 15:20). In August, the position that was once undesirable to me became vacant. I competed for the job and, I was selected. My family and I planned to move there in October 2012. My pastor was saddened by the news but said this is how the mission field is. My emotions were topsy-turvy concerning the new destination, but my spirit was serene; knowing that this was the will of the Lord. Being an active part of the ministries that the Lord created through FAHOW fueled me with unexplainable joy and promoted my desire to do more in the community. I loved FAHOW from the bottom of my heart. If I were a single woman and there was a shower in the church, I would have moved into the building without a second thought. Leaving FAHOW was like a bird leaving the nest for the first time. I was constantly fed and protected by the Lord there. Nevertheless, the Lord wanted me to soar to new heights well beyond my emotional comfort zone.

Before worship service, we pray as a leadership team. On the morning of my ordination, the pastor asked if I would lead the prayer. **At the onset of my prayer, my body was overtaken by spiraling winds. These winds had a cyclone effect that started from my feet and wrapped around my entire body. These cyclone winds were complemented by sounds of rushing winds that were roaring in my ears as I continued to pray (Acts 2:2).** In my spirit, I knew this was God's anointing power. I did not quite understand it yet, but I knew it was from God. There is no one under the sun with this power. I was formally ordained by my pastor on the evening of September 16, 2012, in the presence of family and friends. Do you recall the lady who came to my office, received the Lord as her Savior, and shared her sister's truth with me? She also came to my ordination service with one of her sisters and gifted me with my first pastor's manual.

My life was transformed forever starting with my original purpose for coming to Alabama. I did become a lawyer as I desired. I became a lawyer for the Lord and received my degree from the Holy Spirit! It was revealed that my role was to work with the Lord to set the captive free from all forms of oppression and defend those who are treated unjustly. These are functions of a good defense attorney. The Lord demonstrated His power as both a prosecuting and defense attorney. What a thrill it is to be a partner in the Lord's law firm!

Did you forget about the bondage I felt when I preached as an evangelist? I confined myself to the podium because of my script. This bondage and restriction in my movement were removed by God's anointing power. From the time I was anointed as a pastor until this day, every message He gives me to preach is deposited deeply in my soul and recalled in full. Preparing the message remains, but the use of a script as a crutch was blown away by the cyclone. I can preach with liberty! If you see me preaching today, you will see this bubbly short woman moving fluidly on the pulpit, walking the aisles, and staying on message without a script (Luke 4:18). I believe that the first sermon I preached after being ordained as a pastor was "The Light times four; God the Father, God the Son, God the Holy Spirit and You." There was no tenseness of any kind when this message was preached (Jer. 3:15). You may be intrigued about the contents of the sermon, but we will have to talk about that at a later time. What I will say is this: After this sermon, the light illuminated my life and inconceivably followed me.

Do you think anointing me as a pastor was just to preach with liberty and remove my inhibitions? No, it was not. God was preparing me for the next place He was sending me. **God allowed me to feel His majestic power through the winds when He anointed me during prayer service. This was the same power He used through the east winds to turn the red sea into dry land (Exod. 14:21-22).** The Lord's strong power and might were going to be needed and revealed for the new destination. Stay tuned.

A Place Like No Other

How do you measure a blessing? Is it a gift that you receive? Or is it something else? My experiences have taught me that one blessing is a smorgasbord because of its ability to impact many things (John 4:36 and, Prov. 11:36). The Lord blessed me and my family by sending us to Wetumpka, Alabama. Foolishly, I wanted to leave. I am so thankful that the Lord straightened my thinking and behavior. Contemplate all the breakthroughs, miracles, and blessings we would have missed.

Through the pastor of FAHOW in Wetumpka, the Lord amplified the model He wanted me to replicate as a minister and a pastor. This pastor personified the work ethic, humility, and willingness to be among the congregation that the Lord desired. We were able to freely operate in the gifts that God loaned us and, those entering the doors felt welcome and loved. You did not see any opulent chairs for the clergy. Nor were the clergy seated on the pulpit. This was done to disband a belief that a hierarchal system at the church existed. What a testament to humbleness. This was a blessing to see and principles that I adopted.

The vast ministries that we deployed in the community with a small group of members and the number of souls saved were remarkable. This demonstrates what you can accomplish with a few willing spirits. I cannot ignore the blessings of being ordained twice and experiencing God's power at a higher level. He showered me with His favor and elevated me after demonstrating my faithfulness in times of trouble.

The greatest of all these blessings was my walk with the Lord. In Wetumpka, we became close friends and walked hand in hand. Of all the places that God has taken me, Wetumpka is the place where I clearly heard the voice of the Lord, and, He called me often. My mind was renewed, my walk with the Lord became erect and, my spirit was lifted to immeasurable heights (Eph. 4:23 and, Col. 3:10). All of these blessings came from a place called Wetumpka, a place like no other.

Reflections and Movement Forward (Chapter V)

Question 1: Do any of my actions demonstrate that I deny God (Tit. 1:16 and, Eph. 5:10)?

_____

_____

_____

Question2: When I see injustices or someone being mistreated will I avoid involvement (Eph. 6:13 and, Isa. 1:17)? Examine your history, it may be a predictor of your future.

_____

_____

_____

Question 3: When you give, how is your heart? Do you feel the need to tell others that you gave something (Matt. 6:3-4)? Is there any jealousy in your heart toward others who have what is missing from your life(Gal. 5:20-21, Job 5:2 and, Prov. 27:5)? Examine your heart.

_____

_____

_____

Question 4: Am I willing to operate outside of my comfort zone for the greater good (Rom. 5:3-5, 2 Cor. 1:4-6 and, 2 Cor. 4:8-12)?

_____

_____

_____

Question 5: What reconstruction needs to happen in my mind and/or heart to love unconditionally (Rom. 12:2, Eph. 4:22-25, and, Col. 3:10)?

_____

_____

_____

Question 6: Thinking of my actions and outcomes as fruit, do I produce fruit that will last, and will I continue to produce more fruit (John 15:16 and, Matt. 13:22)?

_____

_____

_____

Question 7: What are you doing with your overflow? Your surplus may help someone through a tough time (2 Cor. 8:14).

_____

_____

_____

CHAPTER VI

WHEN THE HANKS COME MARCHING IN

Preparing to leave Wetumpka, Alabama was a bittersweet time in my life. Moving to a new destination with the Lord was exciting, yet leaving the church was a somber moment.

Closing out all of my unfinished business at work progressed without any wrinkles. During my last week of work, the person whom God was going to appoint to take my position surfaced. I informed the CEO of my recommendation. He planned to appoint her as the interim leader and announce the job for open competition at a later time. I already knew that she would ultimately be chosen because this appointment was well beyond man's authority. God's appointee is a strong Christian and a person that I hired externally two years before my departure. I was charged with anointing her for her new journey. Considering the demonic forces that she was going to be up against, an anointing from the Lord was in order. When she was made aware of the Lord's plan, a look of astonishment appeared on her face, but she was ready for the challenge. We conversed about the role, prayed and, the Lord anointed her through the use of my hands.

Before my final workweek ended in Alabama, the Lord threw me a curveball on my way to work. I was driving and having a great time singing and bouncing to the gospel music playing on the radio station. My music was not too loud to drown out the word of the Lord. Whenever He speaks everything comes to a screeching halt. **Out of nowhere, the Lord said this: "When you get there, there will be hanks there."** Out loud in the car, I said what is a hank? I had no earthly idea what the word hank meant. Are you aware of the meaning of this word from a spiritual perspective? When I got home from work, I dashed to the computer to look up the meaning of the word. The first definition that popped up on my computer in October 2012 was ghosts and demons. This was a stunning discovery. Nonetheless, this is the definition that the Lord wanted me to see. My Savior was letting me know that ghosts and demons were anxiously awaiting my arrival in Louisiana! This also meant that I would need to be prepared for spiritual warfare immediately. In addition to that revelation, I learned that witchcraft and voodoo still exist in Louisiana. None of this spooked me. I already experienced witches and many demonic spirits in my lifetime. The Lord was leading and protecting me and my family. What else could a girl ask for in life?

Before moving to another state, we typically spend a few days with my parents. We would have loved to visit Larry's parents, but they transitioned to glory several years ago. It is unreasonable and difficult to plan a trip to see my family once I begin a new position. We desired to enhance a few things before we put our home on the market. Thus, Larry and DJ stayed home and, I flew to my parents' home. My mother was not feeling her best when I arrived. It was the first week of October and my parents wanted some domestic work done that they were unable to accomplish in the spring. I was more than happy to assist them and volunteer for anything else that they desired.

Once I got back to Wetumpka, a few more things still needed to be completed before we were comfortable with leaving. The additional work took us one day to complete as a team! We hopped in our car in the early morning hours of October 12, 2012. Between being tired from all of the domestic work and the cool breezes from the car window, I was anesthetized and fell into a deep sleep during the drive. When I woke up six hours later, we were practically in Louisiana. If you have been following our path, we continued to go further in the deep south with the Lord. We remained safe in His arms (Deut. 33:27).

Our other car was due to arrive the day after we got to Louisiana. This meant that we needed to get settled in our apartment and notify the transporters of our arrival. We had a prearranged apartment in a gated community at government expense awaiting us. However, we had a little difficulty securing our keys. They were not located as indicated by the apartment management. Later, we found out that the apartment complex and management office was on heightened alert. Someone came into the office and murdered one of the managers. This was a little unnerving. As in the past, our apartment was very nice and passed all of my levels of suitability. Our second car was delivered at the agreed-upon time. We noticed an odd emblem on the vehicle that transported the car. When we got closer, we identified that it was a Christian emblem. Our car was transported by a Christian organization. God was safeguarding everything for us (1 Sam. 2:9)!

My new position started on a Tuesday since Monday was a holiday. Sometimes, a little nervousness develops on your first day in a new position. I think it is the unknown coupled with a desire to give a great first impression that sparks this nervousness. I did not have a drop of nervous energy. I was very relaxed. My previous stint as a consultant allowed me to meet all the key players from the administrative and clinical teams. In addition, I worked with the staff who were now going to be my subordinates previously as well. Some of my newly acquired staff escorted me to my car with tears in their eyes when I departed the last time. My, how things change! The warm welcomes that I once received entering and exiting the hospital no longer existed. Instead of handshakes, I got cold shoulders and rolled eyes. My existence was now detestable for no other reason than my relationship with the Lord (Matt.10:22 and, Prov. 29:27).

I was just at this hospital a few months ago. What changed? The Holy Spirit that dwells in me was going to have a permanent resting place in the building. This was an unwelcomed change for the demonic forces that were freely roaming at will in the hospital. Now they had to contend with the power of the Almighty that they could not defeat no matter what power they possessed. From the moment I stepped foot in the hospital building, the persecution commenced. Satan deployed an array of tricks and utilized a legion of demons with faces that I knew to attack me (Mark 5:9).

My direct line supervisor was the CEO and a Christian. I had barely put my purse down in my new office before being summoned to discuss the CEO's priorities. The major concerns stemmed from a department that was critical to the health and recovery of patients who received care in that unit. The severity of the issues presented dictated a thorough investigation. This type of investigation would be a huge undertaking and require skilled staff to accomplish the work. This was my first day on the job and my plate was already full. Most assuredly, I had to hit the ground running with all cylinders in motion. Before leaving the CEO's office, I was hit with a by the way comment. Remember that I mentioned to you that our apartment complex was on heightened alert because a manager was murdered? The person that killed the manager was the spouse of one of my employees. Preparing for potential media fallout and an emotionally wounded employee was added to my full plate. On day one, I was facing demons, drama, and a difficult assignment. Since God led me to it, I knew I would get through it (Phil. 4:13 and, 1 Cor. 10:13). God has the power to win every battle with no effort and no assistance. Nevertheless, no one gets a free ride in war. Like David in his battle with Goliath, you and I are expected to be armed with faith for every battle. Did you think that the stone killed the giant (1 Sam. 17:45-47)?

My first order of business was to determine the knowledge and skillsets of my staff. The results were abysmal. However, there was one diamond that shined through the rubble. This employee demonstrated the requisite skills needed for the investigation. The questions I raised to the other staff members were a foreign language to them and quite disturbing for me. The complexity of the review would be a deep dive through large data sets and records. It was unrealistic to think that two people could adequately conduct the level of review needed in a reasonable time. Teaching the staff new skills was a must before an investigation could be launched. It was a ghastly task because most of them had no desire to learn something new and they had no desire to work period.

The one talented person on my team worked extremely hard. As a peer, the competent employee did a great deal of the training, and I did most of the analyzing, assessment of results, and all of the report writing. As this was taking place, I was recruiting highly skilled staff. The staffing level was under par. Successfully hiring new staff would increase the knowledge and competency level of the department. The findings from the investigation were the gravest that I had ever encountered in my career. My report was given to the CEO and led to a national review and strong consequential actions. The aftermath formed additional fuel against me. Like Alabama, I was fighting for the weak and those who could not speak for themselves on a grander scale (Prov. 31:8 and, Jer. 22:16). The battle scars I received from this trial were many. During the same period, my staff planned a brunch as a meet and greet venue. My expectations were communicated during this brunch and translated into misery for them. One employee became indignant, stormed into my office, and incited violence. I did not take the bait, but I took appropriate action.

Before I knew it, I was under investigation. More wolves came out during the investigation with hopes of devouring me (Matt. 7:15). One of them was a high-level executive who was furious that she had to remove a clinical leader because of a national review that I ignited. People that I never met or interacted with conjured statements that were implausible. The enemy wanted strength in numbers to create a false sense of credibility. The fabrications were countless and baseless! The newly hired staff were unfairly thrust into my storm because of their association with me. The Lord was right (as always). The demonic forces were running wild, but I did not think that they were going to meet me at the front door!

Since Satan was unsuccessful in destroying me in Alabama, he formulated a large-scale attack against me in Louisiana. This time, spirits that were eviler than those I experienced in Alabama were alive and well in Louisiana and tormenting me as often as possible (Luke 11:24-25). Satan and his entourage wanted me to know that they were encamped in the building. Persistent haunting and howling sounds came from the walls in my office and the pipes in the ceiling. This building was haunted and, it was enough for a person to quit their job and run out of the building as fast as they could. Do not think for a second that Satan forgot about our escapade in my bedroom in Alabama or the souls that were saved there.

The Lord warned me! The investigative board was playing charades. Their verdict was decided before any evidence was weighed. In their eyes, I was guilty regardless of the undisputable submitted evidence to the contrary. The chairperson who should have been the most neutral member and, the voice of reason on the board, did not bother to open or read the package sent to her that would exonerate me. Undue pressure was placed on the executive leaders at the local and regional levels to take administrative action against me. What evidence did they have? There was none. There was no cause to take any disciplinary action, no cause to alter my salary, and no cause to change my position level.

What could they do? What they decided to do was put me in exile. They removed me from my office, placed me in another building, and changed my organizational alignment outside of the state of Louisiana. If they had the authority, I would have been placed in a prison cell and chained. I had to travel to the regional office in Mississippi regularly to work and be subjected to a high level of disrespect. All of this was a humiliation tactic, but it did not work. I was hard-pressed on all sides, but not crushed; perplexed, but not in despair; persecuted but not forsaken, struck down but not destroyed (2 Cor. 4:8-9). Their plan was supposed to degrade me, but it made my work life easier. My scope of work was of a higher complexity without being a supervisor and, I was a consultant to the interim leader appointed to take my place. This person came to my office regularly for guidance and sometimes detailed instructions. They implemented a foiled plan which was hilarious. God tells us that He has chosen the foolish and weak things of the world to confound those who think that they are wise and mighty (1 Cor. 1:27 [KJV]).

The Bible also tells us that they have done these things because they do not know God or Jesus Christ (John 16:3). To know the father, you must have a relationship with Jesus. Absent a relationship with the Lord means that Satan is their master. With that being said, what do you expect from them (John 8:44)? Their father is a liar what more could they be? A wicked person listens to deceitful lips; a liar pays attention to a destructive tongue (Prov. 17:4). Being on the wicked bandwagon was fun for them and, several wagons were moving in every direction. While I was in exile, I came to work every day with a smile, operated with a spirit of excellence while extending my expertise to all.

Never forget who your real supervisor is. Always offer your best despite the circumstances. This could have been a redefining moment for me if I did not have the peace of God and the wherewithal to guard my mind and heart (Phil. 4:7 and, Prov. 4:23). Victory for them would have meant an aura of self-pity and shame characterized by my head hanging low as I walked with bitterness in my communication. They lost the battle. The victory belongs to the Lord! Do not let others or a job function dictate who you are. We are who God says we are. Do you know who you are? The Bible tells us that the Lord has made us Kings and priests (Rev. 1:6). If you are thinking that women are not included in that sentence, your thoughts will be different when I share with you what the Lord told me when I posed that question to Him years ago. After reading Revelation 1:6, I said: Lord you only have roles listed for men. His answer was: "I have no second position"! All of His children have the same royal inheritance. There is no gender inequality with God. Let us not forget that God does not show favoritism (Rom. 2:11 and, Acts 10:34).

Are you an exile in this world? If you believe that this world is your home, you are not an exile. However, if you know that heaven is your home, you are indeed an exile. When God called you out of the world of darkness into the light through your union with

Jesus Christ, you became an exile (Col. 1:13 and, 1 John 3:14). As born-again believers, this world is not our home (Heb. 13:14)[4]. This world is a temporary residence for us that is owned by Satan. I am and you are real estate agents for the Lord. We offer prospective buyers an opportunity to live in a mansion for eternity for free! Yes, you can be placed in exile and be an exile at the same time. If you need proof, just look at my life. The proof is in the pudding.

The Sanctuary

In the midst of it all, Larry and I were house hunting again. The luxury of living at the expense of the government was expiring and, we were beginning to feel compressed in the apartment. My mother could not understand why we were buying homes every place we moved. I told her that it was part of the fun of moving to a new location. Like the company transporting our car to Louisiana, The Lord gave us a Christian real estate agent as well. She took us to see more houses than I can count. All of them were nice, but they were either a cookie-cutter model or lacked the charm that I was looking for in a home. Your heart tends to tell you right away if it is the ideal one. Our options appeared to be diminishing. One night, our real estate agent called and shared that she was working with a builder who had a home that was near completion. She believed that this house had all the amenities we desired and, she was instrumental in the design. I fell in love with the house the first time that we walked through it. To ensure that we were making a wise decision, Larry and I toured other homes and found ourselves comparing them to the one I fell in love with the first time. Needless to say, we chose my first love.

Guess what? Our home was built by a Christian builder who was cheerful and would stop by to say hello occasionally. Would you look at the hand of God? We moved into our new home on January

31, 2013. Shortly after we acquired it, we realized that there was something special about this house. Our new house address had patterns of sevens and fives that further solidified it as our choice. Rays of light would enter the home through the windows and form spectacular prisms of beautiful colors that would remain for hours. Beautiful birds would mount and chirp under our front door every morning. Although the birds were lovely, they also brought a great sense of peace with them. My attraction and intrigue with birds led to purchases of bird sculptures and figurines to decorate our home. Our friends told us that our home felt heavenly and majestic. In time, we understood why. God gifted us with a sanctuary that we would need for the raging storms ahead.

Leading The Blind To The Harvest

Now that we secured a resting place, it was time to find a church to fellowship. Visiting prospective churches this time was different. Introducing myself as a pastor and an evangelist was met with mixed emotions. Initially, I struggled with the use of titles before my name. The last thing that I want is to be perceived as a person with a puffed-up ego by using my ordination titles. God helped me to combat this struggle. He let me know that using these titles forms an olive branch for those in need. On the other hand, Some clergy members were elated when we visited while others thought I had a hidden agenda.

We fellowshipped with the selected church three times before we decided to make it our church home. The pastor of the church was very young and recently appointed by the church's board. The building was very big and, the pews were largely empty. The church was in the heart of a diverse community with thousands of people. My research indicated that the vast majority of the community did not go to church. Why were the church pews empty? On the surface, it appeared as though the pastor was leading the operations of the church. However, the board watched every sneeze he made and micromanaged all of his plans. The board members sat in a particular location every Sunday. No one dared to sit in their seats or invade their space.

A sign was on the wall as you exited the church. It said that the mission field starts here. This meant that the mission field was outside of the church. This sign excited me. I wanted to get involved with their evangelism and outreach programs as soon as possible. There were none and the sign had no value in my eyes. Sunday school classes were just being formed, but the church was in the community for years. An annual New Year's Eve event for the community was the poster child for outreach. This was a good idea, but the members and leaders complained that it was poorly attended. Where was the evidence of fruit? If it was any, it was hidden. In essence, the church was dead (John 15:4).

The new pastor and his wife seem to have the right level of zeal to spark enthusiasm and activity. The absence of outreach programs amid a huge, unchurched population grated my spirit (Eph. 4:30). Without a doubt, this was a reason why the Lord sent me to Louisiana. Was this the only reason? Time will tell. Using the research that I conducted, I formulated an executive briefing of the community's demographics, gaps and presented it to the pastor with a few proposals. He was moved by the information and thrilled with my ideas. At the same time, he shared that he was planning a missionary trip to Belize and asked would I be a part of it. I said yes and was thinking at the same time, why do you not see the huge untapped mission field and harvest in our backyard? Was his blindness real? Do I discuss my concerns with him now and potentially hurt his feelings or, should I wait? My choice was to wait for God's timing.

Community Barometer Check

In a couple of months, the Lord touched the hearts of a few members. They became eager to venture into the community with me. The pastor was one of them. This would also give him visibility in the community to promote trust. I provided some just-in-time evangelism training and, came equipped with some resources to launch the outreach program. The two-by-two model that we know of in the Bible is what we used to witness on Saturdays (Mark 6:7). Many subdivisions were near the church. Every community that I visited felt abandoned and creepy. Demonic strongholds were deep-rooted in the soil, but the work of the Lord was not blocked. I was always welcomed with open arms. Sometimes, the gospel was interrupted by things that were going on in the home. When that occurred, I just prayed with my eyes open. Most of the time, the problem would be resolved quickly and, the Holy Spirit would restart where we left off.

The Lord saved several souls. Many of the new converts were reluctant to come to our church. Some shared rumors and others shared past experiences before the new pastor arrived. I was able to convince most of them to give the church another opportunity to demonstrate their love. I kept their remarks in the back of my mind and observed the behavior of the church leadership as visitors entered. There was no point in creating a false alarm or bringing forth issues that occurred with another pastor. During my witnessing opportunities, I asked what did they feel that they needed from the church. A reoccurring theme was an education gap and not having enough money to make ends meet.

Closing Gaps

A church or ministry is effective when it meets the needs of the community. You have to determine the needs to meet them. Feedback from the community, schools, and information gathered from data gave us targeted priorities. As a whole, the state of Louisiana ranked last or near the bottom in education from the years 2012-to 2015. Unfortunately, this has persisted. As of the year 2021, this state has an overall education rank of fifty[5]. This means that they are next to the worst in the nation. In the spring of 2013, the Lord inspired me to create a program called Homework +. The plus sign represents the Holy Cross. A team of volunteers which included the pastor joined my education improvement crusade. We provided tutoring for a wide variety of subjects. Some of us tutored at the church while others tutored at the students' homes throughout the week.

My tutoring started with one child and pronged into all the children in the household. Beyond the tutoring, I was allowed to witness to the children and their parents (often the mother). This program was instrumental in growing the church. The students along with other family members started coming to church in groups! The church body was excited about the growth. Now, we needed more Sunday school classes, but we did not have enough teachers to meet the needs for a brief time. The excitement alone kindled creativity in several members. We planned other activities to reach the community. At this point, the pastor had a reality check. The mission trip to Belize was canceled and, our backdoor mission field became a priority. I did not have to mention the subject matter.

As I continued to minister in the community and tutor, the pervasiveness of food insecurity issues slapped me in the face and could not be ignored. No matter where I went, it was a problem.

All of the families had no additional resources or places to turn to for help. You simply cannot go to a store to buy groceries with no money, nor can you repeatedly go to a food bank. There were limitations on everything that they could receive.

It is tough ministering to someone who has a growling stomach, hungry, and is barely clothed. If a brother or sister is poorly clothed and lacking in daily food, and one of you says to them, "Go in peace, be warmed and filled," without giving them the things needed for the body, what good is that (James 2:15-16)? Aside from this being a barrier to ministry, these gaps needed to be eliminated. The Lord has repeatedly echoed the necessity to address hunger and other needs. He also states in the Word that what we do to the least of them; (the poor and needy) we do it to Him also (Matt. 25:35-36, 40 and, Matt. 10:42). Every time I was confronted with this issue, I went home and made food baskets for them from our cabinets and freezer. I also alerted the church of the needs. Food donations increased, but it was not enough to meet the ongoing needs.

The holidays were approaching and, I wanted to give out some Thanksgiving Day baskets. Some members of the congregation were eager to be a part of this effort. Based on our donations and supply, we could gift ten families with baskets. One of the board members suggested that I contact one of the schools to determine who could benefit from the baskets. I wrote a letter to the selected school and asked for a list of ten families. After being notified that the list was completed, I went to the school to pick it up. As I began to review the list, one hundred families were noted. Oh my God! I have one hundred families, but only ten baskets. What am I going to do? I called on the name of the Lord to solve the dilemma. At His direction, the families with the most children in the household would receive the baskets. Taking the baskets through the community was extremely hard for me. How in the world can anyone feel good about passing a house that you know has hungry people inside? I cried like a baby every time I passed a house on the list. I trust that the Lord met their needs and, they had a good Thanksgiving dinner.

We continued to expand our food closet. Some of the families that came to the church to get food did not attend any church. Nevertheless, we were able to minister to many and plant seeds. If you are saying I do not have much to give, consider this: One bag of beans or a can of food could stop the hunger of a family for one night, promote sleep, and foster learning the next day for the children in the home. Every morsel of food that one eats from your donation equals a spoonful of love. As a child of the Most High God, I could not ignore what my eyes were beholding. Turning a blind eye would be a stench to my soul (Prov. 28:27). The Lord will honor and bless your giving (Prov. 22:9).

Modern Day Pharisee and Sadducee Operation

God urges us to remain watchful. I think that I have mastered that principle and, it is incorporated into my daily living. Most of the leaders of the church marveled at the growth spurt. The motivation of some members was unwavering. They volunteered to serve or lead any outreach or Sunday school activity. On the contrary, the board members were often absent from any activity that the church sponsored. If they did attend, they would come late and make a grand entrance or dash in for a photo opportunity. Mingling with the community or rolling up their sleeves to help were beneath them. They were members of the church who professed to love and serve the community in words only.

I solicited their involvement especially when I launched an outreach program for the elderly. There was always an excuse as to why they could not assist. Additionally, their non-verbal cues provided further evidence of their lack of interest. In their minds, they were aristocracy that distinguished themselves by special seating arrangements. Why is Sabrina asking us to do the work of pagans? People do speak without saying a word. If you want to know what someone thinks, watch their non-verbal cues such as their eyes and body movements when you ask a question.

Based on their lack of involvement, I was amazed that some of the board members attended one of my evening evangelism workshops. I recall that one of the board members said to me: "We have been waiting for you." Those became prophetic words in a few months. My training was applauded, but did they come to learn? I will let you make that determination. Something was festering in the church and, it was not of God. A foul odor was spreading through the church like a wildfire. It did not take long to determine where the stench was coming from within the church.

One Saturday afternoon, one of the members and I were at the church designing many activities for Sunday school and other ministries. The pastor came in with a bamboozled look on his face. Within an hour, he said that he needed our support to tackle the board. He had met with the board and, they wanted to change the music and eradicate some of the outreach programs. You could hear the fear of the board in the pastor's voice. Ultimately, he was afraid that they would recommend that he be removed from his role if he did not do the things that they said. He wanted us to serve as leverage when he disagreed with their demands. I had no problem honoring his request and, I do not think that the person present with me did either.

When the pastor pushed back, the board pushed back even more. I am told that the board members saw me as a person that was eroding the traditions of the church. To them, my approach was too modern to include evangelism. Can you believe it? The evangelism technique I used then and today is nationally recognized and well established. What is the real agenda of the board? Whatever the board said to the pastor of the church at his last meeting with them worked. His demeanor and involvement in outreach changed radically. He stopped tutoring because he became sickened by the quality of the homes and the kids' behavior. Yet, he had an alternative. He could have tutored the children at church. Like the board members, he became too busy to minister in the community.

My ordained title as a pastor surfaced as a thorn in the board's side. Perhaps being an ordained evangelist was a problem for them also. According to the pastor, the board felt that I was there to take command of the church. Are you kidding me? I was as interested in pastoring that church as I was interested in standing on my head. The pastor's lack of confidence in his ability as a pastor and his lack of tenure caused him to struggle with that thought also. He stopped referring to me as Pastor Hughes and I confronted him to determine his mindset. He stated that this was not a problem for him, but his actions said otherwise. The narrow-mindedness of the board and the pastor was obvious. A person can hold an office of a pastor and not pastor a church. Shortly after this episode, we had a guest minister come to the church to preach. The goal was to diversify the church and be representative of the community. The current state of the church was far from it.

I recommended the guest minister. The person that I referred was my pastor from Alabama. He was anointed to preach, teach and sing. Before his arrival, I loaned the Louisiana pastor some of his sermons that were recorded on DVDs. I am sure that the Louisiana pastor allowed the board to listen to them. Otherwise, my old pastor would not have been approved to come to the church and preach. My old pastor came with his wife and armor-bearer and, invigorated the church body and visitors with his extraordinary scripture-based teaching. I shared with my old pastor the struggles I was facing with the church and, he was dismayed. A positive buzz remained in the church for a few weeks after the Alabama pastor left. We needed positivity in the air because the board members were spewing hatred and negativity at the same time.

The growth that we were experiencing was disintegrating and, I figured out why. I observed more than one board member talking about the type of visitors and members that they did not want at the church as the visitors were entering the building or being seated! How hurtful and shameful. They rejected people that had tattoos, people who wore certain clothing, smelled a certain way, unique hair colors or styles were tabooed, and more. Truthfully speaking, they were rejecting a particular generation and anyone poor. Who did they think lived in the community? Oh, I forgot, they did not go into the community. The board's behavior is why the pews were empty when I came to this church!

Unfortunately, what I witnessed confirmed the comments made by some of the people I visited. The board members were modern-day Pharisees and Sadducees and were slowly but surely inducting the pastor into their circle and way of thinking (Matt. 23:12-13 and, Luke 6:42). They were hypocrites that played church and did not love the community. No harm is generated from loving your neighbor. It is the fulfillment of many godly principles (Rom. 13:10). What happened to the motto of come as you are? What happened to the belief that we are to love our neighbors as ourselves (Mark 12:31)?

A church should be better than the best hospital in the world. People come to church to get well not to become sicker when they exit than when they entered. Rejection and humiliation can cause physical and mental sicknesses. Furthermore, The Greek translation for the word "church" in the New Testament is ekklesia. The phrase "a called-out assembly" is the literal translation for ekklesia[6]. The

Bible confirms that as a church body we are called out to serve and love(2 Pet. 2:9-11, Matt. 5:13-16 and, Heb. 10:23-25). This makes perfect sense because we are made in the image of God and, He is one of love and action. You do not have to tell a person that they are not wanted. Your actions and non-verbal cues will speak for you. The board was speaking loudly and clearly.

One day after morning worship, the pastor was having a boisterous lackadaisical conversation with one of the elders. They were making jokes about other churches that had big chairs on a stage to make themselves look supreme. The pastor remarked that he was glad that his church was not like that. He was not talking with me so; I did not interject myself into the conversation. What I did do is give him a look that said are you serious! This church operates like that minus the chairs. All of it was a farce and, I was furious with what I was seeing and hearing from the church leadership. The hanks were not just at my place of employment, they were floating around the church masked as leaders of the church. Disgusted with what I witnessed; I went to the pastor to handle the matter.

A woman from the community called me on my cellular telephone on an early Saturday morning. She needed some food for her family. I asked her to meet me at the church. I was given keys to the church previously to freely enter the building. When I got to the church, I went straight to the kitchen to prepare the food basket. She came shortly after I finished preparing it. We spent some time talking about the Lord before she left. I stayed in the church after she departed to finalize a project. At some point, the pastor and a board member came into the church. If they were in the building beforehand, they must have parked their cars elsewhere because the church parking lot was empty when I came.

A heated conversation was brewing between the pastor and the board member, but I was not sure where they were located. Their conversation got louder. It got so loud; I could distinguish every word that was being said. I believe that the Lord wanted me to hear the contents because their discussion was about me. It was more of the same, nonsense. The core of the conversation was my ordination title of pastor and the fact that another pastor was not needed to lead the church. For some reason, the pastor came to my location and was startled by my presence. Right away, I made him aware that I heard the entire conversation and repeated some of the statements.

His jaw dropped with embarrassment and, he started apologizing. Then, I realized that he must have informed the board of my concerns and what I witnessed relating to some of them rejecting and ridiculing visitors. This caused the argument. When people are caught red-handed in an act of wrongdoing, sometimes they make up a ridiculous excuse for the action or will blame someone else for causing them to do it. What about saying I am sorry? This board member whom the pastor was arguing with within the church needed to find something to act out her frustration. My ordination title was the frontage that she and other board members used to combat their exposed behavior. Loving and following the Lord does mean that you stand against unrighteous behavior from anyone (Rom. 2:8).

This pastor straddled the fence. If you could hear the pastor speaking during the dialogue with the board member, it would have sickened you. He was always on the side of anyone who was in his presence no matter what occurred. He was reaping the harvest from the work that the Lord was doing, but he wanted to keep the board happy at any cost. The cost was at the expense of the community. One would think that a church that sits in the center of many housing areas would be a beacon of light and a place of refuge for them (Dan. 12:3 and, Matt. 5:14). It is sad to think and say that most of the people in these homes were not wanted in the church.

Whatever the board said was the law at that church, but it did not have to be that way. The pastor had the authority to override their decisions. Regrettably, he was not strong enough to make a stand against their hypocrisy.

As all of this was coming to fluorescein, I had far more pressing issues on my mind and in my heart. Some of my family members' health was deteriorating in Delaware. I was flying home regularly to be a part of their health care plans. The church matters would have to be revisited at a later time. The Lord was watching and, my spirit let me know that He was repulsed by the behavior of the church leadership. The wrath of God is not anything to take lightly (Rom. 1:18). Soon His thoughts will be known.

Reflections and Movement Forward (Chapter VI)

Question 1: If God told you that He was sending you to a place where demons and ghosts dwell, how would you respond (Luke 6:46, Luke 9:23, and, Luke 10:19)?

_____

_____

_____

Question2: Think about someone who has some level of authority over you. It could be a parent, a supervisor, or a landlord. What would you do if you witnessed them committing a crime or doing something that was not right? Now answer the same question if that person was someone you liked (1 John 5:16, Eph. 5:11 and, Num. 15:30).

_____

_____

_____

Question 3: When your resources are thin and someone has a genuine need, how will you address the need that was brought to your attention (Luke 3:11)?

_____

_____

_____

Question 4: How would you handle someone you loved or respected who presented you with gossip and slander of any kind (Eph. 4:29 and, 2 Tim. 2:23)?

_____

_____

_____

Question 5: When you become aware that your self-confidence is low, how do you determine the source? What steps would you take to improve it (Phil.3:2-3, John 5:15, and, Isa. 41:10)?

_____

_____

_____

Question 6: If you see a person being rejected or humiliated, how would you express love and help that person to heal (Rom. 12:9-10, Rom. 15:7, and, Phil. 2:3)?

_____

_____

_____

CHAPTER VII
CARMEN'S WAY

The trials that I was encountering in Louisiana did not phase me. At the age of fifty-two, my trials were many, yet my blessings and victories were enumerable (Deut. 28:3 and, Eph. 1:3). Being a partner in the Lord's law firm sharpened all of my senses to keenly detect and expect the wiles of the enemy (Dan. 2:22 and, 1 John 5:4). Matters of the heart are entirely different. I was reared in a very close-knit family nucleus. Our closeness and love for one another have stood the test of time. As a grown woman, I sat on my mother's lap from time to time. I was not that ninety-five-pound young woman anymore, so the lap time was brief. Family gatherings and vacations were commonplace for us no matter where I lived. Until recently, all of my siblings made Delaware their home. A day did not pass without talking to my mother and often my sisters on the telephone. My mother and I would talk for hours about everything under the sun.

The sisterly bonds have remained well cemented. Cecilia is the eldest, I am next in line, Crystal is the knee baby and Carmen is the youngest. Each one of us has unique qualities and some commonalities. One of the things that we have in common is the love from and for our mother Beatrice Thomas. Our mother has long been considered the phenomenal rock of the family. Not only is she the rock, but she is also the glue and source of excitement. It was odd to see my mother lying on the couch for a long period. This meant that she was not feeling well. My October 2012 visit with her before I moved to Louisiana marked a pivotal change in her health. From that time forward, she began to lose weight and not a single diagnosis could be determined by a variety of specialists. She was concerned about her weight loss and the rest of us were also.

My sister Carmen's physical beauty turned a lot of heads. She did not use or need make-up to be beautiful; it was natural. Her beauty was not the only thing that would grab your attention. Carmen was naturally funny and, she never tried to be. It was just her way. She talks with her hands, makes odd facial expressions, and uses different tones in her voice to get her point across. If an odd event occurred, you could expect a story with animation from Carmen. She would have you in stitches. Have you ever laughed so hard that you had to run to the bathroom? This is the kind of laughter that Carmen brought into the room.

Secretly, my dad called me around 11:00 pm one night to share that my mother was not eating. He wanted me to wait until the next day to call her. I followed his instructions and talked to my mother the next day. She explained that she could not tolerate food and many tests were scheduled in June and July to identify the cause. My daily calls continued and, it appeared that she was on the right road to wellness.

Carmen rented an apartment that was a good distance from our parents' home. Because she was very concerned about our mother's health, she did not stay at her apartment. Carmen would go to work and stay at our parents' home in the evening. Remember Carmen's miracle baby named Shalonda? At this time, she was nine years old and attending a charter school. Shalonda stayed with her grandparents because Carmen's new apartment was outside of the school's district. My parents loved having Shalonda there.

One day after work, I received an unanticipated call from Carmen. She said that mom was not doing well and, I needed to come home. Carmen further stated to me that you know that the Lord gave you that healing power so if something happens to mom it is going to be all of your fault. This was Carmen's way of imparting a sense of urgency. I kindly told Carmen that the same power that dwells in me, dwells in her (Acts 4:30). Nevertheless, the seriousness in her voice could not be disregarded. To some, her tone may have been harsh, but it was not to me. This is what she felt. If your loved ones are not able to be candid with you without being scorned, do you value their friendship? Secondly, the Bible tells us explicitly that anyone who does not provide for their relatives, and especially for their own household, has denied the faith and is worse than an unbeliever (1 Tim. 5:8). The King James Version states that such a person is worse than a failure.

I know how fragile and sensitized Carmen's heart became as she continued to see the changes that were taking place in our mother's body. Thus, I asked my dad what he thought and, he said I think you need to come home. I requested two weeks off from my job in Louisiana and got on the next plane smoking on Saturday, July 13, 2013. My church families in Louisiana and Alabama as well as friends were praying for my mother's wellness. Cecilia picked me up from the airport and drove me to our parents' home.

My mother was resting on the couch when I got there. Digesting food was a significant problem for her. Pain followed every time she digested anything solid. I was able to motivate her somewhat. She started moving around the house more. Even though there was no diagnosis, something physiological was awry. Her weight loss was dramatic. Larry and I simply purchased her new clothing to maintain her impeccable appearance whenever the need arose. Her physical body was changing, but her wit and mind were razor sharp.

By day, I went with my parents to every health care visit that my mother had scheduled throughout the city. Comprehensive tests were conducted on our mother. Yet, nothing was ever discovered or diagnosed. By night, we praised the Lord. I held Bible study on most evenings. This was Carmen's idea. If we were not reading the Bible, we were singing gospel music. Before coming home this time, we had Bible study over the telephone as a family too. Carmen and I also slept in the same bed at night and, we would embrace before we went to sleep. This brought back fond memories of our childhood. Additionally, I found myself preparing lunch in the evenings for Carmen to take to work. She never asked me to do this, yet, she was very thankful for it. This visit was the first time that I was able to spend a great deal of personal time with Carmen and, I loved every minute of it! What a difference God has made in Carmen's life. She deserved recognition for the changes, and I freely gave it (Prov. 15:23). Having this quality time with Carmen allowed me to experience her positive changes and get energized by the laughter that she naturally created (Ps. 126:2). Laughter is a good antidote for stress and tension. My Delaware family was unaware of my trials at work. Larry was also spared many of the details. Satan's craftiness did not need to be promoted nor did I want to create an emotional burden for anyone. I was in good hands.

The Cast Out Intruder

On July 24, 2013, we had a great Bible study. Afterward, we relaxed, chatted, and laughed with our mother on the couch. Mom was feeling better, eating a little more, and participating in the Bible study. We went to bed before midnight. I remember that Carmen and I went to sleep with our arms touching each other's backs. **In the wee hours of the morning, a gigantic demon appeared in the air and hovered over Carmen's head while she was sleeping!** She never saw it. Its' appearance was a cross between a big hog and a buddha figure with short legs. It wobbled, but it remained positioned over Carmen's head. At the sight of it, my spirit hurled scriptures from the depths of my soul. **That demon was cast out with all of the force and authority that the Lord empowered me to use (Mark 16:17).**

What you also need to know is that my eyes were never open. My spirit identified and illuminated this demon before my eyes and, scriptures flowed from my spirit immediately. This was the work of the Holy Spirit in totality. Carmen is a born-again Christian who made me aware that she was being plagued by a demonic force, but I never understood the gravity of this force until that day. The following morning, which was Thursday, I informed my mother of what I witnessed with all of the graphic details. When Carmen came home from work, she said I heard all of the words and scriptures you were saying last night. I wish that I could do that. What did you see? I would not tell her despite the number of times she asked. What I did say was: "Carmen you are set free." She told me, yes, I know. The Lord told her before I did that, she was set free (John 8:36).

After we ate dinner, we had Bible study. For the rest of the evening, we just relaxed. Our nephew Jerome stopped by for a few hours and joined in the fun. Carmen did most of the talking and, I did most of the listening. She shared her plans for her and Shalonda. Her direction seemed to be on solid ground. This was the last evening that I would have with Carmen before I traveled back to Louisiana on Saturday. Carmen was not going to come to our parent's home on Friday after work. She wanted to go to her apartment for the weekend since she had not been there for a while. Before Carmen went to bed, she wanted more of Jesus. She asked me if I brought any sermons or music with me that she could listen to before she went to sleep. I did not have anything to give her. Then, she started browsing through our mother's collection to find something that she had not listened to in the past. I am not sure what she found to quench her thirst. We embraced and, I talked to our mother a little while longer before calling it a night.

An Unforgettable Time

I felt that my mother was getting better even though there were no solutions. She was far more ambulatory and active when it was time for me to depart in comparison to my arrival. My mother insisted on taking me to the airport. Shalonda came along for the ride; therefore, I was able to get a few more kisses and hugs from her before saying goodbye. My flight home was uneventful. Thoughts of the precious time I had with my parents and especially Carmen warmed my heart. The love that I have for my family and the love that they show me has a soothing effect on my heart and soul. Love transports and covers your heart and soul with peace. Did you know that the Bible tells us that love also covers a multitude of sins (Prov.17:9)? Why do you think that this is true? My synopsis is that when we love someone, we are apt to forgive something that he or she does, or we are willing to work through their difficulty with them (James 5:20). Sometimes, the love that you experience from your loved one is the only memory you will have of that family member. Keep your love for them alive (Rom. 12:10 and, 1 Sam. 20:14-15). The two weeks I spent with Carmen are unforgettable and carved a special place in my heart.

Returning to my family in Louisiana and the sanctuary that the Lord gifted us with was always a pleasure. In our ensuite, a big stained-glass window was on the wall adjacent to the bathtub. This was an eye-catching attractive feature. I looked at the window every time I took a bath. A dramatic addition to this window took place. For the life of me, I do not know when it happened. I went into the bathroom to take a bath when I returned home from Delaware. Low and behold, three sets of angel wings were embossed on top of the stained-glass window! Fascinated with what I was seeing, I ran to Larry's man cave, grabbed his hands, and guided him to the bathroom to see the angel wings. Larry just raised his eyebrows and nodded his head. I did not expect much more.

Later, I showed them to Cecilia and Michelle when they visited. Like me, they were fascinated with the angels. Were they guardian angels for Larry, DJ, and me? Perhaps they were, but they were not present when we purchased the home. Why did they appear now? Something was telling me that these angel wings were symbolic of a deeper meaning. Once the angel wings appeared, they remained in the same place. Knowing my God, if the angels represented something else, He was going to tell me in due time. Rest assured; these wings were not going to be forgotten.

We went to church the next day. All the members of the church including the board members asked about the well-being of my mother and indicated that they were praying for her. The board seemed overly gracious on this particular Sunday. Based on what I witnessed and heard, I was waiting for the other shoe to drop. Faithful are the wounds of a friend, but kisses from an enemy are deceitful (Prov. 27:6 [KJV]). Well, the shoe did not drop that Sunday. I called my mom when I got home and, she was doing fine.

I went back to my place of banishment on July 29, 2013. My boss and others expressed sincere concern for my mother's health too. However, nothing had changed on the job. Later that evening, I called my mother for our routine daily conversation. I needed to ask her something and called her back around 9:00 pm. Carmen answered the phone and we chatted for a few minutes. Before she gave the telephone to our mother, she said, **"Sabrina, I want you to know that I love you and I always will."** I told Carmen that I loved her too. We frequently express our love for one another. This time, her sentiment touched me differently. Her words caressed my heart, felt sacred and more precious than ever. I still cling to these words to this day.

When The Circle Is Broken

Carmen gave my mother the telephone and left the house with Shalonda to catch a bus to her apartment. The bus stop was a short walkable distance from my parents' house. My mother and I were in the middle of a conversation when it was abruptly halted by an incoming call. When my mother came back on the telephone, she was crying and said she had to hang up because Shalonda called and informed her that Carmen was just hit by a car. What! I had just spoken to Carmen less than forty-five minutes ago. All of the family that lived in the area rushed to the scene, but Carmen was already en route to the hospital in critical condition by ambulance. Carmen's daughter Shalonda was with her mother but, she was not injured. **Carmen's nine-year-old miracle child administered Cardiopulmonary Resuscitation (CPR) to her with a profuse amount of blood pouring from her mouth. She subsequently called for an ambulance, alerted the police department and our family within a short time of the accident. We are told that Shalonda's action sustained her mother's life.** As a fifty-three-year-old woman, I do not think that I could have maintained my sanity or composure after seeing the accident. Yet, a nine-year-old child was able to withstand it all. God's anointing power and grace over Shalonda's life were still apparent. **The Lord used her in a mighty way that night and beyond!**

I was in Louisiana wailing and rocking back and forth in my chair. No one was allowed to see Carmen on the first night that she was admitted. I know that I became a pest. I was on the telephone talking to someone in the family all day and night. The full extent of Carmen's injuries was not known for two days. I pleaded to the Lord to let my sister survive. Highlights of the accident were on the news and the internet. After locating the story online, I could see the belongings that my sister had in her hands at the time of the accident scattered all over the highway. Then, God led me to another link that had a picture of Carmen lying on the ground. She was not bleeding at this time. The Lord pulled me in closer to the picture and, I could see Carmen smiling as she lay on the ground. This was immediately following the accident. While I was staring at my sister's face, the Lord said: "I was there then" (Ps. 28:7 and, Ps. 94:14). He was letting me know that He was at Carmen's side at the time of the accident. This certainly explains why she was smiling. What I realized later is that the Lord never left her side. One of the things that Carmen had in her hand was a book written by TD Jakes called Wake-Up. Carmen's accident did awaken the family to many aspects of life.

Constantly waiting for updates regarding Carmen's condition and being separated from my family during such a troubling time became too overwhelming for me. I packed my bags and booked a plane reservation. If I could not see Carmen when I got there, at least I would be able to provide some level of support to my family. I purchased some anointing oil from a Christian bookstore and, my friend Lori Rayborn gave me some Holy water that she acquired from the Jordan river to take with me. Satan did all that he could to block my flight from departing (1 Thess. 2:18). My plane's takeoff was delayed several hours. I finally arrived at 2:00 am. The time was immaterial to me. I was going to the hospital anyway. Carmen was in the Intensive Care Unit (ICU) and, I wanted desperately to see and touch her. I apprised Cecilia of the plane's delay and, she notified the ICU that I would arrive very late.

Cecilia picked me up and we went straight to the hospital. I put my clergy collar on because most of the time clergy are permitted in the ICU after hours. Also, this would be helpful because Cecilia and I did not know if the message about my delay was passed on to other shifts. We were allowed to visit Carmen for as long as we desired. I talked to Carmen from the time that I entered her room. She was unconscious and could not speak. In my spirit, I felt that she was able to hear me. As I read scriptures, there was a modulation in her heart rate and other vital signs. Carmen was enjoying the Word of God! Other family members noticed the same thing when they read the Bible to her. I anointed her entire body and her room with oil and Holy Water.

As a family, we met with Carmen's medical team. Her team did not come with good news. Carmen's skull was removed because of brain swelling. The neurologist displayed Carmen's Magnetic Resonance Image (MRI) which told a dreadful story. The majority of her brain was determined to be dead. Carmen's heart was in great condition and, she was breathing on her own. **The doctors were baffled by Carmen's ability to breathe on her own since her breathing center was not functioning. On the MRI, this portion of her brain was allegedly dead.** You and I are not baffled by this. The Lord was in control and, Carmen was fighting for her life with every fiber that existed in her body! We were not giving up hope either. We praised the Lord and prayed for Carmen's recovery around the clock. It was not a day or night that she did not hear one of our voices or feel our warm touches.

One of the ICU physicians was an atheist. In my mind, this is incompatible with the medical profession. She told us that the best thing we could do for my sister is to let her die. This was not medicine that I could digest. Our concern with the physician's position and the possibility that she may be stifling my sister's wellness was escalated. We are a Christian family and wanted our position to be well known; we want Carmen to live. Another meeting was held and what the atheist physician said was repeated. She left the room wounded which was not my intention. If she was not willing to implement life-saving measures for my sister if she became further distressed, we did not want her on Carmen's care team. This physician no longer had a primary role in my sister's health care. We did see some improvements in Carmen's mobility and shouted every time. Carmen was moving on occasion. We thought she was in a coma, but we found out later that Carmen was in a vegetative state. The latter state is worse. God was in control and, we entrusted our faith to His unwavering hand (Heb. 10:23).

I cannot emphasize enough that in all situations, you must remain watchful and prayerful. Challenge words and comments that disturb your spirit and, test other spirits that are among you. (1 Thess. 5:21 and, John 4:1). Do not let smiling faces, white coats, and suits fool you. They can cause you harm. Sometimes the harm that they inflict may be graver than your known enemies. If my family and I did not interject our Christian beliefs and remain watchful, some health care measures may not have been used by those with the belief that Carmen was beyond healing, and that God nor Jesus exists (Rom. 10:14 and, John 6:64-65). Do not let a spirit of superiority paralyze you. No power is greater than God.

Sometimes, the clinical team got Carmen out of the bed and placed her in a chair. During these times, Crystal did witness some movement from Carmen. Every day our mother would say: "Carmen, follow the light". This was another mechanism that my mother used to get Carmen to continue to trust in the Lord and fight for her life. This was the first time in my life that I felt destitute and helpless. I had nothing in my mortal being that could change my sister's outcome. Our hope was in the Lord alone (2 Cor. 4:18). All of the clinicians of different disciplines became aware that we placed our trust in Jesus Christ to heal Carmen. We know that someone who entered Carmen's room was changed by the spirit of the Lord. How could someone not be changed? The Lord's presence, gospel music, scriptures, and prayer-filled Carmen's room every day. Often, a clinician was in the room as this was taking place. Seeds were planted. We may never know who had a life-changing experience, but the Lord knows. Our role is to plant the seed. The Lord does the cultivation (1 Cor. 3:6). Our faith goes well beyond what our eyes can see.

In Her Image

Carmen had several friends that loved her dearly. Some of them were her colleagues. One afternoon when I entered her room, a close friend and his wife were visiting with Carmen. I asked him his name and smiled when he stated it. Carmen thought highly of him. He told me that Carmen was the attorney on the job. He shared that Carmen passed on the advice that I had given her on how to handle certain situations. He thanked me for it. I talked with the two of them for at least thirty minutes. They felt like family to me. Only two chairs were in the room for visitors. The guy offered me a seat, but I declined. I stood at the foot of Carmen's bed the entire time of their visit. **Before I knew it, I was moving my body and hands as a form of expression as if I were Carmen. I felt like Carmen's spirit was superimposed in mine. I was speaking for Carmen!** This was an astonishing wonder from the Lord. My actions expressed how happy Carmen was that they took the time to visit her. I also shared a few humorous quotes that Carmen often said and, they exchanged some of her witty comments. This was a lighthearted time and, Carmen would not have had it any other way. I know Carmen could hear every word and her spirit was smiling inside. I will be forever grateful to the Lord for His kindness and for including me in His wonder.

Carmen's Radiant Glow

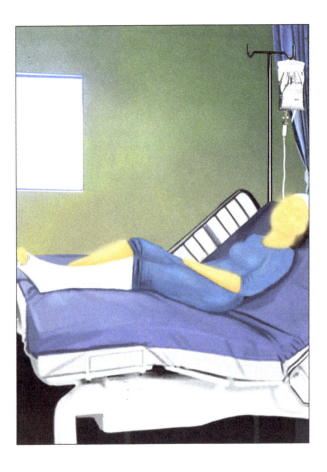

During the accident, one of Carmen's legs was broken. Repairing her leg was postponed until she was considered to be in a stable condition. The ICU physician called my mother when the surgery was scheduled. We waited until the surgery was completed before we went back to the hospital. Carmen was still in recovery when we arrived. My family and I were nearby when they wheeled her gurney back into the room. We followed behind them. As we entered the room, our eyes nearly popped out of their sockets. What our eyes were beholding was spellbinding. **Carmen's body was glowing like twenty-four karat gold from the top of her head to the bottom of her feet. The gold had the brilliance of a fire when it is blazing hot.** Seeing this brilliance reminded me of Moses' conversation with the Lord through the burning bush and the radiance of his face when he came down from Mount Sinai with the two tablets of the covenant law. The bush was ablaze but not consumed. Carmen's body was ablaze and glowing spectacularly. Like Moses, we were marveled and moved closer to Carmen to visualize this miracle (Exod. 3:2-4).

Instantly, my spirit knew that she was having intimate spiritual conversations with the Lord and, she was enjoying His company! Like Moses, Carmen's skin became radiant and glowed because she was in the presence of the Lord during and after her surgery (Exod. 34:29 and, Ezek. 1:27). Halleluiah! This visual will never be forgotten! Do you remember the young lady who died and, her body glowed for days? I could visualize her radiance as her sister portrayed it in my Alabama office. That young lady glowed after death. My sister was glowing and, she was full of life! It is possible that someone other than our family became enamored by her radiance and worshipped the Lord. I never thought that I would behold such a miraculous event in my lifetime!

Seeing Carmen's radiance and her beautiful smile added some tranquility to our family briefly. Just when we thought that she was on a road to healing, Carmen suffered a cranial bleed that required another surgical procedure to correct the problem. We were on pins and needles during the surgery. Thanks to the Lord, the surgical intervention was a success. Carmen's two children remained strong, but I was a mess. Lord, how many more devastating blows could Carmen withstand? Her will to live was impressive. Her heart and lungs continued to function well and bewilder the physicians. The wounds from her accident healed and most of the surgical scarring faded. Her beautiful face was unblemished. However, her brain activity did not improve, but we remained hopeful. Hope is another word for faith. Experiencing the faith of another may become the source of strength you need to press your way through a tough time (Col. 2:5 and, Rom. 4:40).

Our church families and friends across the country continued to pray. Aside from the global prayer, the Lord used my colleagues and friends in the Federal government in several states in a mighty way. They donated their vacation time to extend health care coverage for my sister. This extension of love came at a critical time. The realization of Carmen's condition was sobering; she was not going to be the same anymore. Our family circle as we once knew it was broken. With this thought, we started looking for long-term care facilities that would be able to accommodate Carmen's needs upon her release from the hospital. This was a laborious task, to say the least.

It was now the end of August 2013 and, Carmen's condition was unchanged. Since I had been in Delaware for a month during this visit and Carmen was as stable as she could be, I decided that it was time to go back home to Louisiana. Despite my decision, I still had mixed emotions about leaving. I spent as much time as I could with Carmen before I left. I let her know how much I love her and that we were taking care of her daughter. Carmen's son is a grown man. He needed our support but not our help. Every time I came into Carmen's room, I stayed upbeat. This was a unique day. I could not hold back my tears and, I know she could tell that I was crying because my voice was squeaking. After reading some scriptures with her and singing a song, it was time for me to go. The inflection in her vital signs let me know that she heard me and enjoyed our time together.

Our Lord does hear every petition we make to Him and every tear we shed. In every circumstance, we need to offer thanksgiving to the Lord. Praises to the Lord should not be reserved for what we perceive to be good times (Num. 20:16, Heb. 5:17, and, Phil. 4:6). We were blessed that Carmen was alive.

The Dance of A Lifetime

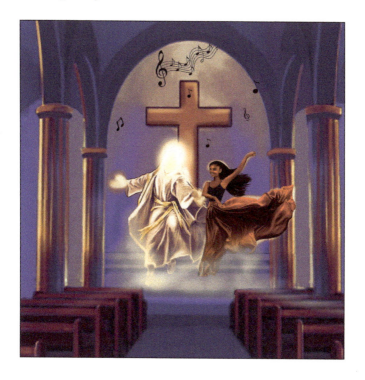

Cecilia took me to the airport from the hospital. Larry picked me up, greeted me with a big kiss, and a hug. When I got inside our home, I felt like the house was hugging me too. I was physically drained and emotionally spent. Nothing or no one could heal my pain except the Lord (Isa. 33:2). I went to bed early with plans of going to church in the morning. Because I had not attended church for a month, I came early in case there were any unfilled needs. After greeting the members that were present, I made a beeline straight to the altar. I had the altar and the church sanctuary all to myself. I closed my eyes and focused on Jesus. The Lord knew what I was going through.

I prayed and praised the Lord verbally and in song. Gospel music was playing as an interlude before the church service. Many of the gospel songs that I like were being played. This stimulated my praise to a higher level. Then, one of my favorite songs started to play. The song was: "Praise Him in the Middle of It." The focus of the song is that you should praise the Lord no matter what you are going through. My praise and worship to the Lord went through the roof. I began to dance like you would not believe. All the parts of my body were in motion (Ps. 149:3). My heart was so heavy. Praising the Lord is what I needed to relieve the weight of my pain. The more I praised the Lord, the lighter my heart would feel.

Hold on to your seat! You are going to be blown away. **As I was lifting my hands and swirling around, I opened my eyes. God the Almighty, joined me in the dance!** This was inconceivable. Yet, it was happening before my eyes. God was wearing a long, majestic robe with a hood on it. He was faceless and brilliant white light formed the shape of His face. All of the places where His extremities should be were glowing brilliantly like neon lights. **It is true, God does inhabit the praises of His people (Ps. 22:3 [KJV])!** You know what else, God can dance and, He was dancing as vigorously as I was. The Lord turned my mourning into dancing and joy (Ps. 30:11)! My Lord danced with me through the entire song. The miracles and wonders that God allowed me to be a part of or witness kept increasing. **This miracle was a dance of a lifetime and an everlasting memory!**

After the song was over, I realized that members of the church, as well as the pastor, were in the sanctuary with me. I tuned out my surroundings during my praise and worship. Heaven only knows when they entered. Judging by their facial expressions, they were present for some of the dance and was patiently waiting for me to finish my praise. I am thankful that no one interrupted my dance with the Lord. Being my extraverted self, my dance with the Lord and all the particulars were shared with my family and close friends with great fervor. This dance alone had the power to propel me through any storm that was coming my way. On Monday, I returned to work with a song in my heart and a big grin on my face. Being in exile remained, but I was showered with empathy from many. Some of my prior staff who were Christians, came to my office to lift me at a time when I needed it the most (Rom. 12:8 and, 1 Thess. 2:11). They also took the time to bring me up to speed with changes that were taking place in their lives.

Pay Attention To The Time

My tutoring and other ministries in the church resumed. Before I went to Delaware, the parents of my students were made aware that my classes would be postponed for a while. They voiced their happiness when I was ready to start tutoring again. News of the program traveled far during my absence. As a result, more students were added to the program. My interactions with the board members were short and sweet for a long time. A resemblance of normality peeked into my life for a couple of weeks.

On Saturday, September 14, 2013, I was in the kitchen weeping as I thought of my sister Carmen's physical state. Swiftly, loud sounds of cymbals began pounding in my eardrums. This was the Lord's way of getting my attention. He knew that my mind was clouded with grief and my emotions rendered me incapable of hearing His voice in a normal way. Once the Lord captured my attention, He said: **"Pay Attention to the Time." I turned and looked at the clock in the oven. It was 5:55 pm.** Because this was the grace hour, I knew the Lord was about to reveal or act on something. I registered the time in my heart and finished what I was doing in the kitchen. Nothing happened and, there were no signs from the Lord that night. I was waiting patiently on the Lord (Ps. 130:6).

The next morning, which was Sunday, September 15th, my mother called me at 8:00 am. She said that the hospital called her around 5:00 am to tell her that Carmen stopped breathing on her own and was going to be placed on a ventilator. Carmen had a major cranial bleed that was far worse than the previous one.

I stayed awake and prepared for church. I laid a black skirt and a matching top on the bed to put on after I showered. After I laid my clothes on the bed, the Lord spoke again. He said: **"Why are you in mourning, it is time to celebrate!"** I said, Lord why are you saying this, I am not in mourning. I looked at my clothing again and realized that the colors of my outfit may be the reason that the Lord was saying that. Black does symbolize mourning in the United States and is the color that is often worn at funerals. I changed my outfit to something a bit more colorful. Still, I was not making the right connection.

My family and I went to church together. I was unaware that the pastor decided to change the service. He got on the pulpit and said, today we are going to celebrate the Lord. The entire service will be devoted to praise and worship. There will be no preaching. Beautiful music and songs filled the church with reverence to the Lord. Still, I was not making any sense of the words that the Lord shared with me in the kitchen or my bedroom.

On Monday, September 16th, I went to work. Around noon, my telephone rang. At this time, I was surrounded by three strong Christians who stopped by to see how I was doing. They were very supportive during my trials. My mother got on the telephone and said that a palliative care physician was with them and wanted to talk to me. He got on the telephone and said that Carmen was dying, when can I get home. I interjected my thoughts and said that you are not God. My sisters were laughing and said to the physician, we told you that she was going to say that. He stressed his point in a very endearing way. I came home the next day and went to the hospital shortly thereafter.

Carmen did not look the same. She was lifeless. In a blink of an eye, all the words that the Lord shared with me a few days ago were now making sense. The Lord told me to pay attention to the time because He was taking her to glory at the grace hour. **Carmen went home to be with the Lord precisely at 5:55 am on September 15, 2013. This is why the Lord wanted me to look at the clock.** The mystery as to why she was breathing on her own when all other indicators said that she should not be; was a sign and a gift for us.

It was a sign that God was in control. When she stopped breathing on her own, it was also a sign that Carmen was with the Lord. Her lifeless appearance on September 17th was further proof of this. The Lord wanted me to celebrate that she was with Him. This is why He questioned my attire and told me to celebrate. The Lord even changed the church venue to be a celebration. These were miraculous acts from the Lord and a display of love that no man could ever replicate. The Lord gifted us with more time with Carmen. At the same time, He was also preparing us during these six weeks for her transition. A few days before Carmen went to glory, all of us came to grips with the fact that she may be departing this life soon. Each one of us was at peace. Coming to a place of peace took some time, but the Lord got us there. My mother said that Carmen was not coming home nor was she going to a long-term care facility. Carmen was in close conversation with the Lord from the moment of the accident and throughout her time in the hospital. I believe that He let her know that she was going to be with Him soon and, her children would be in His care.

A decision was made to remove Carmen from life support on September 18, 2013. This was a formality since Carmen was already home with the Lord. Her son removed her respirator in the presence of other family members. We had a big sendoff celebration in that room that ushered in all the angels from heaven! Someone on Carmen's health care team orchestrated a way to pipe in the gospel music that we wanted to hear. We sang, honored Carmen's deeds, her devotion to the Lord, and her family. I told her well done, you have finished your race (2 Tim. 4:7)! The pastor of my family's church and several members of Carmen's clinical team was an active part of the celebration.

I spotted the neurologist who was caring for Carmen in the hallway. She expressed her condolences and remarked: your sister was a fighter; I do not know how she lived as long as she did with her extensive injuries. I asked her if she remembered the room that Carmen was in when she stopped breathing on her own. She said that she was in room fourteen. Keep this number in the back of your mind. It will resurface again. At face value, the number fourteen replicates seven. Do you remember the Biblical significance of seven? Let me jar your memory. It means something is finished or completed. I always say that Carmen was in room one four. These two numbers equal five. This allows me to also see the Lord's grace in action as well as His completed work. Carmen's placement in this room was God-ordained as well. Her work on earth was completed, by grace, the Lord saved her years ago and took her home to be with Him at the appointed time.

On record, Carmen is noted as transitioning on September 18, 2013. Nevertheless, my entire family knows that she went home to be with the Lord on September 15th. By now, you know I did not omit a single thing. It was the will of God that Carmen transitioned at that time and, it was also His will that I communicate on high the real date and time that He took her to glory. Carmen's wedding reception or homegoing service was held at their church. Like the celebration in her hospital room, it was precious and moving. One of Carmen's close friends who attended the celebration came to me and said that she was having a hard time with Carmen's death, but after she witnessed our faith, she was fine. Let your faith be a source of contagiousness.

I had the opportunity to meet several of Carmen's friends and colleagues who visited her in the hospital. I exchanged telephone numbers with some of them. A few weeks after Carmen's transition, the Lord placed one of her girlfriends on my heart, thus, I called her. She was emotionally wounded by Carmen's natural death. The Holy Spirit took control of the conversation and the young lady accepted Jesus Christ as her Lord and Savior. After our conversation, she told me that my telephone call stopped her from leaving her house and purchasing an illegal substance. Glory to God! In your despair and mourning, you can still offer Jesus and love to someone else. He will turn that despair and morning to oil of joy and a garment of praise (Isa. 61:2-3).

In Carmen's Shoes

Aside from sharing the gospel, the Lord put on my heart to right a wrong. I wanted to see exactly where the accident occurred. I left my parents' home and walked in Carmen's shoes. The street that Carmen and Shalonda had to cross to catch the bus was a dangerous highway. Once the green light was triggered on the crossing light, a pedestrian had to briskly run across the highway to safety on the other side of it. The light would change to red in midstream of a pedestrian walking in the crosswalk. Something was dreadfully wrong with the synchronization of this light in conjunction with the other lights that a driver of a car used to proceed. Also, a portion of this highway had a curve that distorted a driver's view of the crosswalk. This arrangement was an accident waiting to happen.

I felt like the city or state had some level of responsibility for this accident and also had a responsibility to make some corrections. I searched for the name of the state representative who was responsible for the jurisdiction of my parents' community and made an appointment to meet with him. Crystal and I put on our Sunday best clothing and our dad dropped us off to meet with the gentleman. He was saddened by our sister's outcome and joined the fight. Research that he conducted along with mine was enough to get others to listen. Carmen was not the only victim. Several other pedestrians were hit by cars on that highway. Some were critically injured and, some died. Many of their families joined our fight and signed the petition we started. I contacted the local news station and shared my story with a reporter. We planned to meet at the bus stop that was Carmen's destination and across from the highway in question.

As a family, we marched from our parent's home to the location of the accident. My parents observed the difficulty that others were having crossing the street. They refused to walk across the highway and went home to get their car. They parked in a lot directly behind the bus stop. The reporter and representative also struggled to cross the street. The Department of Transportation made some enhancements to signage and the lights, but I wanted the city to build an overpass for pedestrians. This improvement did not take place despite the number of petitions. In memory of Carmen, we had a huge poster of her made and plastered it on a pole nearby the bus stop. When the picture became tattered, it was replaced with a new one. Carmen's son has kept this act of remembrance alive.

Some of you may be thinking; why did such a gruesome thing happen to a child of God? No one wants anyone that they love to hurt. I am no different. I do not have an absolute answer for why the accident was allowed or why my sister died from the injuries that resulted from it. Bad things do happen to God's people. What I can say is this; seeds were planted, lives were saved and, miracles were performed in the process. Through it all, many believed in the name of the Lord and began to trust Him.

John The Baptist was a person in the Bible that I believe shared some of my characteristics. When I read that he was beheaded, I moaned as if I knew him personally. Several God-fearing people and leaders in the Lord's inner circle died horrifically. Their crime was being a Christian. You and I can never erase from our hearts how our Savior died. The Lord was beaten beyond recognition of a human form. He endured suffering greater than any human (Isa. 52:14 and, Isa. 53:5). He did not look like the pictures you purchase from a store. If this happened to our Lord what is the expectation for His followers?

Being a Christian is the best life you could ever ask for as a human being. Do not let fear of being harmed discourage you from having an awesome and eternal relationship with the Lord (Prov. 1:33). There is no better friend than Jesus (John 15:13, Prov. 18:24, and, Prov. 17:17). Fear of any kind creates a path for Satan to operate. The Lord will always protect and guide you. Like my sister, we all have a designated time to die a natural death. Having my sister Carmen in our lives for fifty years is a blessing. Carmen's last words to me were spoken on July 29, 2013. Her words were I love you and, I always will. These words are a gift that keeps on giving.

Decay Removal

For a few months, the board members in the Louisiana church were civil. It did not take long before they reverted to who they are. Attacks against visitors were flying high during the New Year's Eve annual celebration. They were openly mocking the visitors and laughing at them. What the heart is full of, the mouth will speak (Luke 6:45). Their behavior was atrocious and lacked any similarity to humor. My family and I were also being watched like hawks. Our words were being measured and our tithing too! We were just serving the Lord and the community. Why the need to scrutinize us? I do know why. I disagreed with their rejection of the community and their unwillingness to love unconditionally. The board was searching for any ammunition to use against me. One time, I recommended a change to improve the flow of a program and was told by the pastor that just because we are the biggest tithers in the church it does not mean that they have to take our advice. This response came from left field and was the most illogical response I ever heard. What was the real issue and agenda? Why was he measuring our giving to the Lord? The pastor never answered that question.

The poor treatment of our guests and other defenseless members annoyed me to no end. Again, I voiced my concerns with the pastor. He arranged a meeting with the board members of concern, himself, and me. The board members did not come. Instead, they sent the pastor's wife to serve as an advocate for them. This demonstrated a lack of respect toward me and, the wife did not know about their shenanigans. The words from the board member who said that "we have been waiting for you came to light." She did not know how profound her statement would become.

The pastor started the meeting by saying he did not understand why I became so angry. The Holy Spirit took control and, I became the Lord's battle-ax again. The Lord recounted how the words of the board members wounded many, caused them to stumble and feel unworthy of love. The pastor set idly by and watched. He did not defend the people that he was appointed to shepherd (Jer. 23:1 and, Zech. 11:17). God's ax was already at the foundation of the church and, He was in the position to cut down all the trees that did not produce fruit and throw them into the fire (Luke 3:9). After I concluded, I walked out of the church and, my family and I never returned. Although we do not wish any harm on our enemies, the Lord has a way of rescuing the righteous and causing trouble to fall on the wicked (Prov. 11:8).

The church body disintegrated rapidly from that day forward. I had no idea that this was going to happen. Every board member left the church. Some moved to another state, some left due to illness, and were placed in nursing home facilities. The pastor was either asked to resign or removed. God cut down all of the decayed trees. Some other members also left and joined other churches, After God expunged the dead trees, I received a call urging me to come back to the church. A new pastor was installed. My family and I elected to keep our distance from the church. Our work at the church was finished. As it is written in the Bible, we were not going to have fellowship with the fruitless deeds of darkness. Instead, we are to expose them (Eph. 5:11). This was one of my purposes for being at the church. Working with the Lord is always challenging and full of twists and turns. He will graciously direct you through every maze with His light.

Transformative Light

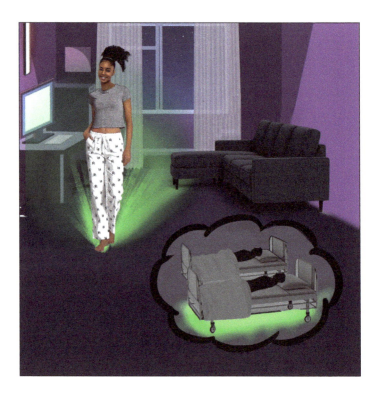

Some of the songs we sang as children in Sunday school are still remembered. On an occasion, you may sing one of them as an adult. I do. One of my favorite childhood songs is This Little Light of Mine. As the song goes, we are to let our light shine (Matt. 5:16 and, Luke 11:36). Did you know that the properties of light that God created for us to explore are the characteristics of a Christian? Light is reflective and, we are to be reflective of Jesus' nature and emulate His principles. Light exposes and eliminates darkness. This is what we do when we share the gospel, spread and conquer evil in the name of the Lord. Everything that happens in the natural world has happened in the spiritual realm first. Only God's infinite wisdom could devise such a correlation. As shared with you some time ago, one of my sermons after being ordained as a pastor was the power of the light. This is when God revealed to me the connection between the properties of light and a Christian. The spirit that is in a Christian does shine. I do not know about you, but I can often discern when a Christian is in my midst. We emit light. Do you remember that guy from my class who said that he could feel that I was an evangelist? It was the warmth from my spirit (my light) that he was feeling. God wants us to transform the world with the light He has given us (Isa. 42:16, Eph. 5:7-14, and, Acts 13:47). The words that my mother shared with Carmen in the hospital linger in my spirit. **She told Carmen to follow the light. The Lord transformed these words into instructions and action for me!**

One early morning in January 2014, I arose from the bed and planted my feet on the carpet in preparation for work. When I stood, a green reflection was coming from the soles of my feet. Our smoke detector had a green light on it. I thought that somehow that light was the source. As I walked toward the bathroom, that green light was following me. **There was a green light shining from my feet with every step. I put my slippers on my feet and just like the soles of my bare feet, the green light was shining from the bottom of the slippers. I walked to the kitchen and green lights illuminated my pathway. The sheer amazement of this spectacular occurrence had me speechless for a few minutes.** The outside light surrounding the perimeter of our home was also illuminated. I asked Larry why did he turn on the outside light. He remarked that he did not turn on any lights. Because what I was experiencing was the light, I knew without a shadow of a doubt, that it was the Lord. He wanted me to follow the light. The Lord did not speak. He simply cast the light as a sign. I called my pastor from Alabama to get his opinion on what the Lord was doing. He encouraged me to pay close attention to the hand of the Lord in my surroundings.

I went to work and stopped by the Starbucks café to get a latte. I kidded with the person who was making my coffee for a few minutes and got on the elevator. By the time, I got off the elevator on the eighth floor, it dawned on me that I had left my coffee at the café. I hopped back on the elevator to retrieve my coffee before it got cold. This time when I got on the elevator, there was a woman in it. Her eyes were bloodshot red as though she had been crying for a long time. She had a sullen look on her face that indicated that something was bothering her. I asked the lady if she was okay. She said that her father was not doing well. I asked her his name and ward number. I told her that I would visit her dad.

My stomach was growling and, I was famished. I said to myself that I will get something to eat and then visit the lady's dad. The Lord spoke immediately following my thought. He said, work first and eat last (John 5:17 and, 2 Thess. 3:10). The Lord had an assignment for me linked to the light under my feet and that lady on the elevator. What could it be? The location of the ward was very close to my office. Once I reached my destination, I went to the nurse's station to find out what room and bed number the patient was occupying. On my way to the patient's room, the room number registered in my brain and stopped me in my tracks. Drum roll! It was room one four (fourteen). This was the same room that my sister Carmen occupied when she took her last breath. I wonder what the Lord is planning this time. I walked into the room and looked for the particular bed number given to me. **This patient's bed was encircled by green flashing lights. It was the same light that was under my feet. He was my assignment and, the light was all about him!**

The patient sat up in the bed when I approached his area. I looked him straight in his transparent eyes. My spirit was telling me that this patient did not have all of his faculties. Softly, I asked him if he believed in the name of the Lord and, he nodded yes. I was led to touch his leg and, I could fill a large mass moving in his body. I prayed and exited the patient's room as quietly as I entered. I believe that the Lord healed him that morning on the spot. The Lord used me as a conduit of His healing. He did not need me, but He wanted me to participate. Later in the day, I saw his daughter again. With a smile on her face, she said that her father was doing very well. I exchanged smiles with her. The daughter of the patient was also a part of my assignment. If I had ignored her, I would not have become aware of her father's issue. Consider this: If I deliberately ignored the woman on the elevator after identifying that she was wounded, I would have been no different than the priest and the Levite that ignored the beaten man on the side of the road. We are to respond like the Samaritan woman who rendered help. (Luke 10:30-36).

Consider The Butterfly

While I was in Louisiana, I had to return to Alabama to attend a court hearing. I told my old pastor that I was coming and, he asked me to preach that weekend. The message that the Lord wanted me to deliver was entitled: Consider The Butterfly. As odd as this title is, its relevance is worth echoing. This message is about the woman who glowed after her death and others like her. Butterflies are so beautiful. I do not know anyone who will kill a butterfly, do you? What about that caterpillar? The opposite feeling emerges, right? I have seen the faces of some adults cringe at the sight of a caterpillar. They are seen as creepy creatures that should not be near you or your home. Often, they do not make it to the next step. They are killed before they can be transformed into a butterfly. Take a close look at a butterfly, a portion of the caterpillar remains when they become a butterfly. That part of their old self will never disappear. However, it is the wings that are generated from the new creature; the butterfly that permits it to fly and even soar.

As believers, we may be guilty of not letting others come into their future because we will not let go of their past. When the Lord saves individuals and changes their habits for the good, why would you flaunt their old addictions and bad habits in their faces or remind friends of their past? This behavior may cause that person to be imprisoned by their past and kill their new spirit. Let this person come into their future with the Lord and fully transform into that beautiful butterfly! God is the only judge. (Luke 6:37). This behavior may also cause a person to stumble and possibly revert to old habits because of your branding and labels. Jesus detests this type of behavior and, you can expect His wrath if this describes you (Matt. 18:6). It is not too late to repent and apologize. Let us focus on removing the splinters and beams from our own eyes (Matt. 7:3 and, Luke 6:41). Like butterflies, transformed Christians carry the baggage of their past with them. However, they only share their past as a part of their testimony to assist others in defeating their giants and managing their raging storms.

Reflections and Movement Forward (Chapter VII)

Question 1: Take ten minutes and think about the goodness of the Lord. Now praise His Holy name at least the number times equal to the events that came in your spirit. How can you elevate your praise at home, at work, and in your community (Ps. 34:1 and, Heb. 13:15)?

_____

_____

_____

Question 2: Lord manifest any event that I have caused someone to not come into their future because I will not forgive their past (Isa. 43:18, Col. 3:13 and, Num. 14:19)?

_____

_____

_____

Question 3. When a person's loved one transitions, he or she tends to have a lot of support. As months go by, the support tends to fade. Ask the Lord to identify someone who still needs support and then, pray about a meaningful way to assist (Isa. 40:1 and, 2 Cor. 1:4).

_____

_____

_____

Question 4: Think about the parable of the Samaritan woman who rendered help to the man that was robbed and beaten. Who do you identify with the most: the priest, the Levite, or the Samaritan woman (Luke 10:30-36)? Ask the Lord if He supports your choice? Be sensitive to a scenario that He may reveal to you that supports His answer.

_____

_____

_____

Question 5. Take some time each week to tell someone instrumental in your development, thank you. Select one day a week to offer help to someone who needs development in an area that you are skilled or gifted (1 Thess. 5:12-13 and, 1 John 3:17).

_____

_____

_____

CHAPTER VIII

RAGING STORMS

Foreshadows of The Trumpet

Ironically, Carmen's transition was a wake-up call for the entire family. We all examined our lives and got all of our business affairs that were incomplete in order. Carmen had her business affairs well intact. In February 2014, I was doing my two-week stint at the Regional office in Mississippi, but still in exile. The only good thing about going to Mississippi was our close friends that live there. Jerry and Dorothy Jones have been my friends for almost forty years and Larry's friends for thirty-five. I looked forward to fellowshipping with them every time I came into town. Like everyone else close to my heart, they were not made aware of the trials I was facing.

My routine telephone calls to my parents never ceased (Deut. 5:16). While I was in Mississippi, I called them during my lunch break and before I went to bed. One evening, I asked my dad how he was doing and, he said he was not doing well. I was shocked to hear him say that. He said he did not know the exact issue, but he knew that something was wrong. The next day, he was admitted to the hospital and, he stayed there for at least a week before he was given a diagnosis. His cancer had returned. Because of its location, it was undetected until it got larger. I called him every day and, his demeanor remained jovial. During a lunch break at the end of February, I went outside to get some fresh air and listen to some gospel music in my car. My mother said that my dad wanted to talk to me. He got on the telephone and expelled some air first. I knew then that he was going to unleash something serious. My dad said that the doctors told him that he only had thirty days to live and, he began to weep. I restrained my emotions and told him that the Lord was in control. I emphasized that he had the winning hand. Whether he lived or transitioned, he was in the hands of the Lord. He decided to be placed on hospice at home. This news was hard to digest. Carmen just transitioned five months ago. Even with this unhappy news, my dad stayed positive. He was telling jokes about his ride home in the ambulance. I had been to Delaware so frequently, that the personal time I could take off had diminished greatly. Therefore, I was torn about the best time to come home. Because I was on a business trip, my mother insisted that I wait. She later gave me clues when it was time to come home.

The Sound of the Trumpet

I arrived on the evening of March 25, 2014, which was a day after my mother's birthday. I was very happy to see my dad and, he was happy to see me also. That night, we magnified the name of the Lord with our praise and worship. I can still see our dad at this moment lifting his hands high in praise and dancing in his bed (Ps. 109:30). He did not sing out loud or talk much. He was preserving his breaths. The morning of March 26th came with some signs that our dad was in transition mode and, the family members were alerted. All that could, rushed over and encircled his bedside.

Crystal played her tambourine as we sang and worshipped the Lord. (Ps. 150:3-4). I remember thanking our dad for everything that he did for me and my family that came in my spirit. His deeds of love were many. The Bible tells us that those who demonstrated perseverance in doing good seek glory, honor, and immortality and, God will give them eternal life (Rom. 2:7). This represents who our dad was on earth. Many people benefited from his kindness. Our dad took a deep breath and sighed. We thought that this was his last breath, but it was not. My mother called his name with great authority and my dad sat straight up in his bed. The way he responded to my mother's call, I believe he thought he was standing before the Lord on judgment day and was ready to receive the Word of God like a man (1 John 4:16-17). It was such a dignified response.

His body laid back down very swiftly as though it was exhausted. Hastily, my spirit said: Pop, you are released to go to glory! Spontaneously, the Lord sounded the trumpet and he transitioned to glory. I always say that the angels of the Lord flew our dad to glory on a jet plane because he transitioned at 7:47 pm. His departure from this life was two days after our mother's birthday. As desired, he transitioned from his home surrounded by people who loved him. Cecilia closed his eyes with coins and, the flood gates of mourning poured like a river. Who would have thought that our dad would transition six months after Carmen did? Lord, our cups of grief are running over. Please take these cups away from us (Mark 14:35-36)! The Lord used all of us to lift one another. I cannot adequately express to you how honored I am that the Lord used me, to share the good news with my dad and be a part of his conversion, years before his departure.

His homegoing service at my parents' church was glorious! Crystal's daughter Macy did a solo praise dance in his honor that commanded a standing ovation. She danced beautifully at Carmen's service, but this dance opened the gates of heaven. The outpouring of love from the Lord and many others soothed our mourning (Matt. 5:4). The big smile on my dad's face at his service is also something that will never be erased from our memory banks. This smile was not there at the time he transitioned. To God, our dad was the sweet aroma of Christ while he was alive and while he was perishing from this life (2 Cor. 2:16). I told my mother that God put that smile on his face as a sign. It was a sign that my dad; David Thomas saw the face of God and, he was with Him in glory. When the perishable has been clothed with the imperishable and the mortal with immortality, then the saying that is written will come true: Death has been swallowed up in victory (1 Cor. 15:54). Hallelujah!

As great as we know living with the Lord through eternity will be, most people do not want to rush their exit on earth. My mother did say that she hoped that I did not see God's face any time soon and, I said I hope you do not either. However, we understand that God has the ultimate control of our exit point and, it may not coincide with our wishes.

The End of Exile

My ministries and trials at work and church co-existed for a while. The beauty of my trials at my job this time was the warning I received from the Lord and the focus I placed on Him during the trial. Focusing on the Lord and not the actions of the enemy made the trial insignificant. In addition to that, the Lord gave me a secret weapon to use. It was kindness. The requests of my enemies were honored with a smile. By being kind to your enemy, the Bible tells us that the coals of fire will pile on their heads (Prov. 25:21-22 and,

Rom. 12:20). When I returned to work after my dad's transition, I was realigned back to the hospital.

A new CEO arrived and ended my seventeen months of exile in March 2014. The beginning of our relationship was a little bumpy, but the path became smooth once we got to know one another. He utilized the talents that the Lord loaned me to the fullest and gave me public recognition at the local, regional and national levels. I designed and taught the hospital's analytics program. Like me, he was fascinated with data and numbers so, he was in my fan club. To this day, we communicate and have mutual respect for one another. As I think about it, I have maintained good relationships with all of my supervisors over the years unless they were proven to be the Lord's enemy.

My alignment with the new CEO was rewarding for me. He allowed me to spread my wings as wide as I wanted. I became a hot commodity. My expertise was requested broadly. One of the influential clinical leaders wanted desperately to align me with his service line. I continued to assist him, but I was appropriately aligned with the CEO. If I was not teaching, I was serving as a consultant. This arrangement was a perfect niche for me. My work life was back on track and my trials there evaporated. The pain of losing my sister and dad did not fade. All of the family were deeply wounded. My concern gravitated to my mother. She was frail and suffered the loss of her youngest child and her husband.

Facing The Inevitable

On the day of my dad's homegoing service, my siblings and I went into my mother's bedroom to help her get dressed. We knew the gravity of her pain and that she had to face the inevitable; the burial of her husband and coming back to their home without him.

When she removed her lounging outfit, I broke down and left the room. My mother had become very thin and, this was not her intention. She purchased a scale and placed it in her bathroom because she was losing weight rapidly and wanted to monitor it. Two years had elapsed since the onset of this issue with no solutions in sight. Her diminishing weight did not impact her ability to think or respond. My mother was feisty as ever.

A few days after my dad's burial, my mother gave me some family pictures of her parents and siblings and said: Take these you will need them when it is my time. I did not want to take them, but I did. After I looked at them, she placed them in a keepsake box where she was storing important things. In my mother's mind, she was facing the inevitability of her death. Larry and DJ drove back to Louisiana and, I stayed with my mother another week longer. Cecilia and Crystal lived in Delaware and were able to assist her. A few weeks later, my mother flew to Michigan to visit her siblings. We thought that would lift her spirits.

From the latter part of the summer of 2014 to September, my mother was admitted to the hospital intermittently for various reasons, again no answers were received. She insisted that she was fine and told me emphatically not to come home. My mother said that she would call me when it was time.

On October 10, 2014, I got a call from my mother. This call meant that my mother felt as though she was going to depart this life soon. I jetted home to Delaware the very next day. I could not wait to embrace my mother and shower her with love. The most I could do at this time was pray. I sincerely felt like my mother needed to be admitted to the hospital and, Cecilia felt the same way. We were going to insist that deeper comprehensive testing be conducted. We had one major obstacle: our mother. She was not going to go to the hospital. Why should she want to go? No tangible actions or solutions evolved from other admissions. We devised a plan to admit her, but we did not have to implement it. On October 13th, she fell in her living room while the visiting nurse was present and concluded on her own that she needed to be admitted. We never told her our plans.

Mom was taken to the hospital by ambulance and admitted through the ED. We were going to make sure that she had a thorough evaluation to get to the root cause of her weight loss. I stayed overnight in the hospital with her and, my sisters went to their homes after a long night. Before going to sleep, my mother stated that she was going to have a test done in the hospital that was originally planned as an outpatient visit. She hesitated to share the reason for the test. Then, mom said that a spot was identified on her lung that the physicians thought was carcinoma. The next morning her physician came into the room and said that he was certain that the spot on her lung was cancerous. I did not absorb his words into my spirit. As Christians, we do not claim defeat.

The day of the procedure arrived and, we prayed at my mother's bedside before they wheeled her out of the room. The procedure lasted two hours and then she went to recovery. Once she came into her room, we entered and inundated her with love. The surgeon came in the room a few minutes later and imparted the great news. Our mother did not have cancer! He said he did not know what the nodule in her lung is, but it is benign! My friends, we could not be happier and, you can guess what I did next. My dancing began in that surgical suite. The smile and sunshine on my mother's face were priceless. God's work is never in vain (1 Cor. 15:58 and, 1 Cor. 15:14). I believe that the Lord was after the heart of the physician who communicated with certainty that my mother had cancer. His heart and mindset had to be changed. I further believe he walked away knowing that my mother was healed miraculously. If he ever doubted God, he no longer did.

I am the one in the family that monitors all the vital signs and reads all of the medical notes. As I was gazing at her blood pressure results, I noticed that it was inclining and the nurses that were supposedly monitoring her at their station were not responding to the change. Her blood pressure was moving to the stroke zone level. I left my mother's room and went to the nurse's station for urgent intervention. They seem to be unphased by the elevation which irritated me. A nurse contacted her inpatient physician to order some medication. At last, her blood pressure went to a normal level within an hour after taking the medication. Lord, thank you for bringing my mother out of the woods.

Mom was now stable and ready to go back to her inpatient room. Cecilia and I decided to go pick up some fast food while everyone else stayed with our mother. We had just hit the highway when Cecilia's cellular telephone rang. It was Crystal screaming and crying her head off! Her pitch was so high that her initial words were not discernable. Finally, we got the message; our mother just had a stroke! Cecilia did a dynamic pirouette with her car and, we returned to the hospital quickly. We dashed out of the car running at lightning speed through the parking lot, the hospital lobby, and to the elevator. That elevator was not moving fast enough for us! Thankfully, nothing or no one was blocking our way when we exited the elevator. Our adrenaline was high enough to bulldoze our way through a crowd.

At last, we got to our mother's room and, she was being transported to the Stroke ICU with all kinds of medical equipment attached to her and a cadre of physicians and nurses flanked around the gurney. My sisters and I grabbed a hold of any portion of the gurney that we could affix at least one hand. Our mother knew that we were at her side by the prayers and scriptures that we were vocalizing. Our mother suffered a massive ischemic stroke that rendered her unconscious. She stayed in a coma for over a week. When visitation was allowed in her room, a parade of people who loved her swarmed inside her room and the waiting room around the clock. The ICU allowed her to have more visitors than usual. Seeing my mother's eyes and hearing her voice after this event was a gift from the Lord.

The first thing she said was: You all prayed me out of heaven early. The stroke did change some of her functions. She was unable to move or use the left side of her body, had difficulty standing, and was struggling with short-term memory. I requested family medical leave(FML) and planned to stay with my mother as long as possible. I could count the number of hours I had remaining to be off duty on one hand. The frequency of traveling back and forth to Delaware for my sister and dad exhausted the majority of my time. I used the ICU's facsimile machine in an office area to submit my FML to my job. As Crystal and I were walking back from the office, one of the nurses who was caring for my mother stopped me and asked if I was a pastor. I stated that I am and asked her why was she asking. She said that she could feel it. This is a familiar response and affirmed that my presence at this hospital was another divine appointment. The love that others had for me was demonstrated by their donations. Because of them, I was able to be off from work without an interruption in pay for months. I was not worried. If I was not a recipient of donations, I was not going to leave my mother's side. The Lord always provides and, I have a husband that takes care of his family. Why do I ever need to worry? We are never to be concerned with having our needs met. If you are worried, it is probably time to reevaluate your faith (Luke 12:28).

The Power of The Number Five

I came to the hospital every day early in the morning and left before nightfall. My sisters, extended family, and members of her church filled in the gaps. The effects of the stroke further weakened my mother's fragile body. Because of her weakness, her lungs and chest cavity would not expand enough to expel mucus from her body. This posed a problem for her oxygenation. She was placed on and off the ventilator multiple times. Being on a ventilator for a long period is contraindicated for wellness. The Intensivist on the unit told us that she was going to need a tracheotomy. This is a procedure whereby a hole is cut in the middle of your throat and a tube is inserted for breathing. This is not a desirable procedure but the only solution for some patients. In my eyes, my mother is not just a run-of-the-mill patient. She is a queen and a child of God. I did not concur with the specialist and did not believe that all other efforts were exhausted. **I told the Intensivist in the presence of my mother's Respiratory Therapist and Cecilia that we are going to wait five days and then extubate her. Note what I did not say. I did not say "try" to extubate her.**

The physician got very angry with me. He said do you know the amount of infection that can happen if that ventilator remains for five more days? I told him that I am acutely aware of what could occur. Right after that, the Holy Spirit began to speak. My spirit said that I serve a God that heals (Exod. 15:26, Luke 10:9, and, Ps. 6:2). I know that He will heal her and allow her to be weaned from the ventilator in five days. My spirit sensed the raised eyebrows of the Respiratory Therapist. I turned around to the therapist and asked him if he believed that the Lord would heal my mother in five days and permit her to be extubated? He said that he did not believe in God. Wow, we have another person who does not believe in God now treating our mother. However, his countenance was unlike the physician caring for Carmen. He was humble and handled my mother with tender loving care. My spirit knew that God was dealing with this guy.

With reluctance, the physician conceded. Honestly, he could not override the wishes of the family in this situation. The Lord moved my eyes to the foot of my mother's bed. There were some buttons on the footboard panel. I looked at the buttons and asked the physician if the bed was a percussion bed. He said yes. I asked why were they not using the functions of this bed to assist with my mother's extubation? He scratched his head and, I said that we want this function used over the next five days. A percussion bed taps the middle of a patient's back. This helps the patient to expel mucous.

Day five arrived and the moment of truth was going to be unwrapped. The Respiratory Therapist and the Intensivist came into the room. The therapist proceeded with the extubation process. **My mother was removed from the ventilator and remained off of it!** The clinicians looked at each other and then they looked at me with their pupils bigger than fifty-cent pieces. Yes, they were stunned! They thought that her oxygen level would decline and, she would have to be put back on the ventilator. It did not happen. I could not pass up an opportunity to testify about the goodness of the Lord to a captive audience. **I reminded them of what the God I serve was going to do in five days and, He delivered! The Lord performed another miracle for everyone to see every time they entered my mother's room!** This miracle was performed so that the Respiratory Therapist who was a professed atheist, and the Intensivist who put his trust in science alone would believe in the name of the Lord and be saved (John 4:48, Matt. 21:19-21 and, Luke 17:5-6). I wonder how their relationships are with the Lord today. Adding this miracle to my testimony continues to glorify the Lord, displays His everlasting love, and accentuates the power of faith.

Physical Therapy was a top priority for my mother's recovery. This service was in the hospital, but you would have thought we were going outside of the building based on my mother's request. Every time she had therapy which was frequent, I had to carry her purse. I said mom why do you need your purse inside the hospital? She told me that I carry mine wherever I go and, she wants her purse wherever she goes. I laughed and carried the purse. Her paralysis on one side also inhibited her ability to stand on her own. Getting the strength to stand with assistance was the first hurdle my mother had to cross. Her determination to get her body back to normal during such a weakened state was quite notable (Act 3:16). Watching my mother in action made me realize where her children's drive to succeed in stormy times is derived.

My mother's perseverance during this therapy was a testament to her faith and her will to defy more odds. She forced her body to move with all her might for each activity. Whenever she had the physical and mental stamina, she put forth an effort to strengthen her body. Her actions exemplified what it means to put your body into submission (1 Cor. 9:27). Many times, the desired outcome was not achieved, but I was always proud of her determination and will to improve. The stroke did not alter my mother's wit or humor. In addition to strengthening her body, my family and I did several things to restore her memory. She had forgotten that our dad was deceased and wanted to know why he was not visiting her. I had to tell her that he died and communicated a tidbit of information surrounding his death to jar her memory. When I walked into my mother's hospital room on the morning of November 7, 2014, she said I know what today is, and said happy anniversary to me. It was my twenty-eighth wedding anniversary. I smiled and felt at that moment that her memory has returned. She started recalling other memorable events that further proved that her long and short-term memory were made whole. We were very thankful to the Lord for this restoration.

Glistening Snow

Before my mother was admitted to the hospital, she completed some home improvement projects and had other projects on her radar screen. My sisters and I wanted our mother's home to be as safe as possible when she returned to it from the hospital. Since I was staying at our mother's home, I checked around the house to see what additional improvements were needed. Cecilia found someone to make these enhancements with ease. I was excited to tell my mother about the plans. Once the work was underway; I gave our mother a report of the progress each day. Improvements were made to both the interior and exterior of the house and, we were very happy with the quality of the work that was performed. I had intended to take pictures of the completed work, but it slipped my mind. One day when all of her children and some of her grandchildren were present, I began sharing how happy she was going to be when she got home because of the enhancements. Our mother blatantly said that this is my home. She was referring to the hospital as her home. We understood her to believe that it was her home until she got better. None of her family thought that the hospital was going to be her permanent residence but that was our mother's true belief.

Christmas was over six weeks away, but our mother was acting like it was next week. Her Christmas list was prepared in her mind. She told Cecilia and me everything that she wanted to purchase for her youngest grand and great-grandchildren. It was cold outside and, our mother wanted to make sure that her great-grandchildren got new coats. She got us in the Christmas mood whether we were ready or not. Christmas is always accompanied by a spirit of joy. All of us started doing our Christmas shopping and decorating early. I asked my mother what she wanted for Christmas and, she said some skinny leg jeans. She had already requested a new artificial Christmas tree that was easy to set up. I ordered the tree and purchased some gifts for my mother that included the jeans that she wanted. We decorated our mother's room and finished Christmas shopping well before Thanksgiving.

In 2013, my mother planned to come to our home in Louisiana for Thanksgiving in the year 2014. Out of the blue, she informed me that she wanted to talk to Larry. I called him and gave her the telephone. She told him that she was not going to make it to our home for Thanksgiving this year. My mother was in the hospital thinking about everything that she had scheduled for the coming months. One of the things that she desperately wanted to do was to praise the Lord in her home church. I remember her telling me one day that she wanted to walk down the church aisle and watch the church body holler. She then stated that the only thing that was stopping her was the intravenous pole and line that she was connected to in her room. **My mother knew that her news of no cancer in her lungs, her recovery from the stroke, and, the fact that she did not get a tracheotomy were miracles. This was enough to make everyone in attendance holler in praise to the Lord!**

On or before December 8th, I walked into my mother's room ready to attend to her needs. As soon as I got near her bed, she was ready to talk. With wide eyes, she sat up and began speaking with her face all a glow. Her eyes were glistening and twinkling like freshly fallen snow. With the utmost joy, she blurted, I have seen my house. Considering all of the home improvements that were made while she was in the hospital, I figured that she had a dream about them. Later that day, she told me to take her purse with me when I left because she knew she was not going to need it. I took her purse and decided to keep it nearby in the glove box of the car that Cecilia allowed me to use during my stay. Knowing my mother, she was going to ask for it again in the next day or two. Over the next two days, the Lord kept my eyes on my mother's face. Her skin was as smooth as a newborn baby's skin. When I combed and brushed her hair, I could tell that it was growing and becoming silkier than the previous week. Her appearance was like someone returning to their youth. The Lord wanted me to have this visual of her in my mind.

When Lightning Strikes

On December 10th, It was Crystal's birthday. Because Crystal planned a gathering at her home that evening, I asked my mother if it was okay for me to leave early. My mother said it was okay but there was a feeling of uncertainty in my spirit because of the subdued tone of my mother's response. I left early and celebrated with Crystal, other family, and her friends. On December 11th, Crystal and I made plans to visit our mother together. Cecilia had a hair appointment and planned to come later in the day. Usually, I arrive before 9:00 am. On this day, Crystal had a business matter that needed to be addressed before we went to the hospital. We arrived to visit our mother at 11:00 am. When we entered the room and laid eyes on our mother, we screamed loud enough to shake the walls and the mounted television. Our mother was sitting up in the bed, but her face was disfigured and, she was unresponsive. I ran out of the room and activated the rapid response team.

No one on this team could arouse her so, the code blue team was activated. Within seconds, the code team came flying down the hall and rushed into my mother's room. **Our mother coded in front of us and, her body was in shock!** I reached my hands between the team members that were actively working on our mother and prayed in my prayer language. Crystal and I both were calling on the name of the Lord. I do not remember who called Cecilia, but I do know she had a relaxer in her hair at the time of the call and quickly had it washed out to get to the hospital. It was like all of the force of the five oceans in the world were crashing through the windows in my mother's room at the same time. The storms in our lives were raging ferociously! Lord this is our mother the phenomenal rock, you can not take her away from us! All we wanted was the Lord to answer our call and heal our mother.

The Lord answered our call with the speed of light. Our mother's face returned to normal and, she began to speak to us as if nothing ever happened. She was placed back on the ventilator during the code. I asked her to wiggle her hands and toes and she moved the ones that would move. Later that day, we met with my mother's medical team. This was the session that I dreaded. The bottom line was not good. My mother's prognosis was death and she, was not expected to live through the night, but she did live through it. The words of pending death were hard for my sisters and me to handle, but we had no choice but to swallow them. Our mother is a Christian and where she was going was not being contemplated except, none of us wanted our mother to be with Jesus now.

The word of God tells us that these things (the scriptures) have been written so that you may know that you have eternal life. If you follow the instructions in the Bible which are to repent and accept Jesus Christ as your Lord and Savior, eternal life is yours (1 John 5:13). My mother did that years ago and lived a corresponding Christian life. If anyone could teach unconditional love based on the way they live, my mother would be the principal teacher. After the meeting with the medical team, my sisters and I reentered our mother's room. She was now in a different ICU. I asked my mother to wiggle her toes if she was informed about her health. None of her toes wiggled. I told her as delicately as I could that her thoughts were accurate and, she needed surgery but was not a candidate for it. Being a nurse, my mother knew this statement meant that she was not going to live.

Immediately following those words, I told my mother that I love her and, she said I love you too. I did not want to say how great of a mother or friend she has been, I did not want to say anything that sounded like it was in the past tense. I was believing that the Lord was going to heal my mother. With those thoughts, I rested on the words I love you. After hearing the news, my mother's church family and friends gathered to express their love for her and prayed inside and outside of her room throughout the night. All of her daughters had some private time with her. Our mother smiled the entire day and night. Mom was thrilled that many people came to express their love for her and, she was never in any physical pain.

The Loudest Trumpet

We stayed in our mother's room all night. All of the medical equipment attached to her made it impossible to kiss or caress her. At 2:00 am on the morning of December 12th, I went to my mother's bedside and said mom you made it through another day. Two hours proceeding my words to my mother, she coded twice. Our mother's wishes were known. Years before this occurred, our family discussed each other's wishes. Our mother told us that she did not want us to continue her life if she experienced three codes. This meant that she did not want to be revived after the third resuscitation. She coded three times in one day. At our wishes, the dosage of medication that keeps her heart going was increased after all three codes. The third dosage was the maximum that any patient could receive.

Throughout the morning and the early afternoon of the 12th, we called my mother's name, checked her eyes and other body functions for signs of life. With no signs detected, It was time for us to make a decision. Crystal notified their pastor who came to the hospital to pray with us. **At 5:00 pm, the loudest trumpet that ever existed sounded!** Our mother went home to be with the Lord on December 12, 2014, surrounded by her daughters and her pastor. Her transition was two days after Crystal's birthday. I did not pay attention to my mother's room number until she transitioned. **Just like Carmen, our mother was in room one four (fourteen)!** The Lord had spoken with grace. Our mother's journey was complete. Her diagnosis was only discovered at the point of her death. Our mother lived over two years with a diagnosis and a prognosis that is usually sustained for a few months. This too was another miracle that our Lord performed.

The last words my mother said to me were I love you too! These words will never be forgotten and are very similar to Carmen's last words to me. A couple of days preceding my mother's transition, the Lord wanted me to see that my mother was going to glory sparkling and unblemished. In the next few days following her transition, the Lord made me aware of some signals that she was sharing that were beyond my thinking. What I realized many years later, I could not have handled any signs that my mother was going to die soon. The Lord spared me from that level of grief. I might be strong, but this would have been overpowering for me. Some of you may say that the unexplained weight loss was the first warning sign. This was not a signal for me, but I am sure it was for my mother. Weight loss has so many root causes that do not point to death. When my mother telephoned me and said that it was time to come home in

October is the first sign that she believed that she was transitioning soon. The signals got stronger, but I still did not perceive that her death was drawing nearer. Telling all of her daughters and grandchildren who were at her bedside that the hospital was her home was a pretty strong sign. Instructing me to take her purse home was stronger.

The strongest sign by far was the vision that the Lord gave her of her house. **The Lord told me that the house she saw with glistening eyes was not her residence on earth. It was a clear picture of her beautiful heavenly home. My mother got a good view of the mansion that she was going to live in with Jesus in glory! No home on this planet can make a person's eyes glisten like snow!** The Lord was preparing my mother for her inheritance in the kingdom that He predestined before the creation of the world (Matt. 25:34)! God's love for my family continued to shine. Neither my mother's, father's nor my sister's body ever entered a morgue. The mortuary that cared for our family came to the hospital or our parents' home to prepare and transport their bodies. My friends, this is favor from the Lord (Prov. 3:3-4 and, Prov. 8:35)!

The Wedding Dress

The time to select the clothing that we wanted our mother to wear for her wedding reception was upon us. Our mother told her children years ago that she wanted to wear her peach chiffon wedding dress for the occasion. Our mother and stepfather were married over forty years ago. Heaven only knows the current condition of the dress. I went into her closet to locate the dress. It was in a torn garment bag that could not possibly protect the dress from fading or dry rotting for four decades. I removed the dress from the garment bag and inspected it. The dress was in mint condition. How unbelievable! The dress was still a vibrant peach color and, it had not deteriorated at all. Not even a fray could be found. It only had one tiny smudge on it. This was impossible for man but not God (Mark 10:27).

Considering the age of the dress, we wanted an opinion from a seamstress on how to clean it. Our mother had a good friend who was a seamstress and lived around the corner from her. She came over to look at the dress shortly after Crystal called her. She told us that our mother's dress could be cleaned easily with Woolite and, she volunteered to clean it. This was a precious gift to us from the Lord! **The vision that the Lord gave me in 2012 of chiffon floating in the wind re-emerged.** Remember that this vision was about the lady that shined like gold and sketched the dress in her journal that she wanted to wear to meet Jesus. The Lord honored our mother's wish and gifted us. If I transition to glory today, I will leave this world believing that the vision of chiffon I had in 2012 was foreshadowing the beautiful chiffon that I would see again through my mother's dress. Both my mother and the other lady had their hearts set on celebrating their union with the Bridegroom in an elegant fashion and, the desires of their hearts were granted by God (Ps. 37:4).

Triumph Over Defeat

If you are struggling with the pain of losing someone near and dear to your heart, I know your pain all too well. My sisters and I suffered the loss of our sister and then six months later, we suffered the loss of our dad and, nine months later we suffered the devastating loss of our mother, followed by the loss of my nephew Jereld. These transitions were compounded by the loss of the two children that Larry and I experienced. Although I am not bleeding anymore from these deaths, the wounds are not closed. Honestly, I do not know when or if they ever will. A specific start and end date of a person's grief does not exist. God does understand that we will mourn and, He has given us the Holy Spirit and associated scriptures to comfort and help us to heal. Sometimes, the Lord will rekindle a fond memory to ease your grief. One time, I cried myself to sleep over the death of my sister. In a dream, the Lord gave me a vision of a time when we were hugging each other. Keep those memories alive. I have peace in knowing that my loved ones have eternal life and simply transitioned from this life to it. Their relationship with the Lord added their names in the book of life which triumphed death forever (2 Cor. 2:14).

In your grief, do not punish yourself. By doing so, you will give Satan joy. If you are like me, I do not want that beast to be afforded anything but what God has in store for him on judgment day. Sometimes, there is a tendency to say what you should have done for, or said to, your loved one before he or she transitioned. I have wrestled with those thoughts myself. What I have come to know is what needed to be said or done occurred. Our loved ones departed knowing our hearts. If for some reason you left something unsettled, talk to the Lord. This may be a time to ask for forgiveness or have a teaching moment. Once, you talk to the Lord, leave that burden on the altar. Your altar does not have to be in a church. It could be anywhere. Punishing yourself will imprison your mind and soul and render you ineffective in many aspects of your life. In your mind, your self-worth may diminish and before you know it, you are in a state of self-pity and depression.

If you fall into that cycle, you will not be able to hear from God, your physical health may be in jeopardy and your full potential will not be realized. This is not God's will or purpose for your life. Through our Lord and Savior Jesus Christ, our pain and grief will not defeat us. Through Him, we are overcomers who will use our experiences to help someone else cope with grief and pain. I am not providing you with lip service. I am imparting to you my experiences with mourning, pain, and overcoming grief. If I can triumph through my experiences, you can also. You have to have a desire to heal and not be defeated. It is not easy and, it may take some time. The Lord will guide you (Prov. 11:14 and, Prov. 15:22).

In the early spring of 2015, another career opportunity came to light in Illinois. I competed for the position and, I was selected. My boss in Louisiana gave me a glowing recommendation, but he did all he could to get me to stay. I grew quite fond of his leadership and, some of his strategies should have been canned. Except it was time for me to part ways with Louisiana. It is often said that you leave your boss and not your position. This was not true this time. I would love to work with him sometime in the future. The same leader that wanted to realign me to his service came to me with a proposition for me to stay. It was charming but not alluring to me. Their respect for me and my talents were greatly appreciated, but there was nothing that could keep me there. Based on my research, I was going to join a team of movers and shakers! It appeared that I would be on a team that would promote the best scientific and administrative me.

Larry and I worked for the same organization and in the same building in Louisiana. We also had the pleasure of working for the same organization in Alabama. This new relocation would also be the beginning of Larry's retirement from any form of work. A little bird (me) told the CEO (my boss) about a week in advance that Larry was retiring on the same day that I was leaving. On my last day of work, my boss walked me to my car. Larry was in the car waiting for me to come outside. My boss shared some kind words with Larry about me. Next, he officially gave Larry his retirement certificate.

Larry got out of the car and, we had a small ceremony followed by a few snapshots. What a sweet moment.

My new job in Illinois was going to be my last Federal position before I retired. In two years, it will be time to hang up my work hat. Larry and I agreed to relocate in July 2015. I loved our sanctuary in Louisiana and did not want to sell it. My negotiation strategy did not work with Larry this time. He did not think it was prudent to keep it. I have to admit that he was correct, but the tranquility that our home offered made it hard. I believe that the angel wings on the window symbolized the transitioning and protection of my three family members who are in glory. This move was something new for us. We were not moving further south but to the Midwest. With this change in direction, what is on the Lord's mind?

Reflections and Movement Forward (Chapter VIII)

Question 1: Little things matter a lot. When is the last time you contacted a distant relative to say I love you? Contact someone outside of your inner circle <u>and</u> someone identified as an enemy within a week to offer a spoonful of love (1 Pet. 1:22 and, Luke 6:32).

_____

_____

_____

Question 2: Take ten minutes and think about the transition of a loved one that was close to your heart. Take a personal inventory of your habits after the loss of your loved one. Has your eating, sleeping, and socialization been altered? Has this persisted? If you answered yes to any of these questions, it is time to seek the Lord. If these habits have also persisted, call someone that you respect and who loves the Lord. Share with that person what you are going through (Rom. 12:1, Job 5:8, Prov. 11:14, Prov. 15:22, and, Ps. 16:17).

_____

_____

_____

Question 3. Being exiled often means you have been forced to live away from your temporary home or workplace as a form of punishment. List the ways you behaved when you were rejected and/or forced to operate or work outside of your chosen place. Review the noted scriptures on how others responded to being in exile (Dan. 6:1-26, Jer. 29:4-10, and, Acts 16:16-38). How is your behavior different from theirs?

_____

_____

_____

Question4: God loves you and wants to hear from you. Determine a way to talk to Him routinely. Consider daily prayer or writing in a journal. Be sensitive to His responses through scriptures and other Christians.

_____

_____

_____

CHAPTER IX

THE NEW FRONTIER

The Unpaved Road

My family and I lived in the south for twenty-seven years before heading to the Midwest region. Although I have roots in the Midwest and grew up on the East coast, I consider myself to be a southern girl. We were unfamiliar with the culture and norms of metropolitan and urban living and always gravitated to the quaintness that small-town living offers. Thus, the Hughes family was starting a new journey on a road that was unpaved. There is always some level of chaos when you are packing and preparing to sell your home. The packing and moving of our household goods was nothing less than a calamity. As with all of our other relocations, the packing and movement of our household goods were at government expense and, they select the company for you. Unfortunately, we had a motley crew packing our belongings. They took frequent breaks that prolonged the packing process. I went into one of our bedrooms to check their progress and, one of them was lounging in one of our chairs as though he was off duty and resting at home.

In conjunction with that team, we had a disorganized moving company that was responsible for loading and transporting our goods.

When it was all said and done, there was some damage to our home that needed to be repaired and furniture that could not be transported with our other goods. The truck that arrived was half full of another family's belongings. The moving company miscalculated the weight of our goods and the amount of space remaining on their truck. This was a nightmare that delayed our departure. It took two days for someone to come back and get the rest of our furniture and another day was added to get someone from their company to repair the damage that was done. The time delay caused us to miss Michelle's doctoral graduation ceremony which was problematic for me. I was hotter than a firecracker and made the moving company aware of the impact of their delay as well as my dissatisfaction. I am told by the graduate herself that our delay was a blessing in disguise because her ceremony was quite a snoozer. What I did not consider were the signals that our complications with moving were sending. Are these signs of what lay ahead? You expect some bumps on an unpaved road, but a road should not have hills and valleys on it.

One night before we left Louisiana, I had a dream that I was in a large room with many artificial tall plants. I touched some of them and they were plastic. All of the people in this room were wearing face masks. They were the kind of masks that you see at a masquerade ball. After a while, all of the artificial plants began to move as if they were given life from something. I woke up and said to myself what in the world did I eat last night that made me have that crazy dream. Is it possible that this dream will have a profound meaning in the future? I guess I will have to wait and see.

After all of our issues were resolved, we began our journey to the Chicago, Illinois area. We left on July 10, 2015, and, it was a scorching hot day. We arrived at our prearranged apartment outside of the metropolitan area in time to unpack our things, take a quick shower and join Michelle's celebration at Tony and Barb's house. After a long drive on a hot summer day and celebrating most of the night, my family and I were worn out. I had one day to rest up before going to work. My rest was going to have to take a back seat to navigation of the area to purchase the things that we needed for the next week. Our first culture shock was the tolls we had to pay within the city limits. If you do not know alternate routes and do not have a toll pass you can go broke just riding around the city. Needless to say, we acquired both quickly.

The Façade

The clock alarm beeped at 5:30 am and, I was not ready to turn the sheets loose, but I had to go to work. Who would dare be late for their first day on a new job! Thoughts of starting a key leadership role at a health care system that was considered the flagship of Federal hospitals energized my morning. All the bells and whistles as it relates to clinical programs and research are said to be here. I could not wait to get finished with orientation, dig into my new role and explore the top-notch technology and programs. As a premier organization, one would also expect a robust analytics program and heavy use of analytical tools that the government used to measure performance.

I was anxious to meet my new boss and see my new office so, I went to the respective area during the orientation program's lunch break. I popped my head into the office of my supervisor who was the interim CEO. He welcomed me into his office and to the organization. At this time, he did not share anything about the department or staff that I was inheriting. Since our meeting was brief, I thought that he would share some insight during our scheduled meeting. He did not share any information at that time either. I guess he wanted me to find out on my own. I got a rude awakening real soon.

Remember, I shared with you in the past that the Lord prepares us for our next step during our previous journey. My experience in this hospital made me appreciate everything I learned from my trials in the last three states. My spirit let me know that an ambush wrapped in a web of deceit was contrived long before my arrival. My unknowns were when and how it would happen. My trials made me understand that it is the Lord who wages war. We are to seek His guidance when we see evidence that it is forming (Prov. 20:18). What I do know is that the Lord will expose the enemy's hand and safeguard me at the same time (Judg. 16:12, Isa. 59:5, and, Prov. 26:26). About a month after my appointment, my boss in a round-about way communicated that an external investigation was going to take place regarding my appointment. What? I probed him because what he was saying was not making any sense. Finally, he said that there was going to be an investigation because it was alleged that I knew someone on the interviewing panel who gave me leverage in getting the position. This was absurd. I competed fairly and the person that served on the panel did not assist me in any way to land the position. I earned this position on my own merits through a rigorous process that included multiple panels. No law is broken by a panel member merely knowing the candidate.

In a conversation with a clinical leader, he spilled the beans. An incumbent who was the interim leader competed for the position and was not selected. According to him, she was loathed by many leaders and, he was not shy about his disdain for her. The incumbent and a partner in crime were at the root of this investigation. This was only the tip of the iceberg. The incumbent remained in my department, worked directly for me, and plotted to make my life a living hell before I arrived because she was not chosen for the position.

The funny thing is that she knew all of the members of each panel, why were her relationships not under investigation? I think that you already know why this was happening. As a reminder, the real reason this occurs is due to the relationship that I and the panel member in question have with the Lord (John 15:18).

A couple of months later, the allegation was a nonissue for me, but the panel member was further agonized by others. She won that battle! Although the matter was a non-issue for me legally, I worked with a cloud over my head for the duration of the time that I was there. Sunshine would peak through the cloud when my competence pulled the organization through some dark and challenging times. The plot continued to thicken and, daggers were being thrown at me from every direction. The Lord intercepted all of them. The persecution I faced in Illinois was ten times greater than in Louisiana. I met with all of my staff separately to determine their strengths, weaknesses, and their opinions on organizational priorities. My conversations with them were communicated with positivity and an earnest desire to get their feedback. Many of them were advocates for the non-selected incumbent and decided to spin my words into a web of lies that led to multiple investigations. No findings resulted; however, I exhausted a ridiculous amount of time to support my actions against these frivolous claims.

Their failed attempts led them back to the drawing board. As a responsible leader, I reviewed every job description and evaluated work products against requirements. The work product of most of the staff was inferior. They were not completing the required work and what they submitted most of the time lacked the necessary level of quality. The evaluation period ended in October for most of them. The prior interim leader could have rated them in July, but she did not. All of the employees' rating period was extended. This meant that I would have to rate them at a later time. I know that you can see where this was going. This extension was another setup. If the employees did not receive the rating they wanted, additional complaints were going to be filed. I worked with the staff enumerable times to improve their competency and work products in advance of the end of the rating period. Some improvements were made, but most of my efforts failed and formed resentment. All of the employees received the ratings that they earned and, a domino of complaints followed because they wanted a rating higher than what they earned.

As these complaints materialized, hospital inspections from external entities were expected. The person who did not get my position hid or distorted information to make it hard for me to access data and determine and prioritize performance improvement strategies. She wanted me and the hospital to fall flat on our faces. If she was not doing that, she was conveniently absent from work and derailed improvements efforts when she was present. She filed a complaint also, therefore those above me, were afraid to intervene even though it was warranted.

I discovered through a conversation with one of the executives that most of my employees did not compete for their positions. They were placed in my departments because of underperformance in other units. This was confirmed with HR and, I received supporting documentation. My department was used as a dumping ground for underperforming nurses. This explained the lack of competency and the staff members' resistance.

My areas of responsibility were complex in scope and included hospital-wide analytics which was right up my alley. To determine the pulse of the organization, I scheduled meetings with leaders identified as movers and shakers that I would be working with very closely. These were meetings that I was looking forward to having soon. There is something to be said about a person who is passionate

The New Frontier

about their area of expertise and executes actions that improve and sustain desired outcomes. In my mind, these are traits of a mover and shaker. Whenever I work with someone of this caliber, my creativity and ideas for enhancements are heightened. Meeting such a person at this hospital was an illusion. Their programs were broken and, they were clueless about the analytical tools that they were required to use. Instead of complaining, the Lord used me to design the analytics program and teach ongoing classes to empower staff. This was a highly successful program that expanded staff knowledge and improved organizational performance.

To my surprise, high technology, bells, and whistles did not exist. The dream I had of artificial plants moving and people with masks on their faces were no longer a mystery. The Lord wanted me to know that this place was a façade. It was not a flagship and, the movers and shakers could not be found. This hospital that was noted as premiere did not have a tenth of the framework of some hospitals identified as low performers. How could this be? This hospital was being marketed by influential people who wanted this place to be seen in the best possible light. The squeaky wheel gets the grease. What they did have going for them were some physicians that did their jobs well.

My persecution continued to incline. One of the interim CEOs who was weak got caught in the enemies' devised scheme (Ps. 10:2). They galloped in this person's office from every hill, valley, nook, and cranny with complaints about me throughout the day. These demons acted like animals hunting down their prey. After this leader stated to me that no merit surfaced to convene an investigation into the allegations, this leader was mentally beaten to a pulp and initiated one anyway. After this person was no longer the leader, the next one in line came and banished me to a cold, dark location far from the mainstream. People would laugh every time they saw me.

The shunning tactics, sneers, or gossip did not weaken my spirit or humiliate me. I was excluded from participating in meaningful work for a few months and publicly told to leave or not attend briefings (Luke 6:22). Banishing me was their loss. My salary and monetary incentives never ceased. I used this free time to study my word, pray and prepare for a professional certification exam.

The Lord told me explicitly what the outcome of the investigation was going to be and what the enemy was going to do next. The Lord said that there were going to be zero findings, but the enemy is going to try to convince you not to return to your appointed position. Everything the Lord said would happen did. At the appointed time, I was not going to be silent (Acts 18:9). Five months after the investigation convened, the interim leader that banished me to the dungeon came to my temporary office and said that I was exonerated and, I could return to my position. He then said: You do not want your old job back, do you? I said I knew that you were going to say that. Yes, I do want my job back and, I want to return to my original office as well.

In a day or two, I ran into the interim leader who initiated the investigation on the elevator. This leader congratulated me on being cleared of any wrongdoing. The nerve of this person. If this leader was stronger, this situation would have been avoided. I responded to this leader with non-verbal cues. Based on this person's body movements, my intended message was received and, this individual was ashamed. It was best to keep silent. My tongue would have gotten me in trouble this time. (Ps. 39:1 and, James 3:6). The Bible tells us that in our anger, sin not (Eph. 4:26). From the bottom of my heart, I believe this person knew the Lord and was lured into a trap. The Lord used my persecution to teach this person some valuable lessons on righteous judgment (John 7:24 and, Zech. 7:9).

Within the next two weeks, the third interim leader was appointed to a full-time CEO position elsewhere. Now, a new permanent CEO was appointed. In less than two years, I had four supervisors. This leader who was now my boss was making decisions about my department and did not take the time to even meet me or include me in the changes. Hearing all the revisions in passing, I made an appointment to meet the new CEO. Based on the lack of findings, my level of authority, placement back in my original role, and my office were righteously restored. I stayed in the dungeon for six months. This person was unable to withstand the pressure of the employees' advocates and concocted another organizational chart that subdivided my departments based on the whining (Eccles. 9:12). Thus, the full level of my authority that was restored to me was short-lived.

The roles critical to the success of the organization were aligned to me. The non-selected incumbent was aligned to the CEO and, she elevated her level of destruction with no action taken by the CEO. Oh, did you think that this was the end of the enemies' schemes? No, it was not. The next scheme up their sleeves was an attempt to give me a poor end-of-year performance rating. Such a rating would taint my career. I was asked to submit a self-assessment based on my performance plan. I responded that I could not create a self-assessment because I was never given a new plan. I must tell you that I knew this day was coming and, I had nothing but pleasure in telling them in a nutshell that they could not rate me. In the end, I earned an excellent rating and received a bonus. The Lord continues to confuse the wise with the little things (Isa. 41:29 and, 1 Cor. 1:20). The enemies' fear tactics never penetrated my mind. When you respond to fear, there is a chance that it will affect your heart. My mind was prepared for action and my spirit repelled any form of fear (1 Pet. 1:13 and, 1 John 4:18).

When I interviewed for this position, I made the executive panel aware that this role would be my last in the Federal Government. Only one of the executives who participated in this panel was still employed at this facility. I am sure that this is not something that this leader retained. In October of 2016, I began planning for my retirement. The goal was to retire with thirty years of service. In April of 2017, I would be able to realize this dream. Little did I know that another gift from the Lord was blossoming. I discretely interviewed for the job, finalized my retirement, and gave two weeks' notification of my departure. My boss resented the timing of my decision and probed me to determine my driving force. Nevertheless, my enemies could not contain their joy. They thought that they successfully drained me and won the fight. They had no knowledge that my retirement was several years in the making and, I did not disclose anything contrary to their beliefs. I said my goodbyes to those that I respected on May 5th and, I started my new position in the private sector on May 8th. Look at the grace of the Lord and the new beginning that He had for me.

New Territory

Being employed by the private sector was a brand-new territory for me. My skills sets were transferrable and the departments that I would be managing were the same as the Federal sector. One striking difference was the oversight bodies. The private hospitals have more eyes watching the organization's performance and patient outcomes. The hospital's mission to provide quality care to a diverse community with social-economic challenges and health disparities won me over. This hospital sits in the heart of a drug corridor in Chicago that further emphasizes the need for accessible health care services and caring leaders. The CEO, who was my boss, was out of town on my first day, but he called to welcome me to the family. His words were a nice touch. The person that was responsible for my recruitment warned me that this organization's performance was sub-optimal and, it was in the window for a triannual accrediting survey. If this hospital's performance was measured by first impressions, it would have failed the day that I started my position with them. The entrance area was in shambles. The walls were dirty and, the wallpaper was torn. The chairs in the lobby and waiting areas were screaming for some bleach, soap, and water. They did not appear to have been cleaned in years. If you think that the chairs were bad, you should have seen the floors. If there is anything worst than filthy, the floors were it. Interestingly, the executive suite left you with a different impression. When you walked into this suite, it was like you were in another world. The environment was very polished with decent furnishings. Why the inconsistency? Time will tell.

The new executive responsible for the environment of care had a big hurdle to climb. The place needed some tender loving care for sure and, I was honored to partner with other leaders and extend my love. It did not take long for me to determine that my areas of responsibility were also in shambles. As I continued to peel back the layers of the onion, over ninety percent of the hospital programs that would be surveyed were completely broken, and, those that were not had some notable deficiencies. I had to sound the alarm to the executive team because the hospital was on fire! The hospital anticipated an unannounced survey visit in January 2018 and, the number of deficiencies was tremendous. We had a steep hill to climb with many leaders needing climbing instructions. Structure, performance improvement strategies, and teaching modules were urgently crafted and implemented swiftly. I had to run like my life depended on it and, I had to influence all of the other leaders to run with me!

As a team, we ran hard and fast, but time was not on our side. The accrediting agency came five months earlier than expected and, we were in dire straits! We had too many deficiencies to overcome in three months. Ideally, boots should have been on the ground conducting assessments and executing improvement strategies continually. If not on a continuum, actions should have been taken by leaders at least eighteen months before the expected survey. Our official report was scathing and, the survey fallout was overwhelming. With over fifty pages of deficiencies to address from the agency, I had my work cut out for me. I am not being facetious. The composite team that I am accustomed to having was not here and the leaders of departments did not have a clue on how to respond to a deficiency. For a year, the team in my departments consisted of one; me. Thankfully, I was able to recruit a few additions to the team. Even with more staff, I worked fourteen hours a day on average and remained buried in a pit of heavy workload. I was not alone; other recently appointed executives faced the same thing with no end in sight. The volume of deficiencies did not match the size of the hospital. No one would ever think that such a small hospital would need so much work! My labor was performed out of love and guided by my faith (1 Thess. 1:3). You and I are always working with the Lord wherever we are.

I did not mind working in high gear or working long hours. The community would benefit from the improvements and most of the leaders knew that their departments needed improvements before the survey and were eager to learn ways to improve. Who would disregard a humble and willing heart? A person with this type of spirit makes me want to work harder to help them achieve their goals. Our God calls us to be good examples and, lead those who are blind to the right direction and solutions (Isa. 42:16). We should always help others to see the light (Luke 1:79).

The Unforsaken

In September 2017, I was making rounds on the clinical units throughout the hospital. Rounding on the mental health unit was on my schedule. Shortly after I arrived, I went to the dayroom to observe the activities of the patients. I could see from a short distance that several patients in the dayroom were lounging, playing games, and watching TV. As soon as I stepped near the door entrance, I was flooded by patients asking me to pray for them and their families. Then they asked me to get them Bibles. I prayed for and with them on the spot. After I departed, I instructed one of my staff members to ensure that the department receives Bibles and, he did. I had never laid an eye on any of these patients. You know that this was the work of the Lord.

The following year in the same month, I rounded on the same unit. This time, one of my employees was with me and witnessed the Holy Spirit in action. I was on my way out of the department and this female patient came out of nowhere running toward me. She grabbed my hands and said that she needed prayer and to be saved because she did unspeakable things. Immediately the Holy Spirit went into action. I located a room nearby for us. The Lord saved her soul after her repentance and, we prayed. You know, mental health patients are often forsaken by man but not God. Many times, they are cast to the side, written off as crazy, and said to be not in control of their minds. This is a form of judgment. My friends this cannot be. I am reminded of a scripture that says: By grace, I am who I am because of His grace and His grace is not without effect(1 Cor. 15:10). Many of my life experiences could have landed me in a mental hospital. Think about that for a minute. I suffered the loss of two children and the sequential deaths of family members. It was

God's grace that kept me and my family sane. God went the extra mile and gave us resilience as a bonus.

We have to extend God's love to everyone. The gospel you present, the love that you show will profoundly affect the soul, heart, and mind of someone struggling with mental health issues. When you water a plant do you see the effects of the water that day? The gospel is living water that the Lord will spring up (John 7:37-38). Sharing the gospel and God's love is not an interruption of our work; it is our work!

The Spreading of Bad Seeds

In partnership with other leaders and key stakeholders, it took six painstaking months to correct the deficiencies of the triannual survey. Some significant findings were in the mental health department. Yet, this was only one of many coins that needed to be tossed in the fountain of completion. Accrediting agencies do talk to each other and some of them work hand in hand. The surveyors' facial expressions let me know that they were flinching at the physical condition of the hospital and many of our performance outcomes. They thought that our organization was a bad seed. They more than likely shared their thoughts with other colleagues from sister agencies.

In the year 2018, we had thirty-eight back-to-back surveys from multiple agencies. The first one came on the heels of the action plan we submitted in February 2018 stemming from the survey in August 2017. If this sounds physically and mentally taxing to you, it was. We were bushed. However, I was fortunate to work side by side with other executives who felt like family from the onset of my employment. Someone on the executive team always brought sunshine into the room through an encouraging word or a hug. The

CEO was rarely present during our surveys, but he always received a report from me.

In the spring of 2018, the executive team expanded. With this expansion, the CEO's true character appeared and, it was nothing nice. It was as if this CEO was awaiting the appointment of additional executives to support his callousness and public ridicule. The new executives were given blatant favoritism which the Lord dishonors. Their departments were underperforming and, they got a pass. They gossiped and murmured all the time. It is sad to say that they were bad seeds that caused quarreling, deceit, and a vicious spread of wickedness. All of the actions were born of corruptible seed (1 Pet. 1:23). When it became obvious that they were not competent to manage many of their areas, this CEO shifted their work to other executives who were already overburdened with a voluminous workload. Oh yes, I got some of it. They were able to come and go as they please and did not have to worry about pending work assignments. Others like me had to take work with them during time off even when traveling for a funeral. Do you remember my nephew Jereld whom I shared the gospel while I was in Alabama? He transitioned to glory suddenly and I had to take work with me when I traveled to support my family and attend his services because of the CEO's controlling spirit. Most of us dreaded the weekly executive meetings. It was the CEO's whipping post time. One Christian leader received the brunt of the whippings without merit. This was not me this time but, I was not far behind.

My routine work identified some physicians that had practices that adversely affected patients and their families. A few of them were clinical department heads. I did not sit idly by and let the behavior continue. I submitted reports of findings conducted by myself and or my team. In addition to that, I recommended internal and external reviews. At one of the executive meetings, the CEO said that the physicians are needed here. You are to do whatever they say and, get along with them at any cost. The CEO's eyes landed on me during the conversation. This look is meant to ignore wrongdoing. I would not. These were rogue physicians who only cared about their bottom line and were largely the reason for the accreditation failures. Some of them were featured in the newspaper, TV and banned from other hospitals for their unscrupulous medical behavior.

The person appointed for medical oversight got that role because of a friendship with someone at the executive roundtable. He too was one of the newly appointed favored executives. This person was a novice and, the progress that we were making on the clinical side of the house regressed under his leadership. His executive position was on-the-job training for him. Initially, this person portrayed that I walked on water, but the Lord revealed to me his real agenda after a handshake (Luke 8:17). This guy was drowning in deep waters. He did not understand many of the basic concepts to effectively operate and, he needed a way to offload as much of his work as possible. He thought that I was going to be the scapegoat. He and I were like oil and vinegar. I was bought with a price and the work that the Lord was doing through me will not be in vain. The light that the Lord gave me was shining and, their darkness could not overcome it (John 1:5). I was asked to submit a proposal on what it would take for me to acquire some of his programs and, there was a recent executive hired to lead them who could not manage the programs either. My proposal was rejected and, I know why. I proposed a salary increase. This guy and the CEO wanted me to take on all of this additional work for free. This was not going to happen.

When I pushed back, my persecution elevated. This man and the CEO partnered in deceit and wrongdoing against me. Both of them were bullies who used forceful verbal words to impart fear and get others to do their dirty work. The CEO told me that I did not have any fear. That is one thing he got right, but that was said because I would not bow down to him or the other corrupt seeds. The tag team had no plans of doing the right thing and, I would not budge. They enjoyed being in the dark because their deeds were evil. As a soldier of the Lord, I represent the light and will always expose the deeds of the wicked (John 3:19-20).

Those who enjoy living in darkness will always despise you. Believe it or not, it is not personal. It is the Christ in you that they hate. Being friends with the world (wickedness) is being an enemy of God (James 4:4). The opposite is also true. I was okay with these types of people not being my friends. I and another Christian were subjected to harassment and ridiculed multiple times and, we persevered through all of it (Heb. 10:33). At a social event that the executives were mandated to attend, the CEO tried to force me to drink alcohol. I rejected his attempt respectfully but sternly. He later told me that he could not trust anyone who did not drink. I laughed and said that I drink coffee.

Another demonic scheme was festering at the same time. One of the new executives had her eye on a more senior executive role. There was a problem. The position was not vacant. A strong competent Christian that is a friend of mine was in this seat. The CEO was infatuated with the new executive's beauty and could not see her beguiling tactics. If they were seen, they were ignored. She dressed provocatively and stroked his ego to entice him (Prov. 7:21). Does she remind you of anyone that you have read about in the Bible? Anything she said or proposed, the CEO thought was brilliant. Many times, her recommendations were senseless. This demon in heels wanted to destroy all of the alliances of the person whose seat she wanted. If she was successful, she would be able to discredit and tear down the senior executive with ease, but she did not count on

God's presence in our lives. She contrived a report of false allegations against me that was laughable and did something similar to the person she was ultimately trying to take down so she could rise to the top.

Breaking The Chain

The plans of the executive that infatuated the CEO collapsed on all sides. God exposed her hand long before her actions came forth. For some reason, the CEO and his piranha thought that everyone depended on their jobs for survival and would tolerate their bondage endlessly. The writing was on the wall for me. You and I are sacred in the eyes of the Lord. Your commitment and labor of excellence is a pearl. Do not give what is sacred and holy to the wicked to trample over and then devour you (Matt. 7:6). I chose to break the chains of bondage. After talking with my husband, I planned my methodical exit in November 2018. I gradually purged my office and computer of information that no one needed and took my personal belongings home over two months.

My exit was going to be revealed when I departed. If I resigned in advance of my departure, I would have been tortured until that time. I skipped down the steps to give my resignation to a senior executive since the CEO was not on duty. As planned, I left on December 28, 2018, with a smile on my face. As I exited the building, I wiped the dust from my feet (Mark 6:11). I do understand that high-paying jobs may be hard to come by, but the Lord took care of me and, He will take care of you too. Ask Him. The sun continued to shine. The woman who was after someone else's seat did not get the position after all. I believe she left the organization wounded with anguish and full of disgrace (Ps. 38:5 and, Ps. 69:5). She could not outwit the arm of the Lord. The other Christian leader that she tried to destroy executed a plan that blocked hers.

Why did God send me to this hospital? The Lord planted me at this hospital for several reasons. He used me to teach and direct several leaders with compassion. They desired to achieve greatness but needed a road map. By using God's compass, they received sound guidance and hope that they will be able to share with a new generation. One leader, in particular, wanted a glowing accreditation report for his specialized survey. This person was persistent and came to my office frequently to learn. I surveyed every orifice of his department and taught him skills that he did not have. His department did not receive a single deficiency during the survey and, he launched a methodology to assess his program with proven benchmarks. His reports given at formal meetings were no longer the same. They became data-rich with finite action plans. The smiles on his face were worth being at this facility with the persecution. Money cannot buy the gratification you get from knowing that you helped someone along the way. There were others like him.

I also know unequivocally that I was planted at this hospital to pray and share the gospel with some patients in the mental health unit. Being approached by these patients for prayer and salvation tells me that the Lord prepared their hearts in advance of my arrival on the unit. I believe that my work with the Lord at that hospital was winding down after witnessing to the lady on the unit in September 2018. I also believe that my presence and exit were instrumental in opening the eyes of the CEO to Christianity and the wickedness of the person that he was infatuated with for a long time.

Faith Personified

All of my Christian life I have read about walking in and living out your faith. Can you call out the name of someone at this moment who walked in faith no matter what? I can. I had a friend named Bridget Cowan. Some called her Gina, and some called her Bridge. I called her Lola Bridge. We were friends for twenty-five years before she went to glory. We talked on the telephone for hours every week. One day when I called her, one of her other friends who was like a daughter to Lola Bridge was visiting. She got on the telephone and told me that Bridge had lost a lot of weight. Bridge indicated that she did not know why she was losing weight, but she planned to be examined. She had an annual invasive test scheduled for something else. The physician saw something peculiar that sparked a need for an additional test. She was determined to have pancreatic cancer. I flew to Nashville to assist her with getting her business affairs in order, to serve and comfort her. Bridget was my number one praying warrior and gave me a great deal of support when my family members transitioned. If she did not support me in the past, I was going to support her anyway.

When I went online to book my flight, the Lord told me that Lola Bridge was going to receive a golden anointing. In my spirit, I felt that meant that she was not going to be with us much longer. I planned my visit for a month. Her precise diagnosis, prognosis, and treatment plan were scheduled one day after I came into town. Bridget scheduled it this way to ensure that I could attend. We received information that we did not want to hear. My friend had an advanced stage of pancreatic cancer that metastasized to other organs. I led a praying vigil at her home and anointed her body with oil. Her pain was out of control, kept her doubled over, and caused her many sleepless nights. Her suffering tore my heart into pieces.

I did what I could to make her comfortable, but the adjustments seldomly work.

It took a considerable amount of time for the doctor to find and prescribe a medication that would reduce her pain to a tolerable level. That medication stopped working also. On top of that, It was a struggle for her to eat and drink anything. Organic and whole foods were purchased and prepared for Bridget. Most of it was wasted. She went back and forth to the doctor to get follow-up tests and some procedures that were very painful for her. Not once did she complain or blame anyone for her illness. She glorified God in song every day even though she was in excruciating pain. She persevered through her suffering and made time to care for her parents that lived forty-five minutes away from her home, help others with needs, and found time to assist at church (Rom. 5:3). The Lord allowed me to witness all of this to share it with you. Her faith was firmly planted in the Lord. Bridget personified faith!

She was placed in a hospice center less than a week before her transition. Three days before she transitioned, she dined with family and friends. This was symbolic of Jesus' last supper. A mutual friend of ours named Theresa Richardson called me to say that she just witnessed a miracle; Bridget is eating, drinking, and laughing. This was miraculous to see because she stopped eating and drinking. I talked to Lola Bridge that day and she was in high spirits and laughing with me on the video call knowing that the end of her natural life was drawing near. Bridget knew that she was going to be with the Lord forever and, she had nothing to cry about but a lot to shout about. Bridget transitioned to glory at the same hour that Jesus died on the cross in February 2020. The title of Bridget's eulogy was: Even If. This was a perfect title for a person who trusted in the Lord and lived out her faith (1 Pet. 1:9). Lola Bridge believed that even if she lived or died, her trust is in Jesus Christ alone and her praise to Him will be continually in her mouth (Ps. 34:1). Bridget personified what it means to have faith even until death even if she experienced suffering (Rev. 2:10). When you go to heaven, you will be able to identify Bridget from afar. She will be the one flying slower and lower than the rest of us. This is not because she has a lower status than the rest. God gave her a golden anointing! She is flying this way because of that heavy crown of righteousness that she is wearing, inlaid with many precious jewels representing the work she performed with the Lord on earth (2 Tim. 4:8). Fly on Lola Bridge, fly on!

Tell It On The Mountain

In September 2017, Larry and I decided that we were going to stay in the Illinois area and elected to purchase a home. A few days after moving in, my friend Regina Mosley called me. She sounded like she was exhausted and told me that she was frantically looking for my telephone number because her spirit led her to call me. I took a break from unpacking to chat with her. This was the first conversation I had with Regina in several years. She has been a friend since 1993. We met in Nashville, Tennessee shortly after my appointment with the Federal government. We got closer when I became a supervisor in 1996. Regina was my administrative support backbone. I could not have accomplished my management goals without her. Aside from that, Regina was a source of inspiration when Larry and I suffered the loss of our daughter. She gave us a book with inspirational quotes, gifts and called me when I was convalescing to cheer me up.

Regina dropped a bombshell during her call and, she did not know what to do. Her daughter Kristen Cooper got incredibly ill and was rushed to the hospital. She needed immediate surgery because her colon ruptured. A cancerous mass that originated from her ovaries metastasized to the colon and caused the rupture. Kristen's life was hanging by a thread! If there is such a thing as hugging someone through the telephone, I did it. Regina's heart was shattered and, she required the comfort and strength that only the Holy Spirit can provide. I prayed for a while in the name of Jesus and, I commanded the healing of Kristen's body (James 5:15). The Lord rescued her from deadly peril, healed her body, and made her whole (2 Cor. 1:10)! **She is alive, well, and cancer-free.** Glory to God!

On December 26, 2021, Regina called me to wish me and my family happy holidays, and to catch up since we had not spoken to each other in a while. We spent most of our time talking about the things that we are currently doing with our lives in retirement. I told Regina that I was writing a book and, she asked me if she was going to be in it. I chuckled and told her no that she was not. As our conversation continued, we begin to talk about her daughter Kristen's blessings. Regina began to share details of her personal divine experiences during our prayer in 2017 that were never shared. With this detail, she included some of the content from the prayer I uttered to the Lord. She told me that when I was praying, commanding the angels of the Lord, and decreeing the healing of Kristen in the name of Jesus, a brilliant burst of bright light filled her home and illuminated it. I believe that Kristen's hospital room was also illuminated at the same time.

Regina said that the Lord wrapped her in His arms and told her that He was going to heal her daughter, but she had to believe. Regina said that she told the Lord that she believes. (Heb. 2:4-10 and, Mark 5:29). The light that she experienced was one of God's wonders and none other than Jehovah Rapha; The Lord Who Heals. Regina explained that she has shared this wonder and miracle countlessly and continues to tell it from the mountain top so others will believe in the name of the Lord and be saved or healed (Mark 5:19

and, Acts 4:20). Regina's faith was strengthened and, her broken heart was healed by this wonder and miracle. I told Regina that her truth is supposed to be in the book that I am writing on behalf of the Lord. We laughed, knowing that her call was God-ordained. **Oh, that light!**

Reflections and Movement Forward (Chapter IX)

Question 1. Think for a moment what elements of the book speaks to your spirit the most? 1a. Write down why it resonates with you? 1b. Write your plan to apply the principle (s)

_____

_____

_____

Question 2. When you discover that something that you purchased is not authentic as described on a label what will be your response? Now think about how you handle a person who constantly fabricates things to find favor or acceptance?

_____

_____

_____

Question 3. Praying is a powerful tool that we use to speak to God, make our petitions known, and decree things into existence. With the help of your designated prayer warrior think about a territory that needs prayer. Determine what you need to bind and loose in that territory for the good of the people. Pray in the name of Jesus for those things to happen for at least seven days (Matt. 18:18).

_____

_____

_____

Question 4. Write down your plan to get yourself and at least one person plugged into the Source.

_____

_____

_____

Question 5. Dare to be different this year. Activate a one-hour power session with at least three people to pray, read and dissect God's word. Start your reading in the book of James. Rotate the selection of the scriptures and the person leading the prayer.

_____

_____

_____

CHAPTER X
THE WRAP-UP

What a journey this has been and, I have grown spiritually in the process! I never thought that I would be allowed to see my life retrospectively at the age of sixty-two and learn from it. The bigger gain is seeing the presence of the Lord throughout my life and the lives of others. Through this book, you and I have experienced the many dimensions of the Lord. We have had the privilege of seeing and feeling the presence of Jehovah Rohi; The Lord My Shepherd; Jehovah Rapha; The Lord Who Heals; Jehovah Jireh, The Lord Shall Provide; Jehovah Nissi, The Lord My Banner; Jehovah M'Kaddesh, The Lord Who Sanctifies; Jehovah Shalom, The Lord Who is Peace; Jehovah Tsidkenu, The Lord Who is Righteous and, Jehovah Shamah, The Lord Who Is There[7]. The Lord is all of this just for you and me. If you have not experienced the Lord in all of these forms, you are missing a big treat. The great news is that it is never too late to experience every aspect of the Lord.

Choosing to accept Jesus Christ as my Lord and Savior is the best decision that I have ever made in my entire life. Truthfully speaking, it is the best decision anyone can make because there is no life apart from the Lord. The only thing that a person who has not accepted Jesus Christ as Lord can expect in life is death (Rom. 6:23). All roads in the world lead to death. You will not be able to experience God or hear from Him unless you become a believer. If you have not taken this step, today is a good day to do it. It is simple and can be done wherever you are. First, you need to believe that Jesus Christ was raised from the dead and is our Savior (Acts 4:12). Then, you need to believe and confess that you are a sinner and cannot save yourself (Rom. 3:23 and, Rom. 3:10). Tell the Lord that you are sorry for the sins you committed and ask Him to forgive you (Rom. 10:9 and, 1 John 1:9). Once you do that, you are reborn and have eternal life (John 3:3)[8]. I recommend that you start reading the book of Saint John as a new believer and find a Holy Bible-preaching church or assembly to fellowship. If you took this step of life today, Happy Birthday! I will get to meet you one day somewhere around God's altar (Rev. 8:3).

Choosing to walk hand in hand with the Lord is the decision that shaped my character and exposed me to His power, wonders, and miracles in unimaginable ways. Walking with and serving the Lord means that you desire His friendship, His guidance, and correction. This my friends is a transformative step that enables the Lord to use you for His divine purpose. To be His friend, you have to follow His instructions. Yes, this means you must obey Him. When you do not obey Him, you will get into some of the traps that I experienced in life (John 15:14). Take a few seconds to marinade on these statements: When you are converted to a believer the Lord starts a great work in your spirit. Your old self continually sheds and traits that resemble the character of Jesus are added in its place (Eph. 4:21-23). This is a cyclic process that will evolve throughout your lifetime.

This process is probably the most challenging aspect of Christian maturation. Old habits can be hard to break because we often revert to what is comfortable and what we know. When the Lord pricks you about an action or behavior, or your spirit tells you that something is not right, take heed. What you are sensing, or feeling is true and means that it is something that the Lord no longer wants you to do. This is symbolic of denying yourself, picking up the cross of Jesus, and following Him (Luke 9:23). While you are being transformed, you are capable of spreading your light to others who will turn on the light for someone else. This is being used by God. Remember, He will mend, transform and use you simultaneously. We have to press our way through for the higher calling (Phil. 3:14 and, James 1:4). If you are waiting for the day that you are rid of all your bad habits before you follow Jesus, that day will never come.

You have to surrender to the Lord and let go of your internal desire to control. He will do the shedding and changing, but you have to follow His instructions when He prompts you to abandon or act on something. You have discovered that sometimes I have stumbled and, sometimes I have fallen flat on my face. Often, it was due to my desire to control a situation, disobedience, and stubbornness. If someone tells you that he or she has never stumbled or fallen, this person has never sinned. This is far from the truth because no human being is perfect (James 3:2). You and I are only perfect through Jesus Christ (Matt. 5:48).

The loving God that we serve will still use us when we make mistakes. The Lord will pick us up, chastise us because He loves us and wait patiently for our repentance. However, we should not continue to sin because we know that the Lord will forgive us when we repent (Rom. 6:1). If we resist temptation and urges, these interests will disappear (James 4:7 and, Eph. 4:27-28). Turning away from disobedience and a sinful pattern is a sign of spiritual maturity. There has not been a time in my life when I was not tested during an assignment. A test is necessary to strengthen our faith and prepare us for a higher assignment. This is also a reward for spiritual maturation.

The power, wonder, and miracles that I experienced through my life journey are just an inkling of what you and I can expect from the Lord in the future. The Lord continues to drop my jaw in amazement. Do you know that the same spirit that raised Christ from the dead dwells in you? Clergy members are not the only human beings given this power. This means that in the name of Jesus you can heal the sick, raise the dead and move mountains if you have faith (Rom. 8:11 and, Eph. 1:18-20). Are you getting the drift? Obedience, faith, and action work together like hands and gloves and are required to realize your full potential through the power of the Holy Spirit and necessary to be fully used by the Lord.

Before Jesus sat on the right hand of God, He left us with a Christian imperative to raise the bar. Jesus said: Very truly I tell you, whoever believes in me will do the works I have been doing and, they will do even greater things than these because I am going to the Father (John 14:12). Can you believe this? The Lord believes and expects us to exercise greater power, perform greater miracles and wonders in His name than He did. How is it possible to ever do works greater than Jesus? It is possible through the multiplication factor. Think about the number of Christians that exist across the globe. If each Christian uses the supernatural power that he or she has been given, this world will be overcome with light that will never burn out!

When this happens the spreading of our light will become contagious. Miracles and wonders will be a natural extension of who we are in Christ and what we do routinely. The dawning of each day will be punctuated by the conversion of many non-believers. The growth of the new believers will create the need to build more fellowship halls or churches. Let us never forget to praise and worship the Lord! Our plentiful and joyful noises to the Lord will cause the clouds in the sky to leap with joy with us. Demons will be crushed and willingly flee at our sight! Nothing is impossible with God. Tap into the Source; Jesus Christ and let Him use you starting today. He has all of the resources that you will ever need.

ABOUT THE AUTHOR

Pastor/Evangelist Sabrina R. Hughes rarely introduces herself by her ordination titles. She simply goes by the name of Sabrina. It is the Lord who generally lets others know what offices she holds. Sabrina was born in Detroit, Michigan but grew up in Wilmington, Delaware where her spiritual transformation began. At an early age, God equipped Sabrina with the talents to write poetry, plays and boldly speak in a variety of forums. These gifts are still used by the Lord to expand His kingdom.

Sabrina was a Non- Commissioned Officer in the United States Army Military Intelligence Command and served for eight years. Her interest in determining the unknown propelled her educational pursuit in science. This pursuit resulted in her attaining undergraduate and graduate degrees in science with honors. Sabrina loves having fun with family and friends, cooking, creating recipes, and growing the many exotic orchids that she possesses. Sabrina retired from the Federal government as a health care leader.

Through Pastor Sabrina Hughes' eyes, she is an ordinary human being and a friend of the Lord. Her journey throughout the United States and foreign countries has afforded her opportunities to learn about other cultures and love people from all walks of life. Sabrina's passion for evangelism started in her early twenties and her thirst to share the gospel of Jesus Christ is still prevalent in her life. In addition to being an ordained pastor and evangelist, Sabrina has been a church leader, church planter, teacher, and outreach director for over thirty-five years in several churches. **Her mission and vision are to spread the Lord's light and take the world by storm for and with God!** Pastor Hughes wants her legacy to be what she accomplished with the Lord.

ENDNOTES

1. BibleStudy.Org. 2022. "Meaning of Numbers in the Bible". February 2022. https://www.biblestudy.org/bibleref/meaning-of-numbers-in-bible/introduction.html

2. Editor in Chief. 2020. "Proverbs 17:22 Meaning of a Cheerful Heart is Good Medicine". connectusfund.org. May 2019. https://connectusfund.org/proverbs-17-22-meaning-of-a-cheerful-heart-is-good-medicine

3. Corrie Ten Boom. "Faith". July 1971. Heroes and Heroines. February 2022. https://www.hhhistory.com/2022/02/perfect-preparation-for-future.html

4. John Piper. 2011. "Christian Exiles". Ligonier.org. May 1, 2011. https://www.ligonier.org/learn/articles/christian-exiles

5. Adam McCann. 2021. "States with the Best and Worst School Systems". wallethub.com. July 2021. https://wallethub.com/edu/e/states-with-the-best-schools/5335

6. Compelling Truth.org. 2022. "What is the definition of ekklesia"? 2022. https://www.compellingtruth.org/definition-ekklesia.html

7. David Jeremiah. 2021. "The Names of God and Why They Matter". DAVIDJEREMIAH.ORG. 2021. https://www.davidjeremiah.org/knowgod/the-names-of-god

8. Compelling Truth.org. 2022. "The Romans Road to salvation- What is it"? 2022. https://www.compellingtruth.org/Romans-Road-salvation.html

CPSIA information can be obtained
at www.ICGtesting.com
Printed in the USA
BVHW091434240522
637941BV00016B/770